Prairie Seas,

Mountain Harvest

My teacher, her life, her legacy.

Alice Mary (Blair) Marlatt

Back cover photo, repeated within picture section, used with permission
of the Kaatza Station Museum & Archives, Wilmer Gold Collection.

All other photos within the photo section, except where noted, furnished
by the Marlatt, Fitzpatrick, and Stephens families.

Cover design and interior graphics by Urban Fir.

Advice and editing by Silent K Publishing, V Knox.
www.veronicaknox.com

Dedication

For Mum and Dad.

You have your own story, but your generosity,
("Meet me in Melville, Dad?"), and unquestioning support
made this one possible.

Prairie Seas, Mountain Harvest

My teacher, her life, her legacy.

Table of Contents

Introduction

Some details of my first day of school are hazy, but the memory of my teacher's presence is as bright and sharp as the white chalk on the blackboard where she had printed her name:

Mrs. Marlatt

In 1956, Alice Marlatt had accepted a teaching position in Gordon River Camp, a logging community once existing in central Vancouver Island. On my first day in September of 1957, as an anxious six-year-old, I had no idea that, of the many teachers yet to come, Alice Marlatt would be the one whose personality and character would have the most profound effect on my life. For the next six years, her approval was the best reward for good work, good behaviour, and good thinking. Although fearsome when perturbed, she had endless patience for those needing extra help.

No subject was outside her curriculum of life. She taught the horrors of war and the evils of prejudice. She taught cleanliness, diligent work habits, and penmanship. By reading to us, she inspired a love of reading. She taught the meaning of sportsmanship and fair play. She taught us to dance, to recite, to sing; we went to music festivals and won. She taught us to be responsible citizens.

A cornerstone of the community, Alice Marlatt promoted Christmas concerts, Hallowe'en parties, Mother's Day teas, and Remembrance Day observations. She took us to church, to the legislature, and to the provincial museum. She came to our birthday parties. She shared her experiences, her knowledge, her creativity, and her joy. In that logging camp school, although my body was confined to a desk, my mind was set free.

It was long after her death in 1989 when I realized how my education in that one-room school continues to shape my life. In 2003, I had the opportunity to meet many young university students, and I was amazed to find that much of what I had learned in elementary school was either no longer in the curricula, or did not receive the same emphasis. I understood how much I valued my education under Mrs. Marlatt's instruction, and how little I knew of the sequence of events that had placed me in her care. Curious about this, I asked my parents, who had remained close friends with Mrs. Marlatt's family.

I learned that in 1979 at the age of seventy-six, Alice Mary Blair Marlatt had dictated her memoirs to her daughter, Betty Lou Heeg. When Betty Lou sent me the tapes, I heard a voice that, after forty years, was as recognizable and familiar as my own. That voice related a story that spanned from the settling of the prairies through the struggles and innovations of most of the last century. Alice's narration, plus letters, cards, and pictures, revealed her zest for life, and a personality of wisdom, humour, and courage.

Alice Marlatt had lived a full life on the prairies as teacher, wife, mother and grandmother and yet, before her fifty-third birthday, she bought a car, packed her suitcase, and drove to a mountain-ringed life among strangers. She left her family, her friends, and all that was familiar to come to our one-room school in a British Columbia logging camp. For eight years, she taught ten to fifteen pupils in Gordon River, followed by four more years in another lumber industry community.

Why did she leave Saskatchewan? What gift did she possess that her pupils, and their parents, still recall her energy, her diligence, her charisma and her wit? Within her story are clues solving the riddle of her exodus to the west coast and the strength of character that sustained her there for the next twelve years.

Chapter One: Three Beginnings

1979: Leader, Saskatchewan I

Alice wakes to the clang of a frying pan striking the stove, followed by the sizzle and scent of bacon.

"What on earth is Bobbie doing? We don't eat bacon on week days."

No. It isn't Bobbie, but Art, cooking his breakfast before going to the farm.

Alice has moved across the width of Saskatchewan, but she feels she has moved from Halifax to Vancouver. She recently lived in Rocanville, where she shared a house trailer with her sister, Bobbie, but has been transported to the Town of Leader, and the home of her daughter and son-in-law, Betty Lou and Art Heeg.

I'm still not adjusted to this, Alice thinks, and I used to sail through changes without a qualm. Maybe it has to do with my age. I miss Bobbie. I hope Betty Lou is right.

Alice sits up, feeling the waves of disorientation subside. Her mind resettles, like a ship righting itself upon a change in course. She recalls that it is now September, and she has just celebrated her seventy-sixth birthday. Another year has flowed by, but there have been storms between the calms. She doesn't understand why her temper sometimes gets the better of her.

Alice swings her feet to the floor. Musings on birthdays, storms, and changes fade, as her mind takes a bearing on a different line of thought.

Yesterday, Betty Lou asked her to tell her life story, and Betty Lou would like to record it all. Alice said she would think about it.

After breakfast, Alice makes her bed and finds her walking shoes. She knows that a good walk often clears her mind.

The street is empty beneath the morning sun and a dusty crispness hints at oncoming cold weather. The poplars and maples lining the street are turning from faded green to ochre and gilt. Drying leaves quiver and drop in random sprinkles of autumnal confetti.

Alice looks down at the fallen leaves, and then up at the elevators at the end of the street. Like smug prairie bastions, they oversee their domain as if knowing that, if it were not for them, Leader would not exist.

Alice thinks how Leader and she are close in age, but Leader will surely be here long after she is gone. Towns live longer than people, and their stories can go on and on . . .

As for Betty Lou's request, how much of a story is there to tell? Or how little. Really, she thinks, my life has never been remarkable.

Looking around, Alice decides that there have been a few changes since she lived here in 1929. Some trees are bigger, and some are gone altogether in the way of living things, but there is new growth too. Along with saplings, a few new houses replace those that succumbed to human neglect or prairie elements. Some houses stand empty. The prairie has never been easy on its human occupants, whether they followed the buffalo, struggled on homesteads, or toiled in towns.

Yes, a few changes in Leader, Alice thinks, but the surrounding land looks much the same. Dusty roads with attendant lines of fading Russian thistle intersect a checkerboard of gold and black fields. Some fields sport golden crew cuts, and the shorn stems wave in stiff ripples with the morning breeze. The horizon is far off and vibrant against the blue sky. There are no clouds.

Alice shades her eyes and looks west and then east, a quirked smile on her face. She turns for home. She will do as Betty Lou asked and tell her story.

In the afternoon, Alice seats herself at the kitchen table. With a cup of hot water between dry palms, she waits while Betty Lou clicks a cassette into the recorder. Art, home again, hovers nearby, fixes himself a cup of tea, and jokes with Alice about Betty Lou's fussiness to make sure the tape starts exactly at the beginning. Alice chuckles while she polishes her glasses. Her grey eyes are clear, and Art catches their twinkle as she replaces them on her nose. She sips her hot water.

"We are all set Mother." Betty Lou clicks on the recorder. "Where would you like to begin?"

Alice sits up straight and takes a low breath; her voice is firm and deep.

"I will tell you about . . ."

1902–1905: The Beaches of Ontario

Alice Mary Blair was born on September 7, 1903, near Markdale, Ontario to Agnes (Grainger) and Robert Blair. She was the couple's first child and arrived within a year of their marriage.

Alice Mary was born when draft animals and wagons outnumbered internal combustion engines, and the concept of horsepower produced a vision of four legs and a bushy tail. Canada was only thirty-six years young and linked by the lonely strand of Canadian Pacific Railroad.

With the completion of the railroad in 1885, settlers had begun moving west, including many from eastern Canada where populations had grown but the availability of good land had not. Alice's fraternal grandparents, William and Mary Blair, and maternal grandparents, John and Mary Ann Grainger, had established farms in rural Ontario. Their families had thrived, but although the farms were productive, they were not large enough to support successive generations, thus pressuring the male offspring of both families to find other opportunities.

Agnes and Robert knew their baby's future depended on their prudent plans and wise choices. They may have looked to the experience of their parents for guidance, especially that of Robert's parents, William and Mary Blair.

* * *

William Blair and Mary Rainy, born in Scotland, immigrated to Ontario shortly after their marriage in 1856. South of Markdale, they founded 'Sunnybrook'–a one-hundred acre farm on the edge of Irish Lake.

William additionally supported the family as a 'buggy finisher' working for a family named Hurd in Orillia. That is, he painted the carriage bodies and applied artwork as required. He also applied his artistic skills to canvas, and Alice recalled portraits and paintings of roses attributed to her grandfather.

Robert, born in 1870, was second to last of the Blair's eight children. With five sons, the farm could not be equally divided and remain profitable. By 1901, Jim, the eldest son, and his wife Margaret ran the home farm and cared for the senior Blairs. The three girls could marry, but it was up to the four younger boys to make their way as best they could. For a time, Robert worked on the farm of his older sister Maggie and her husband John Graham, but as Robert had inherited his father's painting talent, he also worked at the Hurd's carriage business. At the close of 1901, Robert at thirty-one, had some resources, but a substantial and affordable plot of land in rural Ontario was beyond his means.

Like the Blairs, the Grainger family was of Scottish heritage. John and Mary Ann Grainger had settled in the Creemore area east of Irish Lake where their eldest child Laura was born, followed by Agnes in 1879. Eight more siblings surviving infancy followed Agnes.

When Agnes was fourteen, she suffered a bout of diphtheria, which affected her vocal cords and damaged her soft palate. She was still ailing when her mother spotted Dr. John McCullough driving his horse and buggy down the road, and sent the younger children out to flag him down. Dr. McCullough decided to facilitate Agnes' recovery at his own home in Walters Falls under the care of Mrs. McCullough, proposing that when Agnes was well enough, she could then help in the household.

The Graingers may have accepted this arrangement because they could not afford the doctor's services, and, by the standards of the times, Agnes was old enough to earn her keep. Agnes recuperated and then worked in the McCullough household for most of the next nine years. At the urging of her mother, she once tried a better-paying job in a cotton mill, but she loathed both the work and the unpredictable temper of the owner. Agnes returned to the McCullough home where she remained after the Grainger family heeded the call of prairie land.

The Graingers pursued their Saskatchewan dream early in 1902 without their two eldest daughters. Laura had married, and Agnes continued her arrangement with the McCulloughs, who considered her a member of their family. Little did Agnes know that finding love would take her away from the McCulloughs, and the relative civilization of rural Ontario, to the rigors of a prairie homestead and reconnection with the family she had left over eight years before.

When Agnes was twenty-two, she travelled to Markdale to help Laura recover from a difficult delivery. Laura and her husband, Bill Wilkerson, lived with Bill's adoptive, and widowed father, 'Uncle Tom'

Grainger. This visit was one of several points of fate on which pivoted the sequence of events leading to the birth of Alice and her story.

Earlier in the same year, Robert had suffered a bout of lead poisoning from the paint used on the Hurd's buggies. He had gone home to his parents' farm to convalesce.

When somewhat recovered, Robert visited his friend Tom Grainger who introduced him to Agnes. Good friend Tom may have had something of the matchmaker in his nature, as when Robert and Agnes met there was a definite spark. Robert's visits became more frequent, and the smitten pair were soon a local item.

When Laura regained her strength, Agnes returned to the McCullough's home. It was not long before Robert was actively courting, in Alice's words, "the beautiful young thing." Through hard work, at possibly the risk of his health, he had acquired a "spanking team and a buggy with a top." He drove a round trip of forty miles to woo Agnes.

Will he come? Agnes thought. It was such a long way from Irish Lake.

She tapped flour-dusted fingers on the rail of the front porch, leaned out and looked up the street. She pushed a strand of hair into the bun at the back of her head, straightened her back and took a deep breath.

Muffled in the Sunday afternoon hush between the after-church chatter and the refined hubbub of Sunday dinners, the town was silent. Surely, she would hear the clip-clop of trotting hooves from a long way off? The spring air smelled of green things sprouting, and the shadows shrank with every second. It would be a perfect day for a stroll while the horses rested. She dwelled on the thought of walking, maybe daring to hold hands or go arm in arm . . . the thought of being so close warmed her cheeks and sent tingles up her backbone, as she remembered his last visit and the look in his eyes. . . yes, he would come.

The screen door creaked open behind her, and Dr. McCullough stepped onto the porch.

"So, Agnes, no sign of your young man yet?"

Agnes turned and smiled, but the twitch at the corner of her mouth gave her away.

Dr. McCullough removed his spectacles and waved them in a tight circle.

"Do not worry so. You have been in a perfect rampage of beating and baking since yesterday, and I am sure he can smell spices all the way from that farm. After all, who would not travel forty miles of potholes and dust for some of your johnnycake? And Mrs. McCullough is stuffing the chicken for dinner.

"But, at the moment, I need to know if Robert has divulged how he presumes to support himself and possibly a wife? I take it he won't go back to the Hurds."

Agnes' cheeks burned, but she did not look away. She twisted her apron and lifted her chin.

"He has not. But he is clever and hard-working. I am sure if he is considering a wife, that wife will be well cared for."

At that, they heard the jangle of harness and the clash of eight iron-shod hooves as a team and buggy spun around the corner at the end of the street. Although shiny with sweat, the horses tossed their heads and flicked their tails. Beneath its patina of dust, the buggy gleamed with fine paintwork, and within the arc of its black leather top a lean young man gripped the reins, his bared forearms brown and knotted with muscle. Standing and leaning back, he dragged the team to a stamping halt in front of the house. Accepting that the mad dash was over, the horses snorted and blew with lowered heads. The young man with the intense moustache rolled down his shirtsleeves and donned coat and hat in fluid motions as he leaped from the buggy. He looked up at the porch.

Agnes was unaware she had been holding her breath and let it out in a long sigh.

Dr. McCullough cleared his throat.

"Agnes, ride with Robert while he cools out the horses. Then help put those animals up 'round back. You two will surely have time for a walk before dinner."

Robert's conscientious devotion swayed Agnes who at twenty-three was bordering on spinsterhood, and Robert at thirty-two was overdue to settle down. They approached both of Agnes' families. The Graingers gave their blessing without hesitation, via letter, from their new home in Saskatchewan, but the McCulloughs expressed reservations. Consequently, Dr. McCullough and Robert had a man-to-man chat, which was apparently satisfactory to both parties, as afterwards the wedding date was set for October 8, 1902.

Friends and relatives showered the couple with many gifts, but those from the McCullough family were especially generous: blankets, sheets, china, and lacy beige curtains for their marital home. Said home was a cottage on the back twenty-five acres of the Blair farm–a gift from Robert's parents. Here the newlyweds set up housekeeping and Robert farmed his diminutive holding near the puddle of Irish Lake. At less than a kilometer across, Irish Lake may not have been remarkable enough to earn a moniker of more originality, and was named for the majority of settlers on its marshy shores. This too, became a key turning point in the course of events affecting the Blair family and Alice's story.

In due course, Alice Mary arrived with Grandma Blair officiating as midwife. Agnes and Robert were pleased that their family was off to a strong start with the prompt arrival of a healthy baby girl, and as both came from large families, each had good reason to assume many siblings would follow Alice.

Apart from the worry that his farm might not support a large family, Robert worried about his neighbours. A staunch Presbyterian amid a community of Irish Catholics, he feared that Alice, or any other daughters, might eventually meet and marry a Roman Catholic. As Alice was an infant, his apprehension might have been a trifle over-proactive, yet the farm had limited potential to support the anticipated large family. With their future uppermost in his mind, Robert would have taken notice of the posters and pamphlets expostulating the opportunities of the prairies.

Upon completion of the railroad, the CPR and the government of Sir Wilfrid Laurier had been plunged into real estate speculation. Both entities entreated potential settlers to buy or homestead their tracts, and as there were growing markets for Canadian wheat, Canada, and those owning millions of acres of empty prairie, needed more wheat-producing farmers. The west was open for business, with land aplenty. Notwithstanding the fact those empty acres had not yet proved suitable for grain crops, attractive offers of land were posted in Canada and Europe.

Although the graphics and claims on posters and pamphlets were overblown, if not downright false, between 1896 and 1905 more than one million immigrants flocked to the untested soils of the prairies, enticed with the bait of land. Some pioneers homesteaded the government tracts whereas others purchased outright from the CPR. Either way, the lure of land was hugely appealing in countries where it was unavailable, or plots were small, or other advancement was unattainable due to depressed economies. Land was hope.

Robert's opportunity to explore prairie possibilities came in August, 1904. He joined a 'Harvest Excursion' to the town of Moosomin. Harvest Excursions were joint efforts by government and railroad to attract labourers to bring in the crops. The CPR offered reduced fares for groups of workers to travel on a 'Harvester Special,' and governments invited farmers to register worker requests stating wages and accommodation. A good man with a team could make up to five dollars per day or up to two dollars per day for straight labour. Unafraid of hard work, Robert took advantage of the offer, working for his in-laws, the Grainger family, as well as his older sister, Lizzie Dorsey, and her husband who had already set stakes on a piece of prairie land.

Robert loved the entire experience: cutting, stooking, threshing, and loading the crop into granaries. Impressed with the beauty of the prairies, the bounty of the harvest, the abundance of land, and the opportunities owning a piece of this land could provide, Robert decided to move his family west as soon as possible.

Robert hoped to push off from Ontario before the following spring of 1905, but there were many things to consider before packing could begin. One of these was the birth of baby Laura, arriving November 16, 1904, and named for Agnes' sister.

Canadian winters are rarely conducive to convenient travel, but in the 1900's, the logistics were even more complicated. The best option was by rail, but Robert and Agnes could only afford the lowest fare in one of the CPR's 'colonist cars.' These were equipped with light, a small cook stove, and slatted, non-reclinable seats, but that was the extent of the amenities. There were no facilities for women with children, and winter travel with two babies would have been the height of inconvenience and risk. They postponed the trip until the spring of 1906.

Alice, at her very young age, had no idea the upcoming trip would be the first leg of a life journey taking her to the prairies, to the west coast of British Columbia, and then back to the prairies. She could not have known her life's road stretched ahead with mileposts as teacher, wife, mother, and grandmother. Nor could she have envisioned the prairie homestead of her youth, the Manitoba farms of the depression, or the Vancouver Island logging camp of her middle age.

Corridors of time and distance lay between Alice and the west. And the west coast.

1957: Gordon River Camp–Mountain Seedlings

In an interior valley of Vancouver Island, on a triangle of land at the joining of two small rivers, a logging camp clings to a series of man-made gravel terraces. Clear-cut stumps surround family homes, bunkhouses, workshops, a cookhouse, a community hall and a school. A creation of the company owning timber rights for hectares around, they call the community a 'camp,' yet there is not a tent to be seen. The word is an anachronism hearkening from an era when loggers really lived in tents, and camps were temporary, moving to fresh logging sites at the pace of horses and oxen. Gordon River Camp never saw an ox either, but despite its implication of a flapping tent city at the end of an ox road, the usage of the word 'camp' continues.

A model operation for the times, Gordon River was first reached only by railroad. A few years after its inception, in keeping with advances in timber transport, the railroad was ripped out and replaced with a paved road. Thriving for most of the last decade, the community's residents, and their children, enjoy security, serenity, and the similitude of each season. Each year passes very much like the last.

On this Tuesday morning, Labour Day has passed, and before the sun clears the mountain to the east, loggers issue from bunkhouses and duplexes. Wearing jaunty grins and toting tin lunch kits, they call to each other as they traipse to the assembly yard across from the office. The squat brown building is a temporary anthill where loggers, truck drivers, and foremen, in hard hats and caulked boots, clomp in and out.

Ready to log, the men board yellow-orange trucks, locally known as 'crummies,' for the ride to the work sites.

In solitude befitting its serious purpose, the school sits on a level below the home site, and within it, the teacher opens the door from her apartment to the schoolroom. Middle-aged, with a slim build, erect posture, and grey wavy hair, she walks into the room. Her slippered steps are brisk and sure. She turns on the radio, sets her watch, and sips from her cup of hot water.

Last night, after her arrival from summer vacation in Saskatchewan, she unpacked her suitcase, prepared a bowl of soup, and ate it at her desk in the schoolroom. This would be her second year in this school. She reviewed the roster of children who would arrive in the morning–there would be ten, but it was a close thing. Two of the children were not old enough to enter grade one, and had their parents not agreed to their early start, the school would be two children short of the required ten. Her contract here would have ended after only one term.

The teacher scans the room. It is cool, but with the sun striking the windows on the east wall, it will soon warm. No need to light the oil burner. The desks are aligned, the floor clean, the doormat swept, and all bulbs are alight. Sorted textbooks lay piled, ready to hand out.

She has organized her desk with a bottle of ink, fountain pen, lesson book, a fresh sheet of foolscap for quick notes, and a potted pink gloxinia. She glances again at the board where she has printed her name in large letters:

Mrs. Marlatt

Downing the rest of her water, she returns to her apartment.

The sun is well clear of the eastern mountain when the camp's children awake. A dog barks, a door slams, a baby howls, all blending with the rumbles of a loaded logging truck crossing the trestle south of camp. The sun-warmed pitchy aroma of young fir trees rises above that of dust and the faint smell of oil from barrels under kitchen windows.

The morning smells tickle my nose when I step onto our front walk, and I blink in the bright light. Clutching a new scribbler and pencil close to my chest, I walk to our front gate where my twin friends, Kathy and Kelly, wait in the sun. They shade their eyes, and wave at me to hurry. It is the first day of school, and the twins and I are in grade one.

Mum is close behind me. Camera dangling from the arm holding my baby sister, Jo-Anne, Mum propels my three-year-old sister, Frances. Down the road, three of the four big boys in camp kick dust as they walk our way, and across the road, my other friend, Marilyn, watches from the lane beside her house.

Mum plops Jo on the grass, and calls Marilyn and the boys to join us for the picture. We girls wear new dresses, white socks and polished shoes, and Ray, Randy, and Patrick are smart in starched shirts and pants. The sun in our eyes, we aim squinty smiles at the camera, and with the photo consigned to posterity, Mum waves us away.

Our friend Jeff, who is also starting grade one, meets us at the other end of the lane, and our chattering pack crunches along the gravel road. Lower in the valley a ribbon of mist drifts above the river that murmurs behind its brushy hedge of yellowing alders and cottonwoods. From the top of the school path, I gaze at the trails leading to the river. Marilyn, Ray, Randy, and Patrick run ahead to play with Penny and Wayne in the schoolyard, but we in grade one pause to stare at the school below.

Like most buildings in camp, it is one storey, has brown wood siding and a flat pebbly roof where pieces of crushed glass twinkle in the sun. The row of windows on the near wall is a band of checkered light. It is impossible to see anything inside. A white flagpole stands at the edge of the schoolyard and the Red Ensign lifts in slow flaps, laying claim to all it oversees.

Twitching and tittering, we saunter down the stony path leading to the main door on the far side. Our brave babble wanes, but the shuffle of oxfords on pebbled ground waxes louder with every step. On tiptoes, we creak our way up the wooden stairs to the wide open door. In no hurry to begin school, the others chase and run. From the doorway, four of us peer into a cavern of shadow and light.

The schoolroom is awash with yellow morning sun. From the paned windows on the east wall, rays slant in front of the deep black chalkboard to bounce from the polished beige linoleum and gleaming desktops. The room is like a puddle on a sunny day–impossible to see *bottom and no telling its depth. I squint, blink, and rub my watering eyes. I feel a presence in the room.*

Wearing a pale blue dress, white pearls, and black lace-up pumps, she stands at a white desk in front of the blackboards to our right. The Teacher. Her glasses flash when she spies us poking our heads in the door, and she captures us in the beam of her smile. With one hand on the desktop, the grey-haired lady beckons us forward. My eyes on her face, I jerk across the threshold like a puppet on strings.

We straggle to a halt and stare about the room. In rows facing the blackboard, the desks increase in size from small near the door to the biggest under the row of high windows. The seats and desktops are varnished wood. The legs, wrought in ornate curves of black iron, end in holed feet like gaps between the toes of fairy-tale beasts. The beasts, pinioned to long boards, bow to the high white desk on its dais. All of the seats are flipped up as if daring me to tame one of these creatures.

At the back of the room, enfolded on three sides by bookcases, a half-circle of low wooden chairs looks far more inviting. I stare at the rows of books with bright covers, hinting at equally bright pictures inside.

Hooting and joking as they shove one another, the older pupils stamp up the stairs. I shrink from their noise. I know all of them, but now they are as remote as the eagles that spy on our camp. My mouth is dry. I hope I can say my name when the teacher asks. I stare up at her and swallow. I fidget with my scribbler and new unsharpened yellow pencil. I twiddle it in my fingers and then grip it in what I believe is the correct writing position.

Then, this teacher with the hypnotic smile speaks to us. Her voice rings rich and throaty and carries to every corner of the room. Our puppet heads swivel, and all chatter stops in mid-syllable. Her voice is warm and soft as she shows us little ones to our seats, and becomes more firm as she directs the older students. School has begun.

Our school had no kindergarten, so prior to my first day of grade one I had never set foot in the building. From a distance, I may have glimpsed the teacher as she drove her car or visited friends in camp, but she was only one of several adults rotating in the periphery of my preschooler world. I had no older siblings from whom I could have received instruction, flawed or otherwise, as to what happened in school. Mrs. Marlatt's smile soothed my nerves, and her voice left no doubt as to who was in charge.

A photograph of our class taken in the spring of 1958 shows us assembled on the front door steps. Ten pupils, plus a cocker spaniel, surround Mrs. Marlatt. It is the only formal school picture ever taken, and from the position of the crossed arms, the photographer expended some effort to arrange his subjects, overlooking the fact that the twins seated in front should have been instructed to cross their ankles and pull down their skirts. In contrast to the crossed arms, our smiles are relaxed and natural.

Of the four of us who started grade one, Kathy and Kelly, and I completed our entire elementary school years under Mrs. Marlatt's care. That the twins were there was another quirk of fate hinging on their parents' decision: a decision on which teetered the odds of there being a school at all.

Early in 1957, the school board had sent a plea to the twins' parents requesting their daughters begin grade one in the coming fall at the ages of five and one half. Their parents had agreed. The twins' presence in grade one brought the student body to a grand total of ten; the minimum required to continue the school. And retain the teacher.

At that time, there was a bus running two or three teens to the high school forty minutes away in the Village of Lake Cowichan. Had our school closed and had we joined the teens on the bus, we would have undergone a different school experience, which may well have been as rich and unique as that in our one-room school. But, we would not have had Alice Marlatt.

R.Rigsby

Chapter Two: Prairie Vision

1979: Leader, Saskatchewan II

"It's a lovely picture." Betty Lou leans over the table for a closer look at the sepia portrait Alice holds. It is a shot of William and Mary Blair, Alice's grandparents, on their 50th wedding anniversary. Art, who has been outside taking down screens, wanders in and peers over Betty Lou's shoulder.

"This was taken in March of 1905." Alice touches the faces in the portrait. "I was not yet two and Laura was still a tiny baby.

"Did Grandmother Blair want to go west?"

"Mother was not keen at all. But they didn't go right away, so she had some time to get used to the idea. Of course, there was much to do before they could move. Dad was anxious to go but decided they should wait another year because Laura and I were so young. They left Irish Lake in April of 1906.

"And my Dad was on the same train."

Alice's throaty laugh fills the kitchen.

"Yes, he always got quite a snicker out of that!"

"He was about eighteen though, so easier for him than for your family."

"Yes, it was still chilly for travel. They had Laura and me, and Mother was expecting Raymond. Dad was a determined man."

"Much like when you left Saskatchewan and went to the coast in 1956? That was fifty years later. You sold everything, packed, and drove west."

A slow smile from Alice. She looks away from the photograph, and into a distance not seen by Art or Betty Lou.

"Well that was different," she says.

1906: Setting Sail

In March of 1905, William and Mary Blair celebrated fifty years of marriage. Robert and Agnes joined the festivities, but all the while Robert dreamed of Saskatchewan. Over the summer, the would-be homesteaders prepared for their migration scheduled for the following spring.

Robert disposed of excess implements and sold his land to an Irish neighbour. Not suited to the demands of prairie farming, the dashing team and buggy also went to a new owner. Robert bought stock and equipment, plus fares for family and freight, but retained a cash reserve for the purchase of land. He booked space on the train, and Agnes packed the household goods. The venture west was about to begin.

Although Agnes had discovered she was expecting a third child due in August, this was one matter that couldn't be postponed to a more convenient date. In keeping with the itinerary, Robert Blair loaded his pregnant wife, daughters, stock, implements, and a collie pup called Uno, onto the train heading west April 30, 1906.

Fifty years later, when Alice moved to British Columbia, she might have remembered how her father had chosen to leave Ontario. Like Robert, she sold her property, packed her bags, and set a bearing west. Their reasons for doing so might have differed, but their determination was the same.

Yet, in 1906, Alice was not yet three years old, and a train ride was an exciting and novel adventure. She could not know that her future husband, Ashton 'Curly' Marlatt, aged eighteen, and his older brother John were on the same train. Robert, while strolling through the cars, may have unknowingly nodded to his eldest daughter's future husband. He may have chatted with Ashton. If so, he would have applauded the pluck of the young man who had left Ontario for good, and who was going west to seek a better life. Ashton's destination was the Wawanesa area of Manitoba where his bachelor uncle owned land, and where he hoped to become a landowner too.

Robert was not yet a landowner. His destination was Moosomin, Saskatchewan, where his in-laws lived, and where he intended to install his family while he shopped for a homestead. The vast differences between the wild windswept expanses of Saskatchewan and the tempered fertile farms of southern Ontario did not break the spell of Robert's enchantment with the prairies. His vision projected far beyond the immediate prospect of ploughing the seas of waving grass.

Agnes was less enthusiastic. She had many friends in Ontario and was fond of Robert's family. She could easily visit the McCulloughs and her older sister Laura. In Ontario, her children could grow up with their cousins in familiar surroundings, with shopping and services, and access to schools and medical aid.

Agnes' mother, Mary Ann Grainger, already in Saskatchewan, may have sent warning letters describing the deprivations of prairie farming. These were considerable. The rosy posters of the CPR and Canadian Government depicted lush fields of bounteous crops, orchards of fruit trees, merry streams of pure water, and joyful homesteaders tending plump livestock.

Either the artists had never laid eyes on the prairies, or were following instructions from the spin-doctors of the times, as the realities were far different. Not portrayed were the cruel winters, the frosts (both early and late) the grasshoppers, the blights and rusts, the unpredictable rainfall, the challenges of finding good water, the high costs of goods, and the gamble and risk of prairie farming. The hardy souls who dropped anchor on homesteads where moorage was tenuous, uncertain and a constant struggle, would have been well able to advise relatives left at home. Agnes did not share her misgivings with young Alice, but Alice knew her mother was troubled.

The train rolled west. The family watched the scenery slide by as they chugged away from the farmland and towns of Ontario, crossed the bouldered crest of the Canadian Shield, skirted the edge of Lake Superior, and steamed on into Manitoba. Beyond the blooming city of Winnipeg, the towns became fewer and smaller, and as the prairie opened up, they crossed the Manitoba/Saskatchewan border.

Early in May, the family disembarked in Moosomin, and Robert settled his family in a rented red brick house. While Agnes set up housekeeping, Robert found what he thought was suitable land in the Red Jacket area, farther west. He probably had not received good advice regarding his choice of property as the terrain was, and still is, stony and wet. The family grew with the arrival of baby Raymond in August, but there was no crop in that fall of 1906.

The lack of a crop, and therefore an income, may have been what necessitated a move to the home of Robert's sister, Lizzie Dorsey, north of Moosomin, near the crossroads to the hamlet of Welwyn. From there, Robert, with his money dwindling, went homestead shopping again. He found an established farm outside of Rocanville.

The modest burg of Rocanville had sprouted around a designated elevator site when the railroad had reached the area in 1903. An influx of new settlers had arrived with the railroad, but in 1906, the settlement numbered barely one hundred inhabitants. Robert's prospective quarter section farm was within five kilometers from 'town.' The proximity to a growing community may have fulfilled Robert's vision: fat Holstein cattle and gallons of fresh dairy products located with easy access to a rail station and a local market. Robert bought the property, assuming ownership in December.

In any Canadian province, December is not a propitious month in which to move, and this was especially the case in Saskatchewan in 1906.

Robert travelled ahead to their new 'house,' a crude log cabin devolving in later years to a pigpen. Via sleigh, and in biting cold, Agnes' younger brother Norman drove Agnes and the children to their new home. With too few blankets, Alice was "freezing cold" and Agnes cried "all the way from Welwyn corners." Before succumbing to exposure, they stopped at the Hewgill homestead where the fireside and hot tea helped thaw feet and fingers. Alice, who warmed enough to take in her surroundings, was shocked by the appearance of Mrs. Hewgill's hands–discoloured from applying blacking to the stove. At three years old, she was unable to understand how a person could have black hands. She never forgot the image.

Beyond the fascination of Mrs. Hewgill's hands, Alice noticed two striking cranberry glass pickle jars, and later, as a young teen, she teased Mrs. Hewgill about possibly giving one to her. At a very early age, Alice had an eye for fine *objets*.

The respite in the comfortable surroundings was too brief for Agnes' liking, and too soon, Norman re-ensconced them in the sleigh. The expedition resumed.

While Alice, Laura, and their unhappy mother watched the hind ends of horses slogging through snowdrifts, and shivered under their inadequate covers, Robert put the finishing touches on the welcome wagon. He whitewashed the inside of the cabin and killed a pig. He had pork simmering on the stove when he went to milk the cow, but on his return, was stunned to find the cabin full of smoke and the pan full of flames. Without thinking, he threw his pail of milk onto the burning meat. The grease exploded, and flames burst toward the ceiling, so as Alice quoted, "it doesn't look too good when mother comes in."

This was possibly the understatement of the century. Alice was anxious about her mother, and it didn't help when Agnes placed Raymond on the table and dissolved in a flood of tears. The state of the cabin from the exploding pig was only part of her anguish.

"Look at the snow!" she wailed, at the sight of snow filtering through cracks between logs. Agnes was convinced leaving the comforts and society of their farm in Ontario was madness.

1958: Gordon River–Sailing Through Winter

Long after all denizens of Camp were abed, snow-filled clouds, unexpected and unpredicted, stole in before midnight. They released their fluffy burden and shook themselves out before morning. Although snow at higher elevations is common, some winters come and go with scant snow in the homesite.

"Wake up and see the snow!"

Mum's newsflash prompted an eager arising. Ignoring the frigid floor I scampered to the window and hopped from foot to foot, planning snowy games. Instead of being at work, Dad sat at the kitchen table with a steaming mug at his elbow, and my sister Fran, fingers in her mouth, in his lap. While I was glad to have him home, I knew it wouldn't be good if the snow kept him from work for long.

Still, it was breathtaking. Snow covered everything: trees, fences, roads and alleys, and the top of the neighbour's car. The power poles wore hats of snow, and the swing in our back yard had a cushion. I shoveled Cornflakes into my mouth and left early to make the first footprints.

Beyond our yard, I stopped and listened. Silence. No wind whispers, no grinding trucks, and no friends calling. The trees lining the river had become an enormous white hedge. As I watched, the sun rose above the mountain, and the snow sparked with sequins like those on my mother's best sweater. When I reached the corner of the school, I looked back to see other people following my tracks, and the magic of the morning melted away.

We leaped from the porch into the snow to see who could go farthest, and some of the boys rolled forward in somersaults. We shrieked and threw snowballs. Mrs. Marlatt came out with her broom and swept most of the snow off the steps and porch, and then brushed us

R.Rigsby

too. We laughed, and made sure to stamp and shake before going inside. She had put down newspapers for our boots, and helped us hang the wettest coats over the rail around the heater. Then we took our seats and settled down to work. Occasionally, somebody would stand and look out to make sure the snow was still there. It was.

Now, hurrying to finish arithmetic so I can read for a few minutes before recess, I peek at the book waiting in my desk. I jump when I hear Mrs. Marlatt clear her throat. She walks the aisle by my desk, and although she stops to look at my arithmetic, she then continues to the front of the room and turns to face us. I catch a glint behind her glasses as she looks at me, but the corner of her mouth lifts.

"Before you people go out for your recess, I want to show you a game you might like. It is called 'The Fox and the Geese.'"

On the board, she chalks what looks like a wagon wheel and explains. We should tramp this wheel in the snow and then choose one person to play a fox. All others are geese. The idea is for the fox to catch the geese, which then become foxes and can join in chasing the rest of the geese. We must not step outside the wheel, and the hub is 'home' for the geese. It is a safe spot, but they can't stay there long because that wouldn't be fair nor would it be much fun. Grabbing boots, coats, and mittens, we shoot out the door as if we are already frightened geese.

Before we spoil the field of snow, we form a line and follow one of the boys to tramp out the giant wheel and its spokes. The game is even better than we expected. I glimpse Mrs. Marlatt watching us from her apartment window, and when she opens the main door, we are panting and hot. I hope the snow lasts a long time.

Chapter Three: Prairie Reality

1979: Leader, Saskatchewan III

Alice removes her glasses, pinches the bridge of her nose, and rubs her eyes.

"Mother would climb the attic ladder in the evening and look out the window facing west. I knew she was crying, but she always said she just liked to see the sun go down. Even now, I hate the twilight. I always put the lights on before the sun is gone."

Betty Lou stops the recorder and looks at her mother. It is late afternoon and although the sun is bright, it dips toward the trees lining the street.

"And yet, Grandmother Blair lived all of the rest of her life out here, and I never heard her complain."

"No, no complaining ever, but that first winter was terrible," said Alice.

1906–1911: Blood, Sweat, and Prayers

Alice recalled that what her mother thought was snow on the floor was whitewashed chinking Robert had knocked down in his panic to eradicate the smoky mess. After calming Agnes' tears, Robert cleaned up the remains of the calamity. Over the next few days, the family established a routine, and settled in to endure the prairie winter. The only available wood was green from the standing woodlot on the homestead, and Robert could not bring himself to ask his new neighbours for dryer wood from their property. Consequently, in that winter of 1906-7, the log cabin was cold and smoky.

However, some chinking *had* fallen out, and the cabin was draughty until Robert solved the problem in an enterprising pioneer manner. Chinking was usually made of clay mixed with moss or straw, but that winter, not only was the mud around the edges of the slough frozen solid, but snow covered anyplace where moss might be found. Robert created his own chinking recipe. Instead of mud and moss, he mashed fresh manure with cut up straw and plugged the cracks with the aromatic filler. For extra insulation, he banked more manure around the outside of the cabin–as much as the livestock could produce.

While Agnes and Robert effected home improvements, Alice minded baby Ray and Laura. Although they were virtually housebound for the winter, there was much to do to make the cabin a home and the holding a farm. Agnes cooked every day, and there was always washing, especially with a baby and a two-year-old. How she managed to prepare everything from soap to butter, and sustain enough hot water to launder diapers is exhausting to imagine. Agnes took a long time to adjust to her prairie life, and perhaps she never did, though she never complained, and she never again lived in Ontario. For the first year, at the end of the day, Agnes climbed the rickety ladder to the loft where a window faced west. She may not have been aware that Alice heard her tears.

In spite of having family in the area, Agnes pined for the east and the life left behind. She hadn't lived with her parents since she was fourteen and had a close relationship with the McCulloughs. She believed they should never have left Ontario, and would have been better off staying on their farm on Irish Lake.

Alice knew her mother was unhappy, but Agnes never shared her worries with her children. That Alice noticed and remembered her mother's distress may have been due to unusual perceptiveness and her growing sense of responsibility. From an early age, she was expected to help wherever possible, and although her parents were loving, neither she nor her siblings were indulged.

There was no time for coddling children if the family was to survive. In the spring, while Agnes dug and planted the garden, Robert planted the crop that would be the family's source of income. Using three horses and a furrow plough, Robert cultivated and seeded the two broken fields of the quarter section. After planting came praying that rain and sunshine would alternate in optimal amounts, that rusts and grasshoppers would be minimal, that hail-bearing clouds would sail on to other locales, and that the crop would be sealed in granaries before the first frost. Robert and Agnes, as devoted Presbyterians, soothed their souls in their church in Rocanville and put their hearts and bodies into their land.

In late 1910, after four years of body-breaking toil and unrelenting winters, Robert and Agnes received the distressing news that Robert's mother, Mary, was very ill. The family did not expect her to survive the year. Agnes and Robert decided to go east hoping to spend one last Christmas with Robert's mother, and although sad for her mother-in-law, Agnes received the pronouncement as a blessed parole from the sentence of prairie life. They would stay with Robert's sister, Maggie, and her husband, John Graham.

Train travel still being the most convenient mode of transport, the Blair family again boarded a colonist car at the lowest fare. In a large valise, Agnes, perhaps with foresight based on her experience of the inbound journey, packed provisions: cooked chicken, milk, roast beef, bread and butter. According to Alice, by the end of the trip there was "loads of food left over." The colonist cars had no more niceties than in 1906, but with the slatted seats pulled together as makeshift beds, and enough blankets, Agnes bedded down her family with a modicum of comfort.

Alice recalled having a fabulous time on the train with one exception. At one point the track ran, at what seemed to Alice, precariously close to Lake Superior. Unnerved when Agnes sat next to the window to better view the water below, Alice voiced her fears that her mother might fall out. At seven years old, she was chided for being a "booby baby." Years later, Alice drove through British Columbia, but she recalled that the hair-raising precipices of the Roger's Pass and the Fraser Canyon hardly ruffled her at all.

Although the visit was a gloomy deathwatch, Alice had a wonderful time. The Grahams owned an orchard producing Northern Spy apples, and in addition, they had produced six children: Howard, Wilfrid, David, Mary, William, and Annie. The Graham children were enchanted with their young prairie cousins, and guarded their guests with care while keeping them entertained. Good manners notwithstanding, they could not restrain their hoots of laughter when Alice, Laura, and Ray, on being offered their first-ever apples, ate them, cores and all. Regardless of the inevitable teasing of older cousins, Alice and her siblings "had a gorgeous time" at their Aunt Maggie's.

The children were allowed a wide latitude of freedom while the adults attended Grandma Blair and prepared for Christmas. Alice discovered Aunt Maggie's parlour; a formal room for special occasions, such as entertaining the minister. With a fine carpet and settee, and lanterns with fringed shades, it was the height of 1910 home fashion. In order to absorb every detail, Alice sat alone in the unheated room as often as possible. Her log home on the prairie was rustic and tasteless compared to the sumptuous home of her aunt. However, Aunt Maggie decided the parlour was off-limits to her inquisitive niece and locked the door.

While the parlour was unavailable, the dining room was not, and the meals at Aunt Maggie's were bountiful in a 'land-of-plenty' with its stunning selection of food. Christmas dinner was an array of delicacies; apples were strongly represented. Driven to her daughter's house for the occasion, Grandma Mary Blair made an entrance on the arms of her sons Robert and Jim.

Mary Blair passed away early in February 1911, and Agnes instructed the children in funeral rites and proprieties. This was seven-year-old Alice's first funeral, and afterwards, she and Laura decided to enact their own observations using frozen apples found in the orchard. They buried their loved ones with suitable prayers and then sat singing under the trees. Their other Aunt Maggie, Uncle Jim's wife, was shocked. Having no children, she thought such behaviour inappropriate, but Agnes did not admonish her girls.

The family stayed in Ontario until March. It was another winter of brutal cold in Saskatchewan and not much better in Ontario. Alice found the Ontario winter damper than at home, and the house was not warm, but she was happy to make this small sacrifice in order to play with her cousins.

Agnes would have loved to stay forever, but this could not be. With the coming of spring, they boarded the train for the return journey.

While the Blair family had visited in Ontario, the farm in Rocanville had been under the care of Robert's nephew, Bob Dorsey.

Bob, aged twenty-six, was Lizzie Dorsey's son, and although he worked elsewhere in the summers, he spent his winters with the Blair family. He was today's version of a 'gadget freak' owning both a camera and a gramophone. Alice loved to squeeze the camera bulb when cousin Bob took pictures, and she adored the gramophone.

While Alice and her siblings waited their turn to wind the crank, Agnes and Robert played 'Flinch,' a popular card game of the times. Having reservations about regular decks of cards and their gambling associations, Robert and Agnes considered Flinch a more acceptable alternative. Robert also played the Jew's harp and the autoharp, and could be enticed to entertain the family along with Bob's gramophone. With chores finished for the day, games and music filled snowbound winter evenings.

Throughout the year, the weekly routine concluded on Sunday with the family pilgrimage to the Presbyterian Church in Rocanville.

Conveyed in either the four-wheeled 'democrat,' or the sled, drawn by two horses, they rarely missed a service. Agnes met other women in church and community, and Robert, a skilled carpenter, finished the pulpit and chair for the minister. That the farm was relatively close to town allowed Agnes more occasions to socialize and make friends, which perhaps compensated for the loss of those forsaken in Ontario.

Alice and Laura lacked friends for the first few years, as there were no close neighbours with potential playmates. Thus, being close in age, they were each other's playmate, inventing games that would sometimes include Raymond.

Although usually as angelic as they appeared in the photos taken in that era, Alice and Laura were not above mischief. On a dull afternoon, perhaps when the winter wind blew, they, from the loft, dangled a hook on a string. Agnes was entertaining a guest, and the girls had heard that the lady wore a wig. The guest was oblivious, but Agnes, with that maternal sixth sense, turned in time to see what they were about. She glanced from them to the buggy whip in the corner. The string receded.

Nor were they above hatching fibs to cover misbehavior. One hot day, Agnes found she was out of bluing for her pile of laundry. She thought luck was with her when she spotted her sisters, Ethel and Olive, out on the road to town, so sent Alice and Laura to catch them. The girls walked down the lane with dutiful steps, but once out of sight of the house, and before reaching the road, they sat down in the shade. Nervous of going farther and afraid of being too far away from Agnes, they concocted a lie to explain their failure.

Knowing they hadn't made any effort to flag down her sisters, Agnes was ready with the buggy whip when they returned. This she switched across the miscreants' legs. They had no opportunity to try out their story, or blame each other.

The sting of the buggy whip across the girls legs was applied not so much for naughtiness, but more often for lying about their pranks or tattling on each other. Alice said there were occasions when she was punished unjustly, but she felt that she, as the older child, could not tattle on Laura or Ray. This dim view of lying and tattling stayed with Alice all of her life.

1958: Gordon River–The Blabbermouth

On a weekday evening in late spring, my father dozed in his armchair with his book flopped on his chest and his head flopped on the back of the chair. My father often napped after supper. His work as a high rigger was strenuous, and he was out in all weather, all day, five days a week. As well, he suffered recurring bouts of asthma and bronchitis, which rendered him short of breath, wheezy, and weary. He was twenty-eight years old.

Down the hall wavered the splash of water, my sisters' giggles, and my mother's murmurs as she readied them for bed. At seven years, I washed, brushed my teeth, and got into bed without supervision, and I had enough seniority to merit a later bedtime. Lost in the funny papers of the Vancouver Sun and oblivious to my father's fatigue or my sisters' prattle, I lay sprawled on my mother's braided rug with the paper spread in front of me.

It had been a warm day so there was no thump and whir of the oil burner to mask the odd noise in the yard. Jarring night noises were rare. Screeching traffic, siren wails, stereo music, or human hubbub did not exist in our secluded camp.

When I played with friends on twilit evenings, and we stopped to rest, we first heard only our thumping hearts and gasps for air. Then, we might hear the wind in the trees, or chirping crickets, or frogs peeping in distant ponds. We might hear the 'chirr' of a nighthawk. At any time of the year, we could hear the variable rush of the rivers overlain with the drone of the power plant. Yet, none of these sounds roused my father from his after-supper doze and made me look up from the paper.

Rising with an uncharacteristic frown, Dad dropped his book, jerked open the front door, and stepped onto the porch. I followed poking my head out the door.

"What are you doing? Get out of there!" Dad waved his arm and smacked the rail.

Alarmed boyish voices piped in the dim garden, followed by the spatter of gravel shooting out from under running feet.

"Bloody kids were in the rhubarb!"

He was more shocked by their audacity than angry at the theft of some rhubarb. It was a small camp, and few things occurred that did not make their way to the ear of Mrs. Marlatt.

* * *

In school a day or so later, I have forgotten the raid on the rhubarb. My stomach has let out a few rumbling reminders that lunch hour is near, but having completed my Language questions in "full sentence answers," I am free to read. I look at pictures in one of the newly arrived library books. We receive a fresh box every few weeks and wait our turns for the best stories. This one, called 'Saturday Cousins' looks promising. There are many black and white drawings, and one is of a mule. Not a horse, but close enough.

The fire door at the end of the room is open, and I smell the earthy aromas of our scraped out camp in the clear-cut. The tang of hot red dust, fresh cut logs, and evergreens lingers in the air. Hovering just below consciousness and ever-present, it gives our camp its identity, like the wet-meat smell of the butcher shop in town, or the mustiness of books in the village library, or the dankness of waterweeds at our favourite picnic site at the lake.

Keeping my head down, I glance right and left. Like me, others are finished their exercises and read, or colour drawings or maps, so we don't disturb others who are still working. Turning to the first page, I am soon with the Saturday Cousins.

Mrs. Marlatt rises, and I hear her firm footsteps click to the front of the class. This is unusual. We are waiting for the quietly spoken, "Books away," before we dash out the door and home for lunch. She faces us, straight-backed and straight-faced. One hand is on her hip. We realize something is up and stare at her.

"Before you leave for your dinner today there is something I must discuss."

She tells us how it has come to her attention that certain people have been carousing around camp after dark causing trouble. They have

R.Rigsby

been in yards without permission and have disturbed people. She doesn't know the particulars, but she is not best pleased with this behaviour and it must stop.

Well! I have the particulars! My hand shoots up.

"Yes, Rosemary?"

I launch into the story of the pilfered rhubarb, and I name the three boys who were in our yard. Mrs. Marlatt's expression doesn't change. Her glasses flash as she looks straight at me, but instead of an approving nod and her special smile, the lines from nose to mouth deepen.

"That is all." She dismisses us for lunch.

I am baffled. My revelations have not been rewarded, and I feel my stomach turn over. Before reaching home, I feel much worse.

Out of sight of the school, the boys pounce on me. They are angry. They are also ten and eleven, and big for their ages, while I am an undersized seven-year-old. They stand over me and inform me I am a tattle-tale and shouldn't go around getting people in trouble. I look from one to the other. I twist a fold in my dress and look at my saddle shoe scuffing a rut in the gravel. The boys stand close. They explain they weren't doing anything wrong, they were just taking a short cut through our yard because one of them suddenly heard his father calling. Yeah, that was it, a shortcut. Then, as if suddenly aware time is wasting and they are hungry, they run for home.

Pondering this new information, I trudge the gravel roadway. Dad was mistaken. They weren't stealing rhubarb; they were just cutting through the yard. I don't feel like talking at lunch, but Mum is busy. Between checking a pot on the stove and pulling in a load of dry sheets from the line, she punches down bread dough and shapes loaves. My sisters are more interested in lunch and in pestering each other rather than pestering me. They pay no attention to me picking at my sandwich. The bread sticks in my throat. I decide I must apologize to the boys. I was wrong to open my mouth when I did not know what had really happened.

On the school path, two of the boys walk ahead of me, so I call out and catch up at the corner of the school near the open fire door. Mrs. Marlatt moves in front of the row of windows as she waters her gloxinias, and then she disappears.

The boys wait by a scraggly cottonwood sapling; wavering leaf shadows make their faces unreadable. I tell them my Dad was mistaken, and so was I. I tell them I am sorry. I expect forgiveness, but instead they bend a few branches on the tree and examine the leaves. They look at each other sideways. They don't tell me everything is okay and to forget about it but just shrug and amble away. I follow with slow steps wondering if I hadn't made myself understood.

After school, I wait for the other boy, the eldest of the three, and I apologize to him too. He listens but just mumbles something and hurries off. I feel deflated. I wanted the boys to forgive me and to say they understood my confusion. Instead, they don't want to talk about it. Head down, I walk the dusty path, kicking the odd rock along the way. Then, like the boys earlier in the day, I realize I am wasting time, and if I want to play, I had better run home and change clothes.

R.Rigsby

Chapter Four: School and Education

1979: Leader, Saskatchewan IV

Alice steps onto the porch and inhales until her shoulders rise. This morning is definitely cooler, she thinks.

Like brittle facsimiles of future snowflakes, a few fallen leaves sprinkle the wooden boards of the steps. Alice toes a stray leaf.

I am glad Betty Lou insisted we do this, she thinks. So many memories have come back to me, and I am surprised at what I remember. The memories are like boxes within boxes. As soon as I open a box and discover the memory inside, I dig deeper to find another box. But some boxes are milky glass with no openings, and although I can make out some memories inside, they are blurred. Not everything is as distinct as I would like.

Alice removes her glasses and wipes them with a tissue.

Glasses. Yes, a blessing and a curse. It was certainly a blessing when somebody realized I had the eyes of a mole, but paying for new pairs and cleaning them all of these years has been . . . well maybe not a curse precisely, but certainly a nuisance. Yet, I would have missed much in life had I not been able to see.

Alice fetches the broom and sweeps the leaves.

1911–1913: Life Lessons

After their return from Ontario in the spring of 1911, and after enjoying the more commodious home of their relatives, Robert and Agnes felt the cabin closing in. With six people, including Bob Dorsey, the already close quarters were now claustrophobic. Over the summer, Robert laid plans and assembled materials for a new house.

While Robert began construction, Alice and Laura began grade one in the two-storey, four-classroom Rocanville School. At that time, it was normal for children to start school at seven, but as the family had spent the previous winter in Ontario, Robert and Agnes had held Alice back one year. Also, they thought it best for Alice and Laura to start together, so Alice was eight and Laura almost seven on their first day of school.

Nowadays, via car, Rocanville is barely five minutes away from the Blair homestead, but in 1911 it was too far for Alice and Laura to walk. Needing the 1911 equivalent of a family mini-van, Robert bought a buggy and a good-natured strawberry roan named Dolly. Farm horses were utilitarian beasts and as commonplace then as tractors are now, but Alice developed an early liking for them, and especially for Dolly. The wise mare knew her business, and for most of Alice's schooling, Dolly made the trip too.

Alice's first year was under the guidance of Miss MacMillan whose understanding and ability made a huge impression on the perceptive Alice. This much-respected teacher may have been the model to which Alice aspired during her own teaching career.

Soon after the girls began school, Agnes discovered she was pregnant. Robert and Agnes considered such information unsuited to share with children until it could no longer be ignored, and neither was the process a fit subject to impart to impressionable young ladies. In the spring of 1912, Alice, going on nine, was not impressionable, nor unobservant, but remained unaware of her mother's advancing condition. Alice had no idea she would have a new sibling by late June. The usual schoolyard peer-information-service corrected her ignorance.

One day at the privy, Ethel, one of the older girls, "collared" Alice, and gave her all of the gory details. Alice, affronted by this impromptu lecture on the birds and the bees, asked the informant how the baby got out of her mother's stomach.

"They use an axe," said the malicious Ms. Ethel.

Alice, shaken and fearful, believed her mother could die, but kept her distress to herself. She did not confide in Agnes or Robert, and, like Agnes, she was not one to trouble other people with her fears.

1959: Gordon River–Hell Bound for Repentance

Summer arrived, and for once, warm sunny weather coincided with my father's vacation. My parents packed the station wagon with tent and gear, my sisters, the dog, and me. Miracle Beach, one of our favourite campgrounds, has become our temporary home.

On the beach, I have found an incredible driftwood log with gnarly roots, and one of these looks like a horse's head. From a piece of tent-pole string, I have made reins for my fabulous steed. We have spent hours leaping wide gullies and galloping across a prairie of waving grass. I should be in heaven, but I can barely lift my head.

Friends, who were neighbours when we lived in Chemainus, are camping here too, and I have renewed my friendship with Lisa, who is my age, and her sister Marilou, who is two years older. There is nobody Marilou's age, so she plays with us, and being older, she naturally knows much more than Lisa or me.

Yesterday we waded in the tide pools, and I don't remember how the topic came up, but Marilou mentioned God and how there is a Heaven and a Hell. I learned about Heaven and God in Sunday School in Chemainus, but I don't remember anything about Hell. Marilou told me that if I were bad, I would go to Hell. I looked at Lisa with my mouth open, but she nodded. They said that all bad people go to Hell: a hopeless underworld of eternal smoke and flames, populated with evil demons. I would roast there forever. If I were bad, of course.

Well I know I am bad. I tease my sisters, I throw rocks, I hide my peas in the plant pot on the windowsill, and this spring I forgot our dog in the stumps. Poor Paddy. I left her tied there, went with my friends, and forgot her until Dad came home from work. Because she always waits for him on the porch, wagging and wiggling, he asked me where she was. I felt sick. With supper on the table, I couldn't disappear to get her. I thought I might jump out my window after bed and bring her home, but realized that not only would I not be able to get back into the house, but Dad wasn't about to sit down and eat without finding our dog. I hoped Paddy had bitten through the rope and would be back on the porch any second, but I knew she had not, so I told Dad.

Without a word, he found the flashlight, and I led the way. I knew where to go, and even without the flashlight, I could have found my way along the path between the stumps to the place I had tied her. She was there. Her white apron front and eyes shone in the light. With her usual doggy smile, she pranced on her front paws and leapt about when I untied the rope. The dejection I felt outweighed my fear of the consequences, but I knew I was in big trouble. Paddy, who was no doubt hungry and thirsty, did not seem to bear me any resentment, but Dad was not so forgiving. He took my cherished rope, that had the handy eye spliced into one end, and balled it up in his fists. I knew I would never see it again. I cried when I went to bed, feeling I deserved to be miserable not only for neglecting my dog, but for upsetting my family. I know I am going to Hell.

It was still on my mind when I woke this morning, and I have spent most of the day by myself. I haven't been able to eat, and I am trying to play, but instead of a wild black horse galloping over endless grassy prairie, my horse is just a root. All I see is fire. At supper, Mum asks if I am okay, and I want to ask her about Hell, but if I am going to Hell anyway what can she do?

* * *

We have been home for a few weeks, and it is almost time to go back to school. I have not mentioned to anybody what I learned about Hell this summer, but I am less worried. It feels like a long time ago, and I have come to suspect Marilou may not know everything.

But, from now on, when Mrs. Marlatt leads us in the Lord's Prayer, I will keep my head bowed and my eyes closed.

1912–1913: The Taint of Failure

While Alice worried about her mother and the birth of the baby, the house construction proceeded, and before June, the family moved into their new home. Agnes kept Alice busy helping her paper walls and hang new curtains, but Alice still did not reveal her fears.

On the day Agnes' baby gave notice of imminent arrival, Alice and her siblings were packed off to neighbours, leaving her mother in the hands of the midwife, Mrs. Johns. Baby girl Jessie joined the family June 29, 1912. The following day tornadoes struck the City of Regina, the event described in the Regina papers as "a cyclone." The disastrous anomaly destroyed over four hundred buildings, killed twenty-eight people, and injured many more. The extreme weather event coinciding with the arrival of Jessie may have been prophetic, as Jessie grew up to be a young lady with a mind of her own, and although she did not wreak the havoc of a cyclone, she was spunky and strong-minded.

Agnes was in her thirty-third year when she delivered Jessie. Her survival and quick recovery relieved Alice, and she realized she had been the victim of a cruel joke. Still, women often died in childbirth, and Alice bore her own children in rural Manitoba during the depression when services for expectant mothers were in short supply, and the money to pay for such services, where they existed, was in even shorter supply. To remember how her mother had survived the birth of five children must have been reassuring. That summer Alice, Laura, and Ray filled their days with the usual routine of chores and play, rounded out with the novelty of a new baby sister.

When Alice and Laura returned to school in the fall of 1912, Miss MacMillan was no longer there. Many young teachers, as magnets for young farmers in need of wives, found themselves with husbands and households soon after their teaching careers commenced. A new teacher was in charge. With her knitting in her lap and ruler close by, she smacked whoever was not working on their lessons. It did not enter Alice's head to complain to Robert and Agnes.

She looked forward to the annual Christmas box from 'Grandma' and 'Grandpa' McCullough. The McCulloughs had kept in close contact with Agnes, and were perhaps closer to Alice and her siblings than their actual grandparents.

The McCullough's parcels helped Agnes cope with the expenses of a growing family. Their contributions were a source of luxuries the family couldn't afford or were unavailable in local stores. That year the Christmas box did not disappoint, and one of Alice's gifts was a special pencil, an 'Eversharp.' She took it to school.

This item was much coveted. Alice loaned it to a fellow student, who took more time than Alice liked to give it back. Wanting her pencil, Alice poked her. The hawk-eyed teacher saw her, and Alice received a strapping. Alice refused to say she only wanted her pencil back, and the discipline-bent pedagogue was not one to investigate.

As the school year wore on, Alice became the recipient of more disciplinary action when she began having difficulty following the lines while reading. The more Alice stammered and lost her place, the more the ruler was applied. The despised teacher was one of the few who never married, and Alice later observed this had everything to do with her unremitting bad temper. Under such dubious instruction, Alice failed grade two.

Alice did not say how her family reacted to the news, nor did she elaborate on any teasing she may have received from other students, but the humiliation of being perceived as unintelligent probably stayed with her all her life. Although a full year older than Laura, she was now a year behind her. In the Rocanville School, she may have been the only ten-year-old in grade two.

R.Rigsby

1961: Gordon River–He Who Fails

Crickets chirrup in frantic chorus, a chain saw whines in the distance, and a slow breeze raises hot red dust in lazy spirals on the school path. Because of the unseasonable heat, logging crews are on early shift, and the fathers who live in camp will be sure to find refreshment in the 'men's pool' of the river before going home. In the stumps, the bracken is still the bright green of early summer with many shoots still unfurling, and the air is full of drifting cottonwood fluff from late-seeding trees. Laundry flaps on lines, and a mother with a toddler in tow, bumps a baby carriage home from morning coffee at a neighbour's. Nothing points to the air of excitement within the school as the final day of the school year creeps toward dismissal.

Still confined to our desks, we envision endless days in our stumpy playground: building forts, throwing rocks, running, biking, and acting out all manner of pretending and make-believe. On this verge of summer vacation, the very air pulsates with our anticipation. The fire door is open, and in the rectangle of blue sky, swallows dive and swoop.

After dismissal, I will be as free as the swallows.

Mrs. Marlatt has spent the last few days after class washing everything, including the floors. We helped lug all of the desks from one side of the room to the other, so she could scrub, wax and polish. The aroma of Johnson's Wax fills the air. We straightened books and took down the year's artwork. We pounded brushes, dusted ledges, and wiped chalkboards. Our desks, emptied of papers, scribblers, and crayons, are clean of eraser crumbs, stubs of pencils, and forgotten recess snacks. We polish the seats every day with our own seats, but we have dusted the frames and wiped the desktops. No sticky fingerprints and not a smear of Crayola remains. Mrs. Marlatt will leave for Saskatchewan early tomorrow, and the schoolroom must be ready for the first day in September.

At a word from Mrs. Marlatt, we take our seats and clasp our hands on the desktops. I rub the sweat and grime on my fingers, promising myself to wash at home, even as I smell the green things outside and think about braving the icy kiss of the swimming hole. I am finished grade five, so the last day of school is routine: chores, report cards, and then say goodbye to Mrs. Marlatt. I will spend a few minutes with my friends while we compare each other's reports for the best marks and the nicest comments, but afterwards the entire year will be a fading memory. We all expect to pass to the next grade.

We are amazed when, instead of handing out all report cards and sending us off into summer with good wishes, Mrs. Marlatt hands out one report card only–to one boy. Nodding, but with his eyes down, he takes his report card in its decorated folder, and alone, goes out the door. With her back to us and hands on hips, Mrs. Marlatt watches until the boy is well up the path. It is not yet noon, and the sun casts narrow beams on the row of gloxinias. She turns to face us. We sit unmoving with our mouths hanging open, but the look on her face indicates it would be best to close them.

*She tells us the boy has failed. We hear stern words on what it means to fail and how difficult it is for any student to repeat a year. She tells us we must not, in any shape or form, tease the boy who failed. Some people need more time before they are ready to move on. She will **not** be well pleased if she learns somebody teased the boy.*

We understand. Bug-eyed and nodding, we promise that not a peep will be uttered from any of us.

1913–1914: Perspective on War

It was another teacher, Miss Connor, who realized Alice was in desperate need of glasses and spoke to Agnes. After a visit to Dr. Ferg in Moosomin, Alice received her first spectacles, chosen for their silver rims. Glasses resolved Alice's reading difficulties, and spared her further discipline of the likes of the ruler-wielding teacher. No wonder this particular teacher stood out in Alice's mind as an example of how not to teach.

When not in school, Alice and her siblings each had farm chores, which increased in accordance with their ages. From age eight, Alice made her bed, helped with the milking, and cleaned the separator before going to school in the morning.

Early in 1914, Robert expanded the dairy with the start of what would become a large herd of purebred Holsteins. This early milking duty was the means whereby Alice became a top-notch milker who could produce foam on top of the pail. Tending cattle and helping with chores in winter when the temperature dipped and the wind blew was far different from the balmy warmth of summer, so there was compelling motivation to become skilled and speedy at milking. As she matured, Alice accomplished every task with a brisk economy of motion.

The whole world, including the Blair family, paused in whatever motions were taking place when "the shot heard 'round the world" rang out on July 28, 1914. Alice was not yet eleven when the Great War began, and although there was no immediate impact on the household, she was mature enough to understand the seriousness of the cataclysm. There was no radio, but newspapers reported the clash of the great powers and the succession of events as hostilities escalated. With her fervor for reading, and now outfitted with glasses, Alice read the newspapers and shared her parents' concern for the country and the fates of enlisted friends and family. It made a lasting impression.

1960: Gordon River–Uniting Nations with Hallowe'en

Dag Hammarskjold. This is the name–at least I think it is a name–Mrs. Marlatt writes on the blackboard. We have been discussing the two World Wars and Canada's participation, and have learned how Canada is often a peacekeeper in places where there are fights. We have learned about the League of Nations, and how this early organization, formed after the First World War, led to the United Nations.

I glance around the room and then stand to take a quick peek out the window. Although the sky is the usual grey, and I can't see the mountains, it isn't raining.

Hallowe'en is almost here, and I can hardly wait. This year we will again carry UNICEF boxes for pennies, along with our baskets and bags for treats. We can expect excellent treats because every wife in camp knows exactly how many children there are, and nearly every one of them prepares a plump bag for each of us. Our enthusiasm for trick-or-treating won't be dampened by rain, but we do hope for a rainless night, or at least one of drizzle rather than deluge.

This year I will be a wizard, and my mother, as always, is making my costume. She has found some slinky shiny material that flows when I walk, and she is making a pointy hat out of cardboard. My sister's gumball machine covered in aluminum foil will become my crystal ball, and I will wear a mask of big glasses with a nose and moustache. I will look like the wizard from Disney's 'The Sorcerer's Apprentice.'

*Positive I have the prize-winning costume, I think about the party in the community hall after trick-or-treating. I love our hall. With its high ceiling, walls of knotty pine, and floor of polished fir, the airy space never fails to make my stomach flutter. It will be decorated with orange and black crepe paper, pumpkins, and black cardboard witches on broomsticks. There will be hotdogs and games. I can almost smell coffee and the scents of damp clothing, boiling wieners, and wood paneling. This year I have **not** told my friends what I am going to be. One year Mum worked for days on a pirate costume for me, but I made the mistake of telling a friend. Much to my surprise and disappointment, and probably my mother's too, I was one of four trick-or-treating pirates. Although I thought I had the best costume, the judges didn't agree, and I didn't win the prize.*

Mrs. Marlatt calls for our attention, including the 'little people.' She never calls us anything but 'people.' She told us that, unless we are goats, saying 'kids' is incorrect. My woolgathering on Hallowe'en and language ends when Mrs. Marlatt explains how Mr. Hammarskjold is the Secretary General of the United Nations, which is a very prestigious position in an important organization working to keep peace in the world. The two World Wars were devastating and caused so many deaths that nobody wants another. There are still problems in many parts of the world, and some countries are having trouble becoming democracies like Canada.

* * *

After supper, I sit with my parents as they watch the news. I lean on the lumpy hassock with a book open in front of me, but glance up when something catches my ear. I listen to Bob Fortune, the weatherman on the only channel we receive, forecast more rain in Vancouver. There is no mention of the United Nations, and I wrinkle my nose. I am disappointed, but still I will ask everybody for pennies for UNICEF.

R.Rigsby

Chapter Five: Education and Wisdom

1979: Leader, Saskatchewan V

"Hello Mother." At the sink, Betty Lou fills the kettle.

Alice pauses to wipe her feet.

"Did you have a nice walk?"

Alice chuckles. "Yes, but it's getting so much cooler in the mornings now. And wouldn't you know I can't find that green sweater I just love."

Betty Lou gives her mother a sudden glance. "I think it went to the Missionary Society Rummage Sale when I helped you move here. But never mind, if you would like a green sweater we will find one for you. We may go to Swift Current in a few days, and we can shop then."

Alice sits at the table and looks at one of the cassettes, turning it over and over, reading both sides. Her brow furrows and her expression is intent.

"Mother, do you want to go on with the story today? Do you feel up to this?"

"Yes, I do." Alice sits up straight and folds her hands in her lap.

Betty Lou places a cup of hot water in front of her mother, and Alice begins.

1915: Naming the Bullies

The war in Europe impacted the news and economy, and Alice's family was aware of the hell-on-earth exploding overseas. The 1916 census reveals a long list of soldiers living in the barracks in Moosomin, many of whom would have been local boys. The Blairs felt the reverberations of war, but daily life went on much as always.

The Blair children underwent the usual give and take of the schoolyard, and when Alice was twelve, she and Laura engaged in a bullying war of their own. As always, the Christmas box from Grandpa and Grandma McCullough had been a treasure chest. Along with the usual snowsuits and fabric, the McCullough grandparents had given Alice, Laura, and Raymond "fancy lunch kits." They were made of shiny painted metal and contained cutlery, dishes, and partitions for food. After Christmas, Agnes packed each one with the fare of the day, possibly bread, cheese, a slice of home-cured ham, a piece of johnnycake, and a not-too-withered apple from the Grahams. Alice and

Laura showed their prized gifts to their friends, and then placed them on the shelf in the cloakroom.

Before the shiny kits could be brought forth for lunch, one "green-eyed firecracker" of a girl got there first and "clouted them off of the shelf." Alice and Laura had no time to rescue their gifts before the girl kicked them, breaking dishes and scattering food. Alice did not say how much aggression she and Laura had already endured from this girl, but ruining the lunch kits was the last straw. They went after her. Laura held her down, while Alice pulled her hair. Another girl counted to ten before they let her up. Although this process could hardly have been silent, the screams of young girls in full fighting mode did not reach the ears of teachers who may have enacted a timely intervention. In any case, the damage was done. Not only were the lunch kits badly battered, but Alice and Laura had no lunch fit to eat.

The news of the attack reached the older students in the rooms upstairs, and some "town" girls traipsed downstairs in convoy bearing chocolate bars. With three or four apiece, and with gratitude for such allies, the Blair girls munched through the rewards of the righteous.

The sisters didn't relate the day's events to Robert when he came for them in the buggy, but he noticed the damaged lunch kits. With his usual composure, he handed Dolly's reins to Alice and went into the school. He did not mention the matter on the drive home. After Alice showed her lunch bucket to her mother, her parents had a private conversation, and Robert repaired the damaged kits as much as possible.

The next morning at school, Alice's adversary, pointing to her bald patch, told Alice she was going to tell the teacher that Alice and Laura had pulled out her hair. Alice was scared. Before the recitation of the Lord's Prayer, the girl waved at the teacher and snapped her fingers, to which the teacher responded by sending her to the principal's office. When she came back sniveling, the teacher told her she had received her just desserts.

Although nobody in the Blair household mentioned the incident for many years, Alice later learned that when Robert went into the school, the older girls told him what had happened. In spite of her views on tattling, Alice concluded this story with the observation that she believed they had done the right thing. Justice was served based on witness testimony, rather than the whining of the aggrieved.

1958: Gordon River–Sticks, Stones, and No Names

The incessant rain of the past few November days has slowed to an intermittent drizzle, but with low clouds and no breeze from downriver, this will be a short respite. As certain as it is autumn, there will be more rain.

Life in camp on this Saturday follows the pattern orchestrated by geography, custom, and necessity. Some families have gone to town for supplies, while others enjoy the break from weekday routine at home. There is no overtime for the men today, and no lines of wash squeal over the roadways.

Dad cooks this morning and we laugh as he sings 'The Yellow Rose of Texas' and a few other ditties while he stirs sausages, flips pancakes and plops dishes, butter, and syrup on the table. Dad is not a singer, but his cheerful tunes show his 'all's right with the world' nature. We devour pancakes, and afterwards, my sisters find something to do in their room. Dad, with plans to hunt deer tomorrow, cleans one of his guns, and Mum goes to her sewing machine with her latest project.

With a Hallowe'en sucker stuck in my mouth, and the smell of gun oil in my nose, I don boots and red hooded raincoat, and go looking for my friends. The twins have gone to town with their parents, but I find Jeff at home.

Jeff and I ramble around camp all morning, and then go down to the river to see how high it has risen. As we expect, the waterfall is a roaring torrent. When the river is lower we can cross by way of the rocks above the falls to the island, but today there is not a rock above water. We throw sticks and watch them plunge over our imaginary Niagara Falls. Tiring of this, we resume our ramble following the trail that winds through the stumps below the houses. The big boys appear on the bank above us. One of them throws a rock, and I know we should ignore it and keep going.

We know we should not throw rocks at each other, and we wouldn't dare do it in the schoolyard, but Jeff and I begin throwing, as best we can, rock-for-rock while ducking and dodging. The rocks are not large; most are about the size of a crabapple. The big boys are in a better position, because not only are they on higher ground but they stand on an endless supply of ammunition. Down in the stumps, there are plenty of rocks, but they lie buried in the matrix of sticks, roots and earth.

We laugh and call taunts. I can't throw a ball or a rock for any good distance, so most of my rocks fall short of the targets. Jeff is better, but it is hard throwing uphill. I peer out from under my hood at the 'enemy' and then bend down to pick up a good rock landing at my feet. My hood falls over my eyes, and when I stand up, gripping my rock, I lift my hood in time to see a black blob right in front of my face. The blob looks fuzzy around the edges, but isn't at all soft and thwacks me on the head, just at the edge of my left eyebrow. An explosion of pain in my head is followed by a cascade of blood over my eye.

I yell and clutch my head, but blood streams down my face and down the front of my raincoat, red on red. With the help of the boys, who are now all on my side, I scramble up the bank. Because they saw my mother walking the school path, they take me to Mrs. Marlatt's. I am still yelling when we reach her door, and she must have heard us coming because she has it open when we get there.

Mum looks at my head and applies a washcloth to the cut. I imagine it must be clear across my forehead, but she assures me it is small, but bloody. My sobs subside in unison with my fear. Neither Mum nor Mrs. Marlatt asks too many questions, but I can tell by the look on Mrs. Marlatt's face she knows exactly what we were doing. I don't say a word. Naming who threw the first stone won't earn more sympathy, and by the looks on the boys' faces, they, as well as I, have received just punishment.

1915: Sew Tease Me

The episode of the lunch kits was not a singular event, and perhaps there was jealousy toward the recipients of expensive gifts from the McCullough grandparents. Teasing and bullying were as much of schoolyard life then as now, and Alice was particularly sensitive to this. She told Betty Lou how unprepared she was to handle taunts and bullying, and she wanted to ensure her children learned to manage derision and harassment. Tattling was not an option.

Alice and her sisters were also teased about wearing hand-me-downs and remakes, as the McCullough's boxes often included

Grandma McCullough's retired dresses, suits and coats. Considered outmoded in the east, these were still in excellent condition. Some garments Agnes and her daughters wore, and others they pulled apart. Then, often without a pattern and only referring to the Eaton's catalogue for guidance on fashion trends, they crafted snappy new outfits from the fine materials. Teased about her re-made, re-cycled, or handed-down clothing, Alice learned to ignore the comments. She wore her second hand and remade wardrobe with her head held high.

1962: Gordon River–Second Hand Rose.

Before the sun dries dewy lawns, famished robins sprint through the grass, then halt with heads cocked. They chirp advice on where the best worms stir. Spring has arrived with the robins, and this Monday morning surges with spring promise. Among the stumps, bracken fiddleheads push through the wrack of last season's growth, and rosy buds on flowering current bulge. In the Stephens' yard, sumacs unfurl sensuous leaves, and the Virginia creeper on the antenna post sends out inquiring tendrils. A limb of the fir tree outside a bedroom window brushes the glass with soft bright green needles.

The fir tree scratching my window prods me from sleep, but it's the memory of the dress hanging in my closet that pops me out from under the covers. Yesterday, we visited my grandmother, and she gave my mother a box of clothes from my cousins. In it was the dress.

My cousin wore it, but I don't think it was her favourite. It is light blue, has a white collar, and a row of gold buttons down the front. Although most comfortable in corduroys and running shoes, I held my breath at the sight of this dress. Last night, although we arrived home late, Mum set up her ironing board and pressed out the few wrinkles.

* * *

My new dress receives comments as soon as I hang up my coat. I can't help the smile on my face when I skip to my desk. Mrs. Marlatt admires my dress too. She asks if she can feel the fabric, and I am happy to let her do so. I tell her about the box of clothes from my cousins, and that this dress is my favourite. She smiles and says she also used to receive dresses she just loved and how she felt so very lucky. I should be proud to have cousins who send me nice clothes.

After school, I walk with my friends and tell them this dress is just one of several new garments I have received courtesy of my cousins. In the box are two cardigans, a brown dress, a pleated skirt, and a short-sleeved blouse that will be perfect for summer. There are some shoes too, but these don't fit me, and my mother will either keep them for my sisters or send them to my other cousins. Nobody says anything, and feeling as though more should be said, I say again that it is a very **big** *box, and I'm not sure we have seen everything in it yet. We part outside my gate, and agree to meet in my yard after changing into play-clothes.*

Waiting, in plaid shirt, corduroy overalls, and runners, I sit on the swing and push myself back and forth without putting too much effort into it. Looking at the gravel under my feet, I wonder if we should go down to the river, climb on the slide in the playground, or just run and play horses. Then I hear them singing . . .

"Secondhand shoes, secondhand clothes,
They all call her Secondhand Rose . . ."

My head jerks up. I suppose I should have been ready for this; I have been teased before about wearing my cousins' clothes, but I have never heard this song. They walk through our gate, laughing as they sing, and they laugh harder when they see my face. I stop swinging. In fact, it feels like everything stops. And then, it feels like everything starts again in double-time. My heart beats in my ears, my face heats, and my fingers grasp the ropes as if I am hanging from a cliff.

I look down at my feet. I see the ground exactly where it should be.

It isn't easy at first, but I look up at them and laugh. Then it is easier, and we all laugh together. It is a funny song and a catchy tune and . . . it really doesn't matter. Mrs. Marlatt used to wear secondhand clothes, and she said she was always proud of them.

I'm not sure if 'proud' is what I feel, but my cousins do own pretty clothes.

1916–1918: A Time to Forget

The McCullough's boxes helped during the war years when necessities were not only hard to find but were expensive. Clothing herself and three growing girls, as well as Ray, tested Agnes' budget during good economic times, but when cash was tight, new clothing was at the very bottom of the priority list. Grateful for their generosity, Agnes used or shared everything in the marvelous McCullough boxes: gifts, fabric, clothing and shoes.

Alice and her siblings usually went barefoot in summer, but one year Alice received a new pair of lace-up boots that were the teen girl's dream of 1916. Enraptured with her new boots, Alice wore them one afternoon while playing with her sisters and neighbours.

Their ventures took them to the shallow slough where they launched an empty horse trough to serve as their make-believe ocean liner. Alice took a turn to paddle when suddenly the faulty craft sprang a leak and began to sink. There was no time to paddle to shore. Knowing they would not be replaced, Alice was not about to spoil her new boots, and chose to remain in the sinking trough with her feet propped on the edge. The rest of her went down with the ship. Fortunately, the slough was not deep and the trough hit bottom before it was full. Alice sat in the bilge, feet high and dry, and refused to move until her friends rescued her boots.

Play was important, but as she matured, Alice had taken on more chores at home. In September of 1916, at thirteen years, she was practically an adult. Although her parents protected her from some facts of life, they never babied her or her siblings, and when it came to bearing their shares of work on the farm, everybody pulled their load.

Alice shared the grief of those who lost friends or relatives in the war, and felt other sorrows closer to their family. In 1916, Robert's father, William, died at the age of eighty-one, outliving Robert's mother by six years. Alice did not say if her family attended the funeral, and she might have recalled with some chagrin how, after the funeral of Grandma Blair, she and Laura had buried apples in the orchard and sang under the trees.

Although the times were uncertain, there was no uncertainty regarding the growth of children. Jessie was a child, but Alice, Laura, and Ray were adult-sized, and the family of six, plus cousin Bob when he was home, filled the small house. Before the close of 1916, Robert began work on yet another new house. It was much bigger than the 1912 structure destined to become the chicken coop.

The more elaborate house featured two stories. The front door opened onto a short entry from which the staircase rose to the second floor, and a hall led to the kitchen, the largest room. The modest living room opened off the kitchen, as did a lean-to structure serving as summer kitchen, storage area, and mudroom. Upstairs were four bedrooms but no bathroom. The privy remained outside. In the basement, a new furnace vented to each room, but coal was considered too costly, hence the furnace was used only on the most bitter of winter nights. Notwithstanding Robert's economical attitude to central heating, the newest house was many times an improvement over the original log cabin and its 1912 replacement. Robert, again assisted by Bob Dorsey, attended to every detail with his usual precision right down to the stairway newel post and its decorative cap.

Robert financed the improved living conditions on the success of his growing herd of purebred Holsteins. Where many of his more conservative neighbours grew only seas of grain crops, Robert the risk-taker had sailed into a mixed farming model. The risk had paid off.

During the war years, a time of uncertainty, grief, and fear, Alice grew from a child to a teen of fifteen. Along with her family and their neighbours, she experienced the shortages in certain staples such as sugar and tea, but understood how these inconveniences paled compared to the deaths of those in the forces, or the suffering of the survivors who returned home damaged in body or spirit. They received the news of the armistice declared for November 11, 1918 with relief and hope.

1961: Gordon River–A Day to Remember

On the west coast, the Gordon River pours its tribute into San Juan Bay where Pacific rollers, driven by a southwest breeze, break onshore in explosions of froth. The breeze strengthens and marshals tentative gusts into a confident force. Retreating clouds flee, lose their hold on each other and disperse in shreds. The wind rises up the Gordon River Valley, chasing the remnants up and over the mountaintops until they dissolve into nothingness.

The break in the weather this November afternoon is a surprise. The morning clouds blew away on the warm breeze from downriver, so I stand in the schoolyard and lift my face to sniff the wind. I know it comes from the west coast and I fancy I smell salt water. Dad calls it the 'salt chuck,' and I envision waves pounding a sandy beach. But there is no time to indulge seashore fantasies, as Mrs. Marlatt opens the door and waves us inside.

This afternoon she speaks to the entire school, continuing the topic of nations and statehood. We have discussed how countries quarrel over land, resources, and 'rights,' that sometimes lead to wars. We talk about the sacrifices of Canadian soldiers. In the Great War, there was 'trench warfare' where men, mired knee-deep in filth and mud, fought and died. Few had shelter from the weather, and even so, they were victorious in such battles as that for Vimy Ridge. We talk about Dieppe, the World War II battle where many brave Canadians died on the beach. We observe Armistice Day on November 11 to remind us of the terrible waste of war.

Mrs. Marlatt tells us this year we will hold a Remembrance Day Tea, and we will invite our mothers.

After school, I walk home with my friends. They chatter about what to do next, but I look up at the sky. The wind has died, clouds are creeping about the mountaintops, and there will be more rain before dark. It will be chilly and wet tonight, and I wonder what it would be like to live in a trench far from a warm living room and cozy bed.

* * *

Today we observe Remembrance Day. We have made poppies out of construction paper for each person to wear, and there are more decorating the room. We pushed the desks against the walls to make room for card tables, including my mother's, which Dad carried down last night. They are covered with bright floral cloths and set with china cups and saucers, tiny spoons, and folded serviettes. The tables look as fancy as those in the restaurant where Mum and Dad took us for dinner as a special treat. Each table has a plate of cookies and squares. My mother's baking is there, and I will look for my favourites when it is our turn to sit down. Although she assures us we already have good manners, Mrs. Marlatt reminds us of the etiquette of serving a formal tea.

She goes to her kitchen to check on the kettle, and I look out the window to see a few mothers, wearing raincoats and kerchiefs, making their way down the hill. We will serve the tea and then at 11 o'clock we will have a prayer and a recitation, followed by 'Oh Canada.'

***

Our mothers sit at the tables where there are now be-cozied pots of tea. We giggled as we met them at the door, pinned their poppies, and escorted each to a chair. Laughter, conversation, and tinkling spoons fill the room, but all hush when Mrs. Marlatt, with authoritative clicks of her lace-up pumps, steps to the front of the room. Looking at her watch, she invites us to stand. At exactly 11 o'clock, with arms at our sides, we bow our heads for two minutes of silence. Then Mrs. Marlatt leads us in the Lord's Prayer, and after 'Amen,' we sit down.

Christine, who is very accomplished at recitation, goes to the front of the room. She has a good strong voice and doesn't appear nervous, but, just watching, I am nervous enough for both of us. Christine stands up straight, and with a deep breath, as she has practiced for days, begins:

'In Flanders Fields the poppies blow,
Between the crosses row on row'. . .

Chapter Six: The Craft of Life

1979: Leader, Saskatchewan VI

Leaves swirl in the back yard, fall, and are again whipped into coils. Alice watches as she stands at the counter chopping supper vegetables. She narrated more of the story in the afternoon, and recalled her relief when the Great War ended. She was still only a girl then, with many chores, but her parents had allowed her to follow her interests, and develop a social life in keeping with her maturity.

They might have been a bit more forthcoming on certain aspects of that maturity she thinks, as she dumps chopped turnips into a pot. I used to read at every chance, but not one book was a help in that matter.

I still enjoy reading. And singing. And dancing. I think I can still dance. Nobody has dances as often as before, so I will have to wait for the next wedding and see what I can do.

Alice frowns at the carrots she washes under the tap. She pauses with a carrot in her hand and looks out the window. Instead of swirling red leaves, she sees swirling red skirts.

1918–1919: Words, Not Deeds

Because of their isolation and inherent conservatism, the Blairs had limited entertainment options. Card games, singing, the joys provided by Bob's gramophone, and books, helped pass the winter evenings. Alice loved to read, and was rarely without a book in front of her face.

When winter yielded to spring, Alice's family indulged their passion of the season: baseball. Robert granted himself time-out from the dairy to play with his children, but while Jessie, for one, was a natural athlete and could "run like a deer," Alice was hopeless.

Alice much preferred to have her head in a book, but once gave in to her siblings' pleas to join them. She couldn't hit a pitch to save her life, but on this occasion she got four balls. She was so excited at the prospect of taking a base, she threw the bat behind her, and Robert, taken off-guard, caught the flying bat in his mouth. Two of his front teeth were broken, but Robert pulled the dangling incisors himself saying, "That's alright Alice, I can do without those teeth!"

He went for a long time gap-toothed until Agnes persuaded him to see a dentist. Alice never played baseball again, and never lost her life-long love for the printed page.

1962: Gordon River–Words Indeed

Close-hanging January clouds veil the mountains and weep a misty drizzle. With nary a snowflake, it was another 'green' Christmas in camp, and the snow at higher elevations hasn't resulted in any lost logging days. However, winter is far from over, and any loss of work, and income, will affect the purchase of clothing for growing children, gas for family cars, and food on kitchen tables. None in charge of family budgets are breathing easily yet.

In the schoolroom, nobody is paying attention to the weather, or its possible impact on finances. The only clock in the classroom is on Mrs. Marlatt's wrist, but internal clocks and wavering attentions signal it is almost time for the afternoon story.

I finish my writing exercise, and listen to Mrs. Marlatt teach phonics to some little people. I hear nothing new in the lesson, but I like the sound of her voice and the little kids' giggles. Mrs. Marlatt tells them how an 'e' on the end of a word, like 'cake' is silent, but he is bossy and has a whip. He can crack his whip over the 'k' and make the 'a' say his name. Mrs. Marlatt gives each letter its own voice. The 'k' is whiny and pleads not to be whipped, the 'e' has a crackly voice, like the bad witch on the Wizard of Oz, and the 'a' is only too happy to say his name. The little kids laugh, and flip through their readers to find more words where 'e' is the boss. I remember hearing this lesson, and smile while pulling out a book to read.

With unreliable antenna reception and limited television programming on the one channel we receive, reading is often the entertainment of choice for my family. Although I am in grade six and read well on my own, I enjoy listening to Mrs. Marlatt. It is the best reward for a day's work, and I love all of the books: 'Black Beauty,' 'Beautiful Joe,' 'The One Winged Dragon,' and our current story: 'Anne of Green Gables.'

Mrs. Marlatt glances at her watch. She finishes the lesson with the little people and asks them to print a sentence using a word ending in 'e'. She walks between the rows of desks, talking to people and helping them finish. At last, we hear the words, "Books away." The torpor of the afternoon evaporates as we fold scribblers, slap books closed, cap fountain pens, and shove everything into our desks. Alert and ready, we sit straight in our seats, hands clasped on desktops. The person at the top of the middle row moves back to share the seat with the next person, and Mrs. Marlatt sits on top of the vacated desk with her feet on the seat.

Mrs. Marlatt wears a green dress with a broad collar. The skirt is wide and she gathers the folds about her legs, as she opens the book in her lap. I twiddle my thumbs and watch her face as she finds her place in 'Anne of Green Gables.' I know this will always be a favourite book, and I will always hear how Mrs. Marlatt gives each character a special voice. Marilla's crusty voice is comical, and Matthew doesn't say much, but they are as real to me as any person in camp. Anne's adventures have made us laugh and sigh. I wish this story would never end. The previous chapter concluded with Anne winning a scholarship, and although it isn't clear to me what this is, I understand it is a special achievement. Although Anne is happy, she is worried about Matthew, who is not well, and Marilla, who is having headaches.

Mrs. Marlatt looks up. "I'm going to skip ahead to the next chapter, because this one is very sad. In it Matthew dies."

I feel my stomach go hollow. I had a feeling something bad was going to happen. I let out a big breath, and sit back to listen as Mrs. Marlatt reads. It is the final chapter.

'The Bend in the Road,' is the last chapter in 'Anne of Green Gables.' I sighed when Mrs. Marlatt voiced the last sentence and closed the book. It is a story that has remained long on my list of favourites, and long in my heart. As this book was published in 1908, and reprinted many times, Alice must have read it in her youth. Perhaps the story of this plucky girl who, through strength of character and hard work, overcame teasing and economic hardship to win a scholarship, but who made other choices when circumstances changed, had personal relevance. In our community, there were no momentous changes during those years from 1956 to 1964, and the road of our future looked as straight as any envisioned by Anne Shirley. When Alice Marlatt read to us, she had already experienced many bends in her own road.

R.Rigsby

1919–1922: The Dance of Life and Death

Perhaps because of their relative isolation, the Spanish influenza spared the Blair family. The epidemic first appeared in Canada in June 1918, and lasted, intermittently, through December 1920. Over 50,000 Canadians died, and some prairie residents were numbered in the losses. Alice's family was not affected by the 'flu, yet as farm children, Alice and her siblings knew the meaning of death.

When Alice was sixteen, Dolly had been in loyal service for nine years, but was ailing and could no longer work. The death of animals is a fact of farm life, but Agnes and Robert went out of their way to protect their children from the trauma of losing Dolly. Alice did not say if she had known Dolly's suffering would soon be over.

While she and her siblings were elsewhere, Agnes and Robert took the gun and led Dolly out. Together they limped across the empty fields to a dry well where she was shot and buried. The next day the children walked to school.

On the way home, on reaching the slaughterhouse corner, they met their father leading a young horse. Like Dolly, this animal was a strawberry roan, and they christened him 'Sandy.' Filling Dolly's void, Sandy met all farm-horse expectations, and his docile nature was such that he became the children's playmate, especially in summer. Riding him or hitching him to the stone boat to 'play farm' rounded out the usual summertime games. Patient and accepting, Sandy plodded along with their pastimes.

Among summertime sports passions, baseball was king, but with the passing of autumn anything on ice was, and still is, the winter obsession. Ice is one crop the prairies can be relied upon to yield in abundance. Alice received a pair of skates as a child, but she only skated with a chair on the slough.

Agnes and Robert forbade skating at the town rink, and Alice never questioned her parents' edicts. Perhaps as the eldest, she felt she must set an example, thus Jessie's teenage rebellion shocked her. There were nine years between them, and by the time Jessie was in her teens, Alice was away at school and work. Jessie would not be denied the company of the town rink and went whenever she chose.

Robert and Agnes were not hide-bound disciplinarians, but did not explain their reasoning for their rules. Born when Queen Victoria reigned, Agnes and Robert may have been squeamish discussing feelings or conduct, and they may have been a mite overprotective. With Victorian attitudes at the core of their beliefs, neither were they comfortable discussing the facts of life.

Consequently, the mysteries of female biology were not explained to Alice. Nor did she have older sisters, or cousins nearby, who are often a girl's sources of information, even if it lacks details or accuracy. In her mid-teens, she was shocked to discover her monthly cycle had begun. Unaware of this natural female function, she was sure she was going to die when she "woke up one morning in a mess." She called her mother who assured her everything was all right, and explained this normal part of womanhood.

Still, further explanations on the 'birds and bees' were not forthcoming. Agnes' mentioned her next pregnancy only when she could no longer camouflage her girth with loose dresses and aprons.

"You would think it would be okay to tell a seventeen-year-old girl that kind of thing," said Alice.

Roberta Blair was born on September 8, 1920, almost a birthday present for Alice who had celebrated her own birthday the day before. Alice stayed home to help, but was not as fearful for her mother's survival as she was when Jessie was born. Agnes was then in her forty-second year.

Alice, with newly discovered awareness of herself as a woman, continued to apply herself to sewing and needlework. She loved to dress well and was particularly fond of an elegant wine-coloured coat made during her last year of school in 1922. It draped to below her shins and was therefore warm and practical for winter. Nevertheless, Alice was not above the hi-jinks of high school, even when sharply dressed, and while running from teasing boys who were threatening to put snow on her face, she tripped and fell.

The mucky combination of slush, mud, and who-knows-what-else, stained the lower front of her coat, and the only remedy Agnes could administer was to shorten it to above the knees. Although the coat was less functional, Alice wore it for the rest of the winter and for many years to come.

During her last year of high school, Alice developed a recurring ear infection. Her 'bad ear' sent her to seek treatment from Dr. Armstrong in Rocanville, and as Dr. and Mrs. McCullough had befriended Agnes, Alice became a favourite of Dr. and Mrs. Armstrong. The Armstrongs taught her to dance, and if Alice was dismal at sports, she made up for it by dancing. Alice loved to dance. With newly discovered fervour, she learned waltzes, foxtrots, reels and schottisches. Although Agnes and Robert "never danced in their lives" and only went to dances to visit neighbours, they never objected to their son and daughters dancing.

Reading, singing, dancing and sewing were some of Alice's great loves that she enjoyed for many years. Sewing and reading are private and solitary occupations, but dancing is social and active—a perfect way for a lively young woman to meet people and develop conversational skills. Once she learned to dance, Alice never missed an opportunity, and considered dancing a mandatory social grace. It was also first-rate exercise.

1960: Gordon River–Concerted Dancing

Dancing was part of our 'physical education,' although we never called it that, and when Mrs. Marlatt announced a dancing session, she had plenty of help moving desks. She taught us the waltz, the polka, and our favourite Virginia reel, which always became a frenzy of dervishes. From its home beneath the row of windows, the elderly radio-record player pumped music at the height of its volume while we whirled and spun, and shouted and laughed, until we were red-faced and puffing. Mrs. Marlatt taught us to "skip lightly" and to listen to the music to understand the rhythm and timing.

In Gordon River, the social event of the winter season was the Christmas Concert, for which the school contributed a performance. Mrs. Marlatt wrote the scripts for the plays and every child was included. Each of us acted, danced, sang, had a role in the Nativity scene, or some combination of all.

In the fall of 1960, Mrs. Marlatt decided to include a square dance number in the program, and because my parents square danced in the Village of Lake Cowichan, she drafted my mother to help. That year there were enough boys to partner what had become a majority of girls, so with the acquisition of several records, square dancing began. Mum wrote down the calls, playing the records until she had every word. At first, we practiced the unfamiliar movements without the music, but soon we do-si-do-ed and swung our partners as if we had done it since birth.

Mrs. Marlatt decided the feature square dance must be presented with special outfits. My mother was not only the resident dance instructor, but also became the costume-sewing supervisor. In a flurry of industry in the weeks before Christmas, Mum and her minions added square dance skirts to their costume production.

The girls' skirts, made of bright red cotton, trimmed with white dangling miniature snowballs, were set-off with white blouses and red bows. The boys' outfits of red shirts, black pants and white neckerchiefs complemented those of their partners. After a search in Victoria, Mrs. Marlatt had bought the perfect neckerchiefs. Made of a stretchy crimped material, the pricey items required specific cleaning in order to retain their unique shape. One mother didn't follow the laundering instructions and, just before the big night, the neckerchief was turned into a limp white rag. Mrs. Marlatt was displeased, but there was no time to buy another.

Despite the costume discrepancy, it was 'on with the show,' and on the night of the concert, the square dance segment was a rousing success. It was so appreciated that a square dance or a folk dance, or both, was included in the concerts of the following years.

In the spring of 1963, Mrs. Marlatt entered our school in the Cowichan Music Festival. We girls wore full skirts of red felt appliquéd with designs of twining green leaves and white flowers, and again white blouses and red bows. Our partners wore black pants, red shirts and, this time, *black* neckerchiefs.

1963: Gordon River–Dancing With Our Hearts

Waiting behind the stage for our turn to dance, we are sweaty-palmed and dry-mouthed. We danced in front of our families at the Christmas Concert, and practiced for weeks all spring, but none of us has ever danced for such a crowd as is in the Duncan Secondary School Gymnasium. The din from the mass of people fills my ears, and it is hot and humid. There are at least six other elementary schools entered in the square dance competition, and their dancers must be the tallest of all the pupils in their schools. I turned twelve in February, and I am the eldest, but shorter than my friends the twins who have just turned eleven. Two boys are nine, but another boy and girl and my sister Fran are only eight. There are only three boys in school this year, so my friend Kathy is her sister Kelly's partner. The auditorium is huge and the stage enormous compared to our community hall in camp. We have never danced in such a place. Our schoolroom with the desks pushed back or the platform in our hall would fit at least ten times into this gym.

Mrs. Marlatt stands tall and still, and we cluster about like mute chicks. I couldn't say a word if I tried, and I can hear my heart beating. Mum is on the other side of the stage waiting for the nod to start the record. Mrs. Marlatt gives us her special smile and opens her arms like wings, as if to hug all of us at once. She reminds us to smile, to skip lightly, to keep in the centre of the space, and to look like we are having the time of our lives. We will be as wonderful as she knows we can be.

The music starts. Pair by pair we step from the wings to our places. With taut smiles, we skip into our moves on cue. We know each other very well. If somebody missteps, one of us will cover. We have danced this dance a hundred times. Beyond the swirl of red skirts, I see faces in the audience: smiling faces, nodding in time to the music. When the last note ends, and we line up to make our bows and curtsies, the cheers and loud applause astounds us. The adjudicator awards us first place.

Few in the crowd enjoying the bright faces, skipping feet, and lively tune knew the eight kids on stage did not just represent the best from their school, they were virtually the entire school. There were three more little girls, all six-year olds, including my sister, Jo-Anne, to round out the year's enrollment of eleven pupils. We had competed against much bigger schools, but none of them had Alice Marlatt.

Chapter Seven: Charting the Course

1979: Leader, Saskatchewan VII

Alice steps onto the front porch and buttons her jacket. The morning chill nips her ears, and she minds the icy patches on the stairs. The cold air on her face makes her eyes water and fogs her glasses. She stops a moment to wipe them.

The door to autumn has opened a crack, she thinks, and Jack Frost has slipped through.

At the intersection, she looks down the street to the center of town. The elevators stand like pictures cut out with scissors and pasted against the empty sky.

She hopes her memories are as picture perfect as her view of the elevators, because she wants to talk about leaving home for Normal School in Regina. Perhaps because she idolized her first teacher, Miss MacMillan, she had realized in her teens, as had her parents, she had to teach. Many of her friends looked forward to husbands, families and farming. Those same friends batted their eyelashes at certain boys, and seemed content their futures would be much like those of their mothers and grandmothers.

Alice hadn't disliked the picture of herself as a farmer's wife, but she saw herself in a different picture: one with a classroom of children where warm lights glowed on eager faces. In the background were books and maps, artwork, and lessons on blackboards.

When the Normal School accepted her application, Alice's stomach fluttered at the thought of being so far from home. But, as her parents had worked hard to save money for her education, she could not disappoint them.

Laughing at what a 'nervous Nelly' she once was, Alice stops for another look at the elevators before turning for home.

1922-1923: Single in the City

Agnes' parents, John and Mary Ann Grainger, had been at odds for several years, and by the spring of 1911, Mary Ann had ordered John out. This was an exceptional deed in a community of conservative farmers, and Alice did not disclose what excesses or behaviour, by either party, led to the split. The 1911 census lists the Grainger family with Agnes' brother Thomas, aged twenty-eight, as the head of the household. Also listed are his mother, Mary Ann, and siblings Ethel,

Olive, and Dalton. John, at sixty-six years old, is not on the same roll, and may have found work and lodging elsewhere.

When John Grainger turned seventy-five, he may have been unemployable, and may have run out of survival options.

Sometime before the arrival of Roberta in September of 1920, Agnes and Robert had taken John into their home. Agnes' mother and siblings had criticized the Blair's, and this dispute caused a family rift lasting for many years. John Grainger and Roberta had rounded out the Blair household to eight people, and with these additions, it had become a full house indeed.

In the fall of 1922, Alice, age nineteen, thinned out the group when she moved to Regina. With the completion of grade eleven, it was permissible for her to begin teacher training at the Normal School. This new school, part of the newly founded Regina College, was housed in a handsome neo-Gothic building located at the intersection of College Avenue and Broad Street.

Alice had never been alone in a big city. Regina is not a large city today and was much smaller in 1922, but for a farm girl whose experience of 'town' was limited to Rocanville and Moosomin, it was immense. And intimidating. She travelled alone on the train, and the commotion of traffic and people set her nerves on edge. However, resolute on becoming a teacher, Alice found her rooming house and her school.

Constructed in the early 1900s, the house and its neighbours are part of the expanding City of Regina. In 1922 the two story structure is still settling into itself, with a few creaks in its wood frame skeleton. It has a deep front porch and wide stairs descending to a brick walk set between small squares of lawn edged by flowerbeds and a low cobblestone wall. The cosmos and nasturtiums in the flowerbeds are dying away with the cooler days of fall, but the lilac bushes on either side of the steps have had a good year. Strong new growth has a good chance of surviving the winter.

The house will for sure survive another winter, as it is large and well built. It has eight rooms on two levels and one of the upstairs west-facing rooms is home to the newest boarder, a young lady attending normal school several blocks away.

Her room enjoys the last beams of the setting sun on this late September afternoon. Dust-motes shimmer in the retreating shards of sunlight. The closet door is ajar, and slanting rays reveal a few dresses of a modest design and a burgundy coat hanging there. The coat is made of good wool, but is too short, and when winter sets in with its relentless cold and inevitable blizzards, the owner will certainly risk frostbitten knees. Other garments are out of sight in the dilapidated three-drawer chest. There are few other belongings on display. On the washstand, beside the plain white ewer and basin, a brush, a comb, and a jar of face cream crouch together.

Bracketed fore and aft with unembellished iron bedsteads, the narrow bed displays a quilt in blues and greys. The braided rug beside the bed is also in blues and greys, but this coordination owes more to chance than any deliberate décor plan.

Under the window, a narrow table, of the same vintage as the chest, serves as a desk on which reigns, in harmony with the other well-used items in the room, a kerosene lamp. Its realm, much like its ability to cast a good light, is limited to the desktop, and its subjects are a dog-eared dictionary, a tarnished Eversharp pencil, a bottle of ink, and a capped fountain pen. A straight-backed chair stands away from the desk.

From the rod hang, in contrast with the spare utilitarianism of the space, frilly curtains in shell pink lace. Incongruous in their femininity and fussy impracticality, they lift in a sudden draught from the open window. Pink speckles dance over the bed and furnishings.

Earlier today, the landlady stood in the open door of this room and surveyed the window and its yellowed blind. The boarding house is her sole source of income and she minds the coming and going of every penny. Not given to frivolity or indulgence, as she has many student boarders, she keeps a firm hand on all that goes on in her house.

With her fists on her hips and her head cocked to one side, the landlady looked around the room, then turned and puffed up the back stairs to the attic lumber-room. From a trunk where she keeps spare blankets and linens, she exhumed the frilly pink curtains. She shook them out, pressed them, and, this afternoon, between starting the supper stew and beating the dust out of the entry hall rug, she hung them in the young lady's room. The house emits a creak of amusement.

The young lady who left early this morning is seen striding up the street. Arms full of books, lips set in a firm line, and a slight frown on her brow, she gazes at the sidewalk in front of her marching feet. She wears spectacles on her forthright nose and her long hair is arranged in unfashionable buns over both ears. She unlatches and re-latches the front gate with precise movements. Climbing the front steps, she juggles the load of books and fishes in her bag for her key. Once in the hall, the young lady says hello to the landlady. The older woman nods. Spread in her wing chair with her feet propped on a wooden stool, she relaxes with the 'Morning Leader' newspaper before putting supper on the table.

There are sedate footsteps on the stairs, but the last few steps are accomplished with girlish skips. The young student opens the door to her room. A gleeful laugh rings through the stairwell, and the student, still laughing, leans over the balustrade.

"Thankyou for the lovely curtains!" she calls.

"It was nothing, dear, nothing." Smiling, the landlady turns a page of her paper.

Once sorted out in her rooming house, which was an easy walk to school, Alice began her teaching course. She had enrolled in the short course finishing at Christmas, but then John Grainger died. His estate could not have been huge, but he bequeathed Agnes with money for Alice's education. Perhaps John Grainger thought this would atone for the family discord he had caused when Agnes took him in against her mother's wishes. Agnes wrote Alice and told her to take the longer eight-month course.

When not in class or studying, Alice discovered the joys of urban living. This included shopping. The 'Fifteen Cents' store amazed her, and over fifty years later she recalled the Christmas gifts she bought for her family, including a toy flour sifter for Jessie and a doll for Bobbie. She declared she was not homesick. She felt she had a "sentence to put in," and once her training was complete, she could get on with her life as a teacher. Setting aside her impatience to finish the course, Alice welcomed Christmas break.

She was anxious to go home and "jiggled all the way with excitement" on the train. At the sight of Robert and the sleigh waiting at the station, she said, "Oh, was I glad! What a homecoming that was!"

Alice's relief and joy at going home for Christmas may have been sweeter due to a tentative start at school. Although she claimed she had not been homesick, the sudden changes and the company of strangers likely overwhelmed her. The majority of the students were female, but one of her classmates was a young man by the name of Reg Toole who would eventually meet and marry a future friend of Alice. Alice remembered Reg when, years later, they again met, but at the college she only spoke to him in passing, and she did not "flash around with the fancy girls." Alice did not define this description, but she clearly did not consider herself a "fancy girl," nor did she elaborate on what constituted 'flashing around.' Her one friend was a girl who, like Alice, wore her long hair in buns over both ears. Claiming she "did not have charisma like the other girls," Alice was lonely in their crowd. Her stress may have triggered a cold and a persistent cough.

One day in class, the tickle in her throat had erupted into spasmodic coughs. She had tried to suppress the tickle, but the sputters and snorts only made the cough worse, and she had left the room. When she returned, so did the cough, and this time the instructor sent her out. She had been mortified and was sure she would not be allowed to finish the course.

With her determination– "I am not going to be sent home," – Alice had confronted the instructor. Taken aback, he had assured her he would not send her home, and her condition was surely only temporary. He was correct. Alice recovered her health, and her composure.

Alice's recovery from both infection and anxiety helped her focus on her studies. She graduated with high marks and then began job hunting, applying to many school districts including Sultan, North Battleford, and La Porte. She did not explain on how she chose the schools, but it is likely that school districts would have posted openings at the Normal School. Regardless of how Alice learned of vacancies, she hand-wrote all applications. Allowing for postal delivery, a review of her application, and the formation of a reply, the process could have taken several weeks, but early in summer, she received an offer for Rankin School near La Porte. She was jubilant.

Alice accepted the position since her cousin, Bob Dorsey, and his wife, Jessie, lived in La Porte. Bob had become the 'pool elevator man,' and he and Jessie were in Rocanville on their summer vacation when Alice received the good news. As an opportunity to repay the Blairs many kindnesses, Bob was glad to provide Alice with his family's support in her new neighbourhood.

1923: First Job: A Test of Tenacity

In the fall of 1923, Alice began work at the grand salary of eight hundred dollars for the ten-month school year. With eighty dollars per month to cover expenses and to set aside a reserve for the summer months, Alice had to mind her money. She found a place to live at the Dobbs brothers' home, where she met Isabel, one of the Mrs. Dobbs. Her board bought her an upstairs bedroom through which one set of Mr. and Mrs. Dobbs passed to reach their own room. Since Alice and the rest of the family only went to their rooms to sleep, privacy was manageable.

The Dobbs home was within walking distance of Rankin School. There Alice, young, inexperienced, and nervous, stood before about a dozen pupils. She was shaky on her first day. She said this first class was a surprise in that they challenged her to "figure them out," and she decided this particular group of children had had a "looser upbringing" than her generation. She did not give details, but her new class likely tested their new teacher with childhood pranks: perhaps swapping names and seats, claiming outlandish maladies, or hiding the chalk.

For the first time in her life, Alice faced a group of people whose behaviour and actions were her responsibility. She was required to teach the lessons as outlined in the syllabus for each course, but she wanted to impart to each child a love of learning. She wished to equip them for opportunities they might encounter in higher grades, but she wanted them to enjoy the process. She needed to capture their imaginations, focus their attention, sharpen their skills, and make the experience exciting and fun for all, herself included. This was a make-or-break situation. Her future balanced on her performance, nor could she disappoint Agnes and Robert. It was a daunting prospect and, loose upbringing or not, it was imperative she "figure them out."

Alice's natural assets of good humour, caring attitude, and disciplined work ethic came to the fore. With her pupils soon on track, she began to enjoy her freedom and new routine. This included weekend visits to the home of cousin Bob and Jessie. On Friday evenings after school, Bob drove her to his home where she relaxed in the warmth and hospitality of the Dorsey family, no doubt entertained with music and photo sessions.

Although her job was off to an excellent start, Alice's living arrangements did not work out as expected. Within the first few nights she had discovered her straw mattress came with fellow lodgers: bedbugs. When she had discovered her bedmates, she tried to keep them at bay by keeping a light on. There was a new Aladdin brand kerosene lamp for her to use, but its unfamiliar workings made her nervous. Instead, she had lit matches from her stash kept in a cold cream jar. Each lit match had discouraged the critters for a while, but it was no way to get a good night's sleep. The need for sleep, and her thrifty attitude to burning fuel or matches put a stop to the strategy. Bugs one, Alice zero, in the first round of this battle.

Although it was not a long walk to school, it was a nippy autumn and Alice's short wine coat did a poor job of keeping her warm. Tramping home after school one blustery day, Alice was not only frozen, but terrified when she saw far up the road a herd of cattle charging her way. The wind in her ears sounded like the thunder of hooves, but as the rampaging beasts bore down they revealed themselves as "great wads of tumbleweeds stuck together," rolling down the road. Before they reached her, the wind died, the terrible herd run amok dispersed, and she was able to laugh at her fear.

Alice would have taken on a real herd of stampeding bovines if she could have exterminated the bedbugs. One morning, with her feet so swollen from bites, she could not put on her shoes, and could not walk to work. A Dobbs brother hitched a horse to the buggy and drove Alice to school where her students wondered why their teacher padded about their schoolroom in stocking feet. Of course, she would not tell them, as Alice never discussed any personal matters with her students.

Whether sick, troubled, or hurting, Alice presented the same demeanor day after day. Smartly dressed and accessorized, with back straight, hair neat, glasses clean, and smile in place, Alice faced her students with the same mien, no matter what. Her Normal School training may have instilled this approach, or it might have been due to her perception of professionalism, or simply part of her "stiff upper lip" upbringing in which she shared personal discomfort only if necessary, and only with intimates. Children might become upset if their teacher showed distress, and this would never do.

1963: Gordon River–No Substitute

This Wednesday afternoon in early June is warm, but not warm enough to open the fire door, and the schoolroom is stuffy. No windows open, so on days such as this, it is a choice between a too-fresh draught or fusty closeness. The sun shifted westward hours ago, and the room is now in shade. The overhead lights, with their collection of dead flies in the bowls, emit an insipid imitation of the earlier morning brilliance. With summer mere weeks away, the classroom is claustrophobic. Only a few weeks remain in the school term, yet there is much to do before the year is complete, and, despite the students' restive yearnings, the work will be done. The daily story is a welcome marker that the day is over, and noses may lift from the grindstone.

Mrs. Marlatt reads a chapter of 'Owls In the Family' by Farley Mowat, and I laugh until my eyes water. We have also heard 'The Dog Who Wouldn't Be,' which was equally hilarious, so Mr. Mowat is on my favourite author list. Now in grade seven, I find these stories easy reading, but I often re-read favourite books. Some are as gripping after five readings as they were on the first.

Mrs. Marlatt closes the book. She laughs with us often, but today although she smiled, she didn't laugh. She didn't hear the pun I made about 'hoarse' and 'horse.' Several times today, she removed her glasses and rubbed her eyes.

We wait for dismissal, but instead she puts up her hand and asks for our attention before we go. She tells us she will not be here on Friday, and a substitute teacher will be in charge.

* * *

Occasionally Mrs. Marlatt goes to teachers' conferences, but these are rare, and it is even rarer for her to be ill. We have had very few substitute teachers. It is such a novelty that we are always excited to see such a mysterious creature, and we are eager to please.

The substitute teacher drove down the hill this morning while we were on the playground. Soon after she opened the door and rang the bell even though we were all standing right there.

It has been a busy day, and I have almost finished the work Mrs. Marlatt assigned. Soon it will be to time to go home. The younger people also work on their assignments. Some read, and some colour maps for social studies.

Our substitute teacher asks me, and the grade sixes, to review a list of vocabulary words for further discussion. Since most of these words appear to be from the grade six speller, I know them well. I am confident.

I admire this teacher and so do my friends. She has shoulder length blond hair, wears bright lipstick, and her skirt is shorter than anything my mother wears. I find it hard not to stare at her. She has a nice smile, but she has not smiled very much today, although I have tried to be helpful.

She did not thank me when I mentioned we always do math first thing after recess. She has left the morning's work on the chalkboard, has told me to do work I already knew to do, and has spent much of the day seated at Mrs. Marlatt's desk. This new model, of varnished blonde-stained wood, replaced the old white monstrosity a long time ago, and Mrs. Marlatt moved it from the front of the room to its new place behind our desks and nearer the windows. She has a good view across the room and can spot any lollygagging.

The substitute sits at the desk now. I decide she is probably checking Mrs. Marlatt's instructions to make sure everything is finished.

She tells us to close our books, as we will now discuss the word list. She doesn't leave her seat to stand in front of us, and instead, she props her elbows on the desk. She twiddles a pencil in one hand and runs the other through her hair. We twist in our desks to face her, which we have never done before, and we shift legs and elbows to fit the awkward position. One by one, she asks each of us to explain one of the words she reads from the list. I know all of the words my friends explain, and then it is my turn. My word is 'skulk.'

I know very well what this means, but I can't think of a synonym. I am jittery, and, as often happens when jittery, I can't think. Acting on a flash of inspiration, I jump up from my seat and duck beside the radio-

*record player and then 'skulk' from there to the front of Mrs. Marlatt's
desk. I know the action is perfect, and I peer up at this fascinating
teacher, but instead of saying "correct," as she has to the others, she
tells me to take my seat. She tells me she requested a definition, not a
demonstration, and had not given me permission to leave my desk.*

Permission to leave my desk?

*My face floods with heat. Mrs. Marlatt would have enjoyed my
version of 'skulk,' and she would have laughed. Then she would have
helped me find the right synonym. I sit down and stare at the top of my
desk.*

I felt like an ignoramus, a country bumpkin, but I was also
indignant. And the substitute never did tell me, unasked for or not,
whether my demonstration accurately portrayed 'skulk.'

When Mrs. Marlatt returned, she did not discuss her weekend
away. We did not ask. No doubt our parents knew that Agnes died on
Tuesday, June 4, 1963, at the age of 85. Mrs. Marlatt had gone to her
mother's funeral.

1923-1924: The Root of the Problem.

It was a Friday when the mystified Rankin students stared at
their shoeless teacher. That evening, as usual, Bob waited for Alice after
work. Horrified by the condition of her feet, he and Jessie made her soak
them in a bath of Epsom salts and urged her to find another place to
board. Alice declined. She did not want to make a fuss, and was very
fond of the Dobbs, especially Belle Dobbs.

Belle was a kindred spirit. She had been the teacher at Rankin
school the previous year, but had tendered her resignation when she
discovered she was pregnant. This is what had precipitated Alice's
contract, so the two young women shared their teaching experiences,
their stories of students and parents, and became friends. Alice did not
want to upset Belle and, coming from a prairie homestead, she was used
to making the best of discomfort and inconvenience. Before the end of
autumn, her capacity to endure inconvenience was tested even further
when Mr. Dobbs hired a man to help on the farm. The hired man was
housed in the barn, but his wife and baby son joined Alice in her room.
And in her bed.

Yet, it was not the bug infestation, nor the lack of privacy, nor the polar walk to work that finally pushed Alice over the edge. It was the menu. The Dobbs' garden had yielded a bumper crop of carrots, and Alice's lunch was often cooked carrot sandwiches. Carrots, in various forms, were presented with supper. Soon, Alice could not look at a carrot, and after her trial-by-carrot at the Dobbs', detested this homely root into her old age. Before Christmas, the non-stop carrot diet drove her to seek lodging with the Ewing family.

The Ewings accommodated Alice by pulling up a granary to the side of the house. They cut out a door and plugged the gaps–voila: instant home addition, prairie style. A curtain in the doorway ensured Alice's privacy. Compared to the previous shared quarters, with uninvited bedmates both human and insect, her room was like a luxurious retreat at an exclusive resort. In addition, the Ewings provided transport by way of a buggy and a veteran gelding called Baldy, so in style and comfort, Alice and young Winnifred Ewing travelled to school and back. By Christmas Alice was enjoying her new life, but looked forward to going home for the holidays. The new job had come with some unexpected demands on her spirit and energy. She needed a break.

Today the trip is eight hours by car, but then, by train, it was twice as long. With a 1923 perspective on distance, Alice was a long way from home. On the first day of Christmas break, she leapt aboard the train.

After Christmas and time to de-stress at home, Alice happily returned to work. She met her neighbours, made some friends, and joined her new community in the social life of the district. In the spring, neighbours of the Ewings built a tennis court and Alice learned to play. After her unfortunate baseball trials, she finally found a sport in which she excelled. She played the game for years. Alice finished the school year, and the next September she moved on to Bailey School, another one-room school north of La Porte, but continued lodging with the Ewings.

Mrs. Ewing was a quiet, gentle lady, but her husband was more sociable and liked his friends and cards. On his weekly visits to Eatonia Mr. Ewing would occasionally be detained at the beer parlour, and would sometimes forget to buy all of the supplies. Alice confessed to being afraid of him, and at first declined his offer to play cards. She was brought up with the view that "you did not gamble with cards" and was fearful of "contamination." Perhaps recalling that Agnes and Robert played 'Flinch,' and their morals were still intact, she allowed Mr. Ewing to teach her cribbage. In later years, she played cribbage with her husband and children, as well as other card games, including bridge.

She became an avid bridge player, joining other people of similar bent and helping to organize 'card parties.'

1961: Gordon River–In the Cards

In late February, a diluted afternoon sun does its best to brighten the camp. Blue smoke rises from chimneys of the habited duplexes, but not every duplex has a family. The windows of those vacant are smeared with dust, their lawns are thick with overgrown grass, and paint peels from their porches. Children sometimes play in the untended yards, and today three girls spend the remainder of their lunch hour playing 'Snap' on one sunny porch. Others climb the playground slide, but at a word from a mother, they all race back to school. Until dismissal, the slide, the playground, and the porches will remain as forsaken as the vacant houses.

"Books away."

The words catch me by surprise. I know it is not yet time, but puzzled or not, I am not about to question the early reprieve. Since I finished my language exercise, my books are already away, and I work on my cougar drawing. While other people put away books and scribblers, return library books to the shelves, or gather up crayons, I hold my picture at arm's reach, thinking this might help me see why my tawny cat is not right. He stretches out, fangs bared, chasing an unseen deer. Mrs. Marlatt has shown me how to add shading to my artwork, and I darkened some parts, but something is missing. Maybe she will help me tomorrow. I slide picture and pencil crayons in on top of the pile of books and scribblers in my desk.

I jump as a book thumps on Mrs. Marlatt's desk behind me, accompanied by the cap clicking onto her fountain pen. She clears everything from the top of her desk–another puzzle for the day. I know she often works after we are gone because every morning there is new work on the boards.

Mrs. Marlatt says we will start the story a few minutes early because she would like some big people to help move desks before we leave. Now the puzzle comes together. Yesterday at supper, Mum told Dad about the bridge party at the school and asked if he would please carry down the folding card table after work. At lunch today, Mum was in a flurry of baking: cookies cooled on wire racks and a coffee cake was in the oven. While I forked macaroni and cheese into my mouth, I inhaled scents of cinnamon and cardamom, and counted the cookies.

I squelch thoughts on lunch, cookies, or bridge parties, and sit up as Mrs. Marlatt begins the next chapter of Black Beauty. She tells us how she, and her brother and sisters went to school by horse drawn buggy or sled, and how their horse knew how to get them home, even in blowing snow. On the sled her Dad built a box with holes for the reins to pass through, and sheltered from the cold, they rode to school. I squirm in my seat, and think about my imaginary horse. I stroke a hide like warm satin, smell a rich, hay-like aroma, hear the clop of hooves in thick dust, and see the wind ruffle a coal black mane. I know if I had a horse, I would spend every second with him and never tire of caring for him.

My parents pointed out that horses need plenty of space and plenty of grass, and our yard is not big enough to feed a pony, let alone a horse. In Gordon River, the nearest thing to a field is the playground, which has grass but no fence. Mrs. Marlatt continues with the story, and the school fades away as I join Black Beauty on his adventures. The chapter concludes.

We drag our desks to the window side of the room. One boy wrenches his desk; it tips and a pile of scribblers, loose papers, and books slither across the floor, followed by a sprinkling of eraser crumbs, crayon ends, and a bruised apple. He glances at Mrs. Marlatt, but she just nods her head.

"Pick it up, Mr. Dingleberry," she says, and he packs everything, except the crumbs and the apple, back.

"I think tomorrow you people will go through your desks. It might be time for all of us to do some housekeeping!"

She chuckles. We laugh as we finish moving desks and pick up escaped pencils and papers.

Reaching coats and pulling on boots, we thunder out the door like Beauty and his friends. We can continue our horse fantasies on the playground.

1924-1926: Subject to Improvement

Once Alice resigned herself to Mr. Ewing's penchant for card games, she enjoyed her life with the family. She became very fond of Uncle Jack, the "dearest old man" who helped train the workhorses the family raised. The family's investment in dollars and hard work had produced a matched team of four, and the men spent many hours refining their training. A well-trained team not only contributed to the productivity of the home farm, but also when hired out, earned extra income.

One spring afternoon, with her class intent on assignments, Alice glanced out the window at the bordering Ewing field. A group of horses from the Ross property had broken through the fence, knocked a hole in a granary, and were munching on escaped grain. Alarmed, because too much grain can be fatal to horses, Alice sent the Ross boys home to alert their father. She expected to see Mr. Ross and the boys immediately in the field, and the horses in flight for home. When nobody arrived and the horses continued to fill their bellies, Alice dismissed the class. She and Winnifred hitched up the bewildered Baldy for an express drive home.

Mr. Ewing and Uncle Jack rushed to chase the horses back to Ross property, but it was too late and within a few days some horses died. There was a court case. Already sad about the death of the horses, Mr. Ewing did not want Alice to get involved and would not allow her testimony. The Ewings were found to be responsible, and the Rosses received the Ewing's splendid team in payment. Alice was incensed. She told Mr. Ewing he was too kindhearted, but although dejected by the loss of his team, he would not pursue the matter.

In the face of the hard work, the modest living conditions, and the occasional upset like the horse incident, Alice enjoyed her position, her new friends, and new experiences. She made a host of young friends with whom she attended dances in neighbouring towns, as far away as could be reached by horse and buggy.

Alice loved meeting people almost as much as she loved dancing. She met potential suitors, but at the age of twenty, she wasn't ready for 'Mr. Right.' When she spurned the attentions of a young admirer from a local prominent family, she observed her rebuff "got [her] in the soup." She was further unimpressed with this family because of their practice of discussing her in front of their children, who naturally repeated these comments to their peers. The social politics may have been a factor prompting her to resign her position and return to Rocanville to complete her grade twelve.

At that time, it wasn't necessary for teachers to complete grade twelve in order to go to Normal School and then teach, but Alice wanted her diploma. She chose to return to high school and complete her education.

In June, Alice bid goodbye to her pupils, the Ewings, the Dobbs, and her other friends. Several people, like Belle Dobbs, she added to her list of correspondents and they kept in touch for years. After the farewells, she boarded an eastbound train and went home. This was the first of many adieus to many communities where Alice lived and worked, where she made fast friends, and where she made a lasting impression on all who met her. The leave-taking could not have been easy, regardless of Alice's determination to acquire all of her qualifications.

In the fall, at age twenty-two, she joined a class of grade twelve teenagers, and at the same time accepted a position as substitute teacher at the elementary school. She found it difficult going back to high school and not only because of the differences in age and experience between her and her classmates. The mystery of trigonometry eluded her, nor was she enamoured with composition. On the principal's advice, she focused on history and English, which she readily grasped.

Perhaps because Alice was not strong in mathematics, she felt compelled to emphasize its importance to her students. She understood how proficiency in basic arithmetic led to competence in upper level mathematics.

1963: Gordon River–The Subject of Misery

From their source on the coast, wave after wave of April showers roll up the valley and drench the camp. Like the waves on the shore, there is a short lull before each shower, and camp feels like a beach awaiting the next inevitable wave. The sunny days of summer seem far away, and the recurrent rain, when everybody is so very tired of it, manifests itself in edgy nerves.

My day is not going at all well. Mrs. Marlatt is annoyed with me, and it is my own fault. My homework last night was plain: memorize the times-tables up to ten. I must memorize all of my number facts because everything builds on them, including the ratios that are part of the grade seven coursework.

A few minutes ago, we reviewed last night's homework, and within twenty seconds, Mrs. Marlatt knew I was guessing answers. She ordered me to work on some ratio problems and walked to the other side of the room. I dislike making her cross, but I know I have disappointed her, which is worse.

Up until last year, grade seven was high school, but then the school board changed the rules, and grade seven became part of elementary school. This was great timing for my family. It meant we could stay in camp for one more year, but Jeff's parents decided not to stay and moved away last summer.

Therefore, I am the only person in grade seven, and since Mrs. Marlatt has never taught grade seven in British Columbia, she told me at the beginning of the year we must work hard and cover everything. I must be "fully prepared for high school." All other subjects are going well, except for memorizing poems, and even though I am alone in grade seven, my friends sit right beside me in the next row of desks. Every year we have moved over one row to bigger desks, and I am now under the windows, and farthest from the door.

Times-tables should have been set in my head long ago, but memorization is not easy for me. I have no problem with tables one through five, and of course ten times anything is simple. I am getting better at sixes and sevens, but those eights and nines hit a black spot in my brain without a flicker of light. Last night, if I had studied longer, a spark might have taken hold in the dark, but I am re-reading 'Robinson Crusoe,' a Christmas gift from Dad. I finished it before New Year's, but this book deserved another read. Instead of a multiplication grid, I saw a mysterious tropical island, where a shipwrecked sailor struggled to survive among the palms. I convinced myself I had worked enough on times-tables.

I finish the ratio problems and hope most are correct. I let out a long breath and look at the rain streaming down the windows. Over and over, drop upon drop. I decide to have another look at my problems, and sure enough, I find a mistake. Erasing every smudge, I try again, hoping to see Mrs. Marlatt smile before I leave today.

R.Rigsby

Chapter Eight: The Launch of a Profession

1979: Leader VIII

Alice opens the window in her room, rests her arms on the sill, and chuckles.

At supper, Art joked that she had a good appetite and "the Old Walrus" assured him she has ever appreciated a good meal. She always smiles when she thinks of Art. They have had this "Old Walrus" joke for a long time and she was glad he teased her. Some people, close family included, at times treated her as if she had suddenly developed the thinnest of skins, had no wits, or could no longer understand a joke.

Alice looks at her arms on the sill.

The foreboding chill of the morning gave in to the afternoon sun, and it is a warm evening. Alice ponders how prairie weather rules so much of what happens in their lives. It is always a source of anxiety for farmers, but it matters to town folk too. Everybody prays there will be enough moisture over the winter to ensure a good harvest, that the summer rain will be just right, and that a succession of very hot days will not herald the destruction of hail or grasshoppers. Those not farming rely on productive farmers, and still look to the heavens to foretell conditions from the combination of clouds, scents, and prevailing wind.

Alice looks to the sky now, but it is innocent of suspicious clouds signifying a possible change in the weather. The organic smell of cut grass and dying leaves mingles with that of roast beef and onions.

Supper was late. They had waited for Art, who had been delayed on the farm he works with his brother, Bud.

It won't be long before that farm is put to bed for the winter thinks Alice.

After supper, Art tackled his desk where he shuffled through farm bills and paperwork while Alice and Betty Lou watched television. Alice found her mind wandering and chose to retire early.

Art. He is, she considers, such a good man and he and Betty Lou are a terrific match. All those years ago, when I danced at his parents' wedding, it never occurred to me there would be a joining of our families.

Alice lifts her head and looks westward at a sky of peach-streaked indigo, and eastward where it is India ink with a few sequin stars studding the blue-black veil. Alice clutches her sweater around her *shoulders. Never a plump woman, even in middle age, she has waned somewhat in the last few years and although still sprightly, she knows it is not just her figure that has waned.*

Thank goodness for Art, and for Betty Lou taking the time to record my story, she thinks, and closes the window.

1926: Liberated in Leader, 1920's Style

By June of 1926, Alice had completed her grade twelve, and had applied for teaching positions. She was overjoyed to receive an offer from the Town of Leader. A real town with shops and services, and a larger school of several rooms. She replied at once.

After the train ride to Leader, Alice began her new job and roomed with a local family. With two years of practical experience combined with another year of maturity, her first day jitters might have lasted five minutes. Alice's class of grades three and four was "a bright group," and she reported no teacher-testing or loose upbringing. Because it was then rare, she was impressed to find the principal of the Leader School was a woman, Mrs. Eileen Guild, "a wonderful, understanding, person." In addition, there were other teachers with whom to share ideas, and from whose experience and advice she could learn.

Apart from the improved working conditions in the school, Alice found much about Leader that filled her with joy. People, clubs, dances, tennis games, and card parties, offered a wide choice of activities to fill the social calendar of a friendly and enthusiastic young woman.

Alice made new friends, including colleague Elsie Plummer who soon married a young admirer. Confidence and social maturity had replaced Alice's lack of poise and shyness from the Normal School years. As volunteer and participant, she plunged into community activities, including those sponsored by the local service clubs, such as the Masons and Lions.

When Miss Ethel Stannard, 'Stan,' came to town, Alice met another new friend and soul-mate. Stan was the new public health nurse, and her position in Leader included the perk of a government car. These modern women attended every possible dance, extended their network of friends, and joined in the social life of Leader and any towns within driving range.

One of the social events Alice attended was the wedding of Christian and Emma Heeg. She would have chuckled if she had possessed a crystal ball to foresee this couple's future son, Arthur, married to her future daughter, Betty Lou.

Not worried about the 'yet to come,' Alice and Stan were two young women immersed in the events of the present, and making the most of their freedom as educated and employed women of the world. Thoughts of marriage and family were distant blips on their personal radar screens, and the 1920s were exciting times with new women's rights and new attitudes toward their roles in society.

Women in Saskatchewan had been given the vote provincially in 1916 and then federally in 1919. Robert had always voted Liberal, and Alice followed suit. She voted in every election including that of September 1926, which saw William Lyon Mackenzie King elected as Prime Minister.

Alice believed in democracy, and was fervent about communicating its importance to her students. Not just a right of the democratic process, voting was an important obligation. She believed it every Canadian's duty to vote, and to understand Canada's democratic system.

1963: Gordon River–Governing Decisions

The camp basks in May sunshine on an early weekday morning. The crummies are long gone with their crews of loggers, and sounds of their industry, (muffled whistles and chain saw whines), echo from distant valleys. Sounds of industry (clattering pots and gushing wash water), echo from homes too. Yet, in the school, where normally would be heard childish voices in an enthusiastic rendition of 'Oh, Canada,' all is quiet.

Dad, who is recovering from a broken rib, and I sit in our station wagon, and while he raps his fingers on the steering wheel, I bounce on my seat. My mother is in the house finishing her hair.

Several weeks ago, Mrs. Marlatt decided we older people should go to Victoria and see the "government at work" in the Legislature. The study of Canadian political parties, and their leaders, is a major Social Studies topic. Mrs. Marlatt explained that a person should vote for the party standing for the policies in which they believe and not for the man.

Leaders come and go, but the parties' beliefs don't change, or at least not quickly. I'm not certain on what constitutes a 'policy,' but it's clear this is an important part of democracy.

With a full agenda, we must make an early start. In addition to a sitting of the Legislature, we will go to the observatory, the plant research station, Helmcken House, Craigflower School, and the Provincial Museum. Yesterday afternoon, Mrs. Marlatt repeated that we must be on our best behaviour. We will walk in the museum, and must not annoy other visitors. If we speak, we will whisper. We must not talk at all at the Legislature. This will be a long day and it is important we pay attention to everything we hear and see, as we will talk about it in class for the next few days.

Six of us older students are on this trip, and because we couldn't all fit into Mrs. Marlatt's car, my mother offered to drive. Because of Dad's accident, he can't work, and he is happy to join us. He loves the museum too.

Positive that the museum, which I have visited before, will be my favourite, I imagine its peculiar smell, like woody dust or withered potatoes in the bottom of the sack. I look forward to seeing the exhibits: stuffed animals, shells, antique tools, and Indian artifacts. Most of these are in glass cases with faded print on beige tags.

I look up from my thoughts on the museum to see my friend, Christine, and her brother, Ian, coming out of their gate to ride with us. Kathy, Kelly, and their brother Douglas will ride with Mrs. Marlatt. The younger pupils will stay home, and my sisters will spend the day with neighbours. Last night I shook dimes and nickels out of my bank for lunch, and this morning Mum gave me a fifty-cent piece. This is more than I need to buy a hamburger and a milkshake. I tied my money in a handkerchief. I toss it back and forth from hand-to-hand while waiting for everybody to get aboard and fasten seat belts.

After meeting at the top of the school drive, we are off. Mrs. Marlatt leads the way. Kathy and Doug, from the back of Mrs. Marlatt's car, which doesn't have seat belts, wave and grin. Dad laughs and toots the horn.

It was a great day in Victoria. We managed most points of call on the itinerary, including the museum. I had been there many times with my family, as it was free, and anything free was within the family budget. At the time of our field trip, the provincial museum was housed in a wing of the legislative buildings where most exhibits were in glass cases, except for the giant stuffed bear. At least it seemed giant to me as a child, but on seeing it again years later I realized it was far from big and moth-eaten as well.

At the Legislature, Mrs. Marlatt reminded us to be silent. The warning was unnecessary for me. I couldn't take my eyes away from the regalia, the ornate décor, the rich woods and the golden Mace on its stand in the middle of the room. The MLAs faced each other, and the Speaker sat in a great chair at the far end. Pages, who were all boys, stood on either side, ready to take messages. I stared at the pages, and wondered how one became a page, if girls could be pages, and what was in the messages.

Not everybody was as enthralled. One of the boys fell asleep and rested his head on Dad's shoulder. An officious commissionaire, leaning down from the row above, informed my startled father that the gallery was not for sleeping, and insisted he wake up the boy. Dad was annoyed, but didn't make a fuss and roused the sleepyhead. He was still annoyed fifty years later and whenever we talked about that day, he referred to the long-passed-on commissionaire as a pompous so-and-so. Mrs. Marlatt may have taken the incident as a sign that it was time to leave, and we filed out.

We lunched at a roadside café–with all of us kids lined up on the stools and Mrs. Marlatt, Mum, and Dad in a booth close by. My friends laughed at my pile of change that was too much for a fifty-five cent cheeseburger. They also laughed at my knotted hankie that proved difficult to untie.

After lunch, the tour continued to Helmcken House and Craigflower School. We found the observatory closed, so moved on to the last call on our agenda, the plant research station in Central Saanich. We learned of the golden nematode and the meaning of quarantine.

Afterwards we were to take a ferry from Brentwood Bay in Saanich across Finlayson Arm to Mill Bay. This was to eliminate an hour plus drive south through Victoria and then north on a stretch of highway known as Malahat Drive. Either we missed the scheduled sailing or it was full, necessitating a wait while the ferry plied its way across the inlet and returned. Thus, after the crossing, and driving home through Duncan and Lake Cowichan, it was well after dark when we crossed the trestle into camp.

During the ride home, my mind, like a tape recording on automatic rewind, replayed the sights and sounds of our day, especially that hour in the legislature.

I don't know what business the government of the day debated, but there were neither fiery speeches nor table-pounding shouting matches. Cranky commissionaire notwithstanding, I will never forget that awe-inspiring experience. And I have voted in every election of my adult life.

1927–1928: Calling Authority's Tune

Not only were Alice and Stan well matched in energy and financial resources, they were independent, uncommitted, and devoted to their chosen careers. Their teacher-nurse combo was undoubtedly popular with the local swains, but with their own transportation, they were free to choose which dances or events to attend, and did so. There was nothing to prevent these two vibrant young women to focus on getting the most out of their lives and budgets. They gave up their separate lodgings and moved into an apartment above the doctor's office. In the winter, they skated and Alice expanded her card game expertise to include bridge. Spring arrived and, with Stan, Alice resumed tennis, playing despite putting her knee out of joint. They lived the high life of Leader.

Even Leader's geography had more appeal, as, when Alice had time to look at it, the surrounding prairie was very level, even for Saskatchewan. Alice "learned to love the open prairie" far more than back home.

'Back home,' Agnes and Robert were forty-nine and fifty-eight years old in the spring of 1928. The twenty-two years since leaving Ontario's shores had been harrowing as life was for prairie homesteaders, but Robert had expanded his farm to neighbouring unbroken land formerly belonging to an American investor. He had backed the purchase with his own good credit, but had broken the fields with his own back, assisted by a borrowed Rumely Engine.

Although Robert used horses for farming and transport, he occasionally borrowed a neighbour's equipment for the laborious work of breaking land. Robert had never taken the easy road, Alice observed. He was "a very, very, quiet, hard-working man."

While Alice's life blossomed in Leader, her other siblings' lives continued in Rocanville and beyond. Laura married Andy Arthur, Ray pursued his training and career with the RCMP, and Jessie, a lively teenager, skated, danced, and never missed a party within the vicinity of Rocanville. In the spring of 1928, Bobbie, the baby of the family at seven, stayed close to home with her parents.

Agnes and Robert enjoyed excellent health and were thankful for the prosperity of both their farm and their family. Robert was no doubt relieved that Alice had escaped an early marriage to an unsuitable match in Irish Lake.

Agnes woke to the sounds of Robert rattling around the kitchen and then heard the patter of little girl feet as Bobbie passed their room and skipped her way downstairs. She heard a thump as Bobbie jumped from the third step to the floor. Not so long ago it was the second step. Agnes smiled. All of her children took bigger steps as they grew, and she could not believe Alice was now twenty-four. She remembered Alice as a tiny warm bundle who hardly cried at all. Alice was never a complainer. She had a serious face with big eyes–a face instantly transformed by that unbelievable smile. From whom, Agnes wondered, did Alice inherit her smile?

Knowing Robert had the stove roaring and the porridge pot on, Agnes swung her feet to the floor. She poked her head into Jessie's room and told her to get a move on or she would go to school without breakfast.

"Time and tide wait for no man," she said, "or schoolgirl either."

Jessie groaned and threw back the covers. Agnes smiled and continued to the stairs.

Later in the afternoon, while she washed dishes from the day's baking, Agnes watched for Robert to come out of the barn. As soon as he appeared, she called him to come for a wee bite before fetching the girls from school. He was strong and vigorous, but Agnes worried he pushed himself too hard, and it wasn't a bad thing to take a few short breaks during the day. Robert agreed with a wave and after a quick wash at the sink, took his place at the kitchen table.

While Agnes placed biscuits, butter, cheese, jam, and pickles in front of him, Robert watched her every move and felt his heart swell. She was a good-looking woman he thought, and strong and capable. He knew moving here in 1906 had been hard on her. She had worried about how they would survive in this barren land. The prairies were harsh, and making a living here wasn't easy—leastways for anybody who wouldn't work hard. And they had worked hard, both of them.

He looked out the window at a field of black soil, warming and waiting for seeding, and another field of fat heifers. He thought of the sow and her fresh litter of piglets, and the chickens snapping up bugs and worms in the yard. Gallons of white gold from the morning milking waited for him in the dairy. Sandy, Prince, and the other horses took their ease in the paddock. They won't be easing much longer, thought Robert. In a few days, the seeding would begin.

Agnes joined Robert at the table and took the buttered biscuit he offered. The milk she poured for herself had ribbons of cream throughout. She remembered the cream in the summer kitchen was ready to churn. Once home from school, Jessie and Bobbie would need a bite before beginning their chores. She would get Jessie started on the churn but would finish the butter herself. Every drop of whey must be squeezed out before she salted and formed the butter into the neat bricks she preferred. Bobbie would feed the chickens, but not the pigs. She was too young for that, and the sow, although a good mother was nasty and treacherous. Long ago Robert had warned her never to trust hogs, as he had lost a younger brother to a mean sow. A short time ago Laura and Ray would have been here doing their chores too, but Laura had married, and Ray was with the Royal Canadian Mounted Police.

Accepting another biscuit topped with a dollop of Saskatoon berry jam, Agnes nodded when Robert held up the milk jug, and topped up her cup. Taking a bite of biscuit, she looked around the kitchen. Her eyes crinkled when her gaze stopped at the stack of letters propped on the windowsill.

One letter was from Alice. They had read and re-read it several times, and talked about Alice's latest news and adventures. She was *enjoying Leader: friends, dances, tennis, and bridge parties. She wrote about her school and students. They were all special, and she was convinced one clever young fellow would be a scientist one day.*

The only sour note in this song of joy was Alice's ongoing struggle with a member of the school board, but Agnes and Robert recognized a new maturity and self-assurance in their daughter. They knew, whatever the problem, Alice would find a solution.

Alice loved life in Leader: plenty to do, plenty of people, and plenty of relationships, not all of them positive. In any job, one can expect an occasional hitch with colleagues or managers, but this was new to Alice. She came to realize that a certain member of the school board disliked her, but did not know what she had done to offend. She might have been yet too young to have encountered a person who, from their own biases or misconceptions, form a poor opinion of another person, and constantly look for transgressions to support their opinion.

Alice was normally punctual, but on one occasion, she was late. Her friend Elsie was devastated by the death of her new baby, and Spears, Elsie's husband, brought Alice to their home to help console her. Rain had transformed the roads into the famous prairie gumbo, but Spears had avoided the risk of being stuck by driving his car on the railroad tracks. A neighbour offered Alice a lift back to town in time for her morning class, but too nervous to drive the tracks, he became mired on the road. Alice was only five minutes late, but the school board official hadn't waited and had sent her class home.

On another occasion, this individual made an unannounced visit to Alice's classroom where she was demonstrating the geography of rivers and lakes on a sand table. She had discovered this handy piece of equipment under the stairs and had dragged it into class. For some reason, a pair of overshoes had been left sitting on the edge of the table and had come along for the ride. Alice, intent on her lesson, was unconcerned whether the overshoes had been left by the janitor, or the last person to use the sand table.

The official spied the overshoes. That she had not removed them to an appropriate location for footwear provided him with a reason to berate Alice for this seeming oversight. Alice, now past the point of intimidation by pompous bureaucrats, remained composed. She was well on her way to developing her own aura of authority.

1961: Gordon River–Authority Calls

Bright and cloudless, yet cool–a perfect dawn for those who work outside, and in the staging yard, the ideal conditions are not lost on the groups of men boarding crummies. The outlook promises no slogging in mud, no rain pelting upturned faces, and no lunchtime retreat to shelter. They joke and call as they climb aboard, and with grinding gears, the yellow trucks growl away. The sun won't ease the workload, but will lighten the mood, and more importantly, will firm muddy roads, dry slippery cables, and improve visibility. For this day, the risk of injury will be reduced.

The camp settles down to await the men's return. The camp routine rotates around the coming and going of loggers, and while they are gone, those left in camp get on with other work. In the shop, welders and mechanics keep machinery humming, and in the office, the accountant and timekeeper hum over ledgers and time-cards. Within the homes, are domestic routines of cleaning (something or someone), cooking, and keeping house.

The school day hums along on its own routine, rarely interrupted. Sometimes one of the wives drives in or out of the home site, but nobody in camp drives to the school during school hours. Such an event causes ears to perk.

Today we all hear it. Tires crunch on the school driveway. There is no reason for anybody in camp to use this drive, so we know it must be a visitor from outside. Mrs. Marlatt turns from the board where she writes spelling words for the grade threes, and I stand and peer out the window.

"It is Mr. Saywell." Mrs. Marlatt says, and puts down her chalk.

He is the senior principal of the school district and calls every so often. We know what to do. Two people are at the bookshelves, and somebody is in the washroom, but we finish what we are doing and scuttle back to our desks. We wait.

There is a rap at the door, and then it opens to a portly man with a full smiling face.

We rise together and chime a chorus of, "Good morning, Mr. Saywell."

He returns our greeting, and then he and Mrs. Marlatt speak together for a few seconds. He is quiet-spoken, wears a dark grey three-piece suit and a warm ever-present smile. Listening to Mrs. Marlatt, he looks around our schoolroom, nodding. We know why he is here, and we wait for our turn to read or show our latest work.

I enjoy reading aloud. I am never nervous when I read, but if I must stand in front of the class and speak, I shiver and forget my own name. Mr. Saywell plunks one of the small wooden chairs from the reading circle beside my desk. The chair creaks and disappears underneath him, and I take a breath, inhaling a faint scent of Old Spice. He asks my name and points out the chapter. I am disappointed; the chapter is old work. We are much further ahead in our reader, and I would rather read a newer chapter with bigger words. But I would not dream of speaking out, so I read the passage as Mrs. Marlatt has taught us. Emphasizing certain words, I do my best to "read with expression," and read the dialogue as if it were real people speaking.

*Before I finish three pages, Mr. Saywell stops me with, "Very good, **very** good."*

Then he asks to see my arithmetic. My stomach lurches, but I pull my scribbler from my desk. He thumbs through it. I hold my breath, hoping he does not ask me to recite any times-tables. Mr. Saywell nods and hands back my scribbler, and I breathe again. His knees crack as he stands and carries the chair to another desk.

Mr. Saywell creaks from desk to desk while Mrs. Marlatt resumes her chalking on the blackboard. The buzz of excitement fades. Scraping pencils and rustling papers blend with the murmurs of people reading and Mr. Saywell's rumbly voice. After a while, Mr. Saywell carries the chair to its place in the reading circle. He is finished, and as it is close to lunch, Mrs. Marlatt dismisses us. My coat is underneath two others on a hook, and I wait my turn. On reaching the door, I turn to see Mrs. Marlatt and Mr. Saywell standing by her desk. She shows him the attendance register with its many x-crosses covering the page. Mr. Saywell is still smiling. I have never seen him without that smile.

R.Rigsby

Any school visitation was a rare event, and Mr. Saywell was a favourite caller. On his last visit, he brought us a box of chocolates–no visitor had ever brought us such a treat. Although he smiled, he spoke more quietly than usual. Mrs. Marlatt later told us he had taken another position, and we would not see him again.

The school nurse was also a regular visitor. We had "good manners," according to more than one guest and were always happy and eager to please. Although Mrs. Marlatt expected us to concentrate on our work, and finish every exercise, the atmosphere was far from regimental. She encouraged free expression, such as demonstrating how to 'skulk,' and creative problem solving.

One of her pet peeves was the attendance register. The multitude of crosses on the page were in accordance with the procedure of marking a stroke for morning attendance, and a cross stroke for afternoon attendance. Mrs. Marlatt thought this ridiculous. One should only place a stroke on the page to indicate absence, not attendance.

Therefore every day she would mark the register in pencil if a student were absent, which in our school was infrequent. Then, every few days, as we finished our afternoon work, she would complete the register in ink, and erase the pencil marks, if any. Rustles, coughs, and murmurs were interspersed with the sound of Mrs. Marlatt scratching x marks with her fountain pen and occasional puffs of breath blowing away eraser grains. She never said if Mr. Saywell found her register not updated in the prescribed manner. From what I recall of Mr. Saywell, he would not have considered this a problem.

1929–1930: The End of the Beginning

Alice taught in Leader, and endured occasional supervisory interference for three years. It would have amused her if she had known that fifty years later Leader would again be her home. Here she would spend many afternoons dictating her adventures, including the story of the displaced overshoes.

In the spring of 1929, Stan was transferred to Maple Creek. Alice decided she had had enough tug-o-wars with her adversary at the school board and resigned. Her applications to Maple Creek and Sceptre were accepted, but, to the disappointment of the Sceptre principal, she chose the more appealing position in Maple Creek where she and Stan would again share an apartment. Employment secured, Alice went home to Rocanville for summer vacation.

Toward the end of summer, after a holiday in San Francisco, Stan journeyed to the Blair home bearing gifts: a "salmon-coloured dance dress" for Alice and a child's tea set for Bobbie.

After the Labour Day weekend, the two girls rode the train to Maple Creek, sharing an upper berth. They arrived at six in the morning, disembarked, and each went to their respective jobs. With the stamina of youth, they thought nothing of beginning work immediately after an overnight train ride. During the trip, Stan gushed about a man she had met in Maple Creek.

Alice and Stan set up housekeeping in their bachelor-girl suite, and shortly thereafter Stan brought 'the man' up to visit. His name was Ashton Marlatt–the very Ashton Marlatt who, in 1906, as a hopeful young man of eighteen, had boarded the same train as Alice and her family. According to Alice, this was the first time she set eyes on Ashton Marlatt, or Curly to his friends, and, as was the case for Agnes and Robert in 1902, there was an immediate spark. Stan did not seem too concerned about Ashton, so when the girls met him in the drugstore a few days later, Alice, with a boldness born of newfound confidence, or newly kindled enrapture, asked him to escort her to the Saturday dance. . . and Stan too. Alice claimed the first dance. Stan later chided her for "being a dirty rooter" for "stealing her boyfriend," but Alice countered with the detail "he was only Stan's spare," as Stan was more interested in another man.

From their first dance in September 1929, Alice and Ashton "always went together." Alice claims she did not intend to get serious. Ashton, at forty-two, was a widower with children aged six and nineteen. At twenty-six, Alice was a sparkling young woman who enjoyed riding in Ashton's new Chevrolet and dancing at shindigs as far away as Swift Current and Medicine Hat.

When Ashton took her to meet his son, Albert, who worked in a hardware store in Eastend, Alice should have twigged.

Although Alice, donning her rose-coloured glasses, may not have thought she was serious about Ashton, a certain lady in Shaunavon was. This lady was keen indeed, and it came to her attention that his preference had been drawn to a schoolmarm in Maple Creek. She telephoned Alice and tried to induce her to leave Ashton alone, but Alice wasn't about to be bullied. She may not have thought she was in love, but she was having fun and truly enjoyed the company of this energetic, hardworking, and yes, very good-looking man. Her sharp reply affected a permanent puncture in her rival's trial balloon.

Ashton was a 'blockman' for International Harvester, and his territory ranged from Swift Current to the Alberta border. Essentially a traveling salesman, he was pleased with his career, no doubt envisioning a rewarding future. The shock of the stock market crash on October 24, 1929, might have caused him some disquiet, but New York was a long way from Maple Creek, and he could foresee neither the depth nor breadth of the coming depression, nor the next ten years of climatic disaster.

While on the road, Ashton had regularly called his children, and then there was Alice. He called her every night while out of town. In the days before cell phones, he must have memorized the location of every pay phone in southern Saskatchewan.

One Sunday evening in the spring of 1930, after a week in his territory, Ashton returned to Maple Creek, took Alice out for a drive, and proposed.

Chapter Nine: The Other Parallel–Ashton's Story

1979: Leader IX

Alice dictates for most of the morning, and is hungry for the buns, cheese, and fruit Betty Lou puts on the table for lunch. Betty Lou finishes first and goes out to the porch to pull in a line of wash.

Loving apples since her first taste so many years ago in the Graham orchard, Alice bites into a crisp slice.

She thinks about the story to come: Ashton's story–a good story.

Well maybe 'good' is not the best word, she thinks, since Ashton's life had its storms and dark days. He had wanted me to know everything, and had shared most of it before he proposed.

Later, on winter evenings while blizzards howled and snow piled to the windows, he filled the gaps. While I knitted, he smoked his pipe and we both retold our stories. At the time, I didn't have much of a story compared to Ashton who had already done so much. I have more to tell now, but again, it isn't all happy.

Betty Lou brings in one basket, and takes out another. Alice plucks a tea towel from the pile, folds it into a precise rectangle, and reaches for another.

No matter how many conveniences there are, she thinks, laundry doesn't fold itself.

Between clothesline squeals, Alice hears Betty Lou exchange a few words and jokes with a passing neighbour.

"Well thank goodness I was able to get both loads on the line today." Betty Lou sits down and clacks a new cassette into the recorder. "We were talking about Dad and where he was born and grew up. Do you feel up to going on this afternoon?"

"I do," says Alice, and means it.

I feel energized today, she thinks, and the molasses that sometimes settles in my brain is gone–at least for the time being–and the right words come easily.

"I know your Dad told you many stories about his life, but maybe not everything."

1887-1909: Again, The Eastern Shore

The westbound train of April 30, 1906 conveying Alice and her family from Ontario to the Promised Land, also carried her future husband, Victor Ashton Abraham Marlatt. While Alice and her family continued to Saskatchewan, Ashton (Curly) and his older brother, John, disembarked in Brandon, Manitoba and made their way to the Wawanesa farm of their maternal uncle, Ernest Evans. The boys, with few opportunities in Ontario, had responded to their uncle's appeal for help and envisioned riches in the west. Ashton, although only eighteen, had already packed his life with experiences beginning with his birth in Port Ryerse on August 7, 1887.

* * *

Born to Emma (Evans) and Clayton Marlatt, Ashton was the first sibling for older brother John. Shortly afterwards the family moved to Simcoe where Clayton followed his own father, Abraham, into the pottery business. The family enlarged with the arrival of two girls, Lulu and Alba.

As Ashton and John grew, they helped Clayton at the wheel and kiln. Throughout the winter, they cleaned, glazed, and baked pottery, setting aside the various pieces until summer when they loaded their wagon and went on the road. Hawking pots, pitchers, and crocks throughout the area, Ashton was a travelling salesman before he was ten years old.

At their school, John admired a young lady named Beatrice, and Ashton befriended Joe, the son of an escaped slave. Joe was often badgered, and early in life, Ashton faced the evils of prejudice and the repercussions of standing up to bullies. This early experience may have come in useful when he later suffered other kinds of bullying from his maternal relatives.

Ashton's mother, Emma, was the eldest child of John and Mary Ann Evans, whose other children included Ernest, Florence, Victor and Maud. Being Anglican and devotees of the Conservative Party, Emma's parents disapproved of Emma's marriage to Clayton, as he was not only a Methodist but a Liberal to boot.

When the Marlatt boys reached ten and thirteen, the senior Evans' demanded they live with them in Hagersville, and for reasons not explained, Emma and Clayton agreed. Why the girls, Lulu and Alba, aged eight and three, were not included in this arrangement is not clear. The grandparents may have reasoned that the girls, when they married, would follow their husbands' faiths and political persuasions. If they married in accordance with their grandparents' wishes, they would be saved, but the boys, under Clayton's influence, were a problem. The senior Evans' undertook to rehabilitate the boys from their Methodist and Liberal upbringing.

Ashton and John attended the Church of England with their grandparents, and the boys adjusted to the new liturgy and rites without protest. As for correction of any political bent they may have absorbed from Clayton, they learned the then popular, at least with Conservatives, rhyme:

> Tory, Tory, full of Glory,
> Grit, Grit, full of S___t

Other aspects of their new home-life were not as bearable. The grandparents forced Ashton to wear his Aunt Maud's used shoes. Whether this was due to economizing in the household–since new shoes cost money and if serviceable shoes were available, they should be worn–or for some other reason, is unknown. Ashton hated wearing girls' shoes. He would wear them to within sight of the school, then stash them in the bush and go barefoot in class. Also, Ashton who possessed luxurious curly hair was not allowed to cut it although no reason was offered for this bizarre rule. Over the years, there may have been other instances of disregard or discipline, if not outright abuse.

The boys pilfered coins and schemed to extricate themselves from the tyranny of their grandparents and spinster Aunt Maud.

When their grandparents went to town on errands and while Aunt Maud was distracted, the boys slunk away to the railway track. They leaped into an empty car on the first slow moving freight. The train, either by luck or design, took them to Simcoe where they jumped off and made their way home. Their annoyed grandparents, after a fruitless search, had driven to Simcoe to advise Clayton of the boys' desertion. At first sight of their grandparents rig in the yard, the boys dove into the ditch along the fence line. Their Aunt Florence and Uncle Victor, who had been drafted into the hunt, waited with the horses, but eventually the foursome climbed aboard. The boys kept their heads down until the buggy was out of sight.

With the posse gone, the boys clambered out of their mud-hole and pleaded with their father to let them stay home. Finally, Clayton stood up to his in-laws and did so. The boys were old enough to work, but the pottery business had declined to such a state there was no point in continuing the trade. Clayton took up wallpapering and painting, and at the ages of fourteen and seventeen Ashton and John began their working lives with a succession of menial jobs. The Marlatt family enjoyed only a few years of reunion before the tragic loss of thirteen-year-old Lulu to pneumonia after an accidental fall into Lake Erie.

As always, life went on and for the next few years Ashton and John picked up work, none of it career-worthy, wherever they could, including jobs in a chicken cannery and a jam plant. Then, the summons from Uncle Ernest.

The vision of working in the fresh air of the wide-open prairie seized the two young men who each had a nose-full of reeking raw chicken and percolating fruit. Ashton's boss, on receiving his resignation, offered a better position with more pay. Ashton declined. The young men packed their bags, and on April 30, 1906, joined the other prairie-bound optimists in the doubtful comfort of a CPR colonist car. Ashton never mentioned if he noticed a little girl with steady grey eyes and a serious expression.

Ernest Evans had remained on his parents' farm in Ontario until his late twenties, but as he had two older brothers, his prospects had been limited. He, like many others, had fled Ontario to the mirage of prairie land. In 1906, Uncle Ernest, at age forty-one was a bachelor (who never did marry), and worked his homestead alone.

The notion of engaging his two healthy young nephews, who also had limited prospects in Ontario, must have seemed like a good idea at the time. Perhaps Ernest overlooked the fact that young men who had no investment in an enterprise, might not be as dedicated as expected. Also, as they were young, they might require more social contact.

According to Alice, who had the pleasure of meeting him after her marriage, Uncle Ernest was "a very dry man, monosyllabic" and "you couldn't talk to him at all," and he "didn't talk enough to get married." Although not a gifted conversationalist, Uncle Ernest had no such verbal reticence when giving orders and was a demanding employer: he was "very strict and very anal." Ashton soon found more convivial company and joined the local baseball team at the invitation of one Hank Cory. Uncle Ernest was not about to encourage such diversions at his cost. When Ashton asked his uncle for the horse so he could play ball in town, Uncle Ernest said no, but, if he was driving to town himself, Ashton could catch a ride. Such trips were one-way though, and Ashton had to walk home after his games. The pay and the accommodation were miserly, but Ashton tolerated it for as long as he could, and saved his wages. John went home.

After a final falling out, Ashton deserted Uncle Ernest and acquired a "bit of land with a shack on it," which was probably the abandoned dream of former occupants. At one quarter section, the holding was small, and even after purchasing a cow and a couple of horses it was a pathetic beginning. Ashton augmented the meager returns by working for a family called Jackson for whom he first helped dig a new well. Pleased with his industry, the Jacksons kept him on as their farm hand to the effect he earned a name in the area as 'Jackson's Irishman.'

In contrast with her fiery appearance, red-haired Mrs. Jackson was kind and sympathized with the struggling young farmer. To help him with his new venture she offered Ashton a hen and her clutch of eggs. The hitch was that Ashton would have to come for his hen after dark, as Mr. Jackson was not nearly as charitable, and was "a cranky old guy" besides. As instructed, Ashton sneaked into the henhouse, but his hen and her sisters objected to a stranger rousting them after dark. The ensuing squawks woke Mr. Jackson who, believing a coyote was raiding his henhouse, blasted away with his shotgun. Ashton ran for cover. A few days later, with Mr. Jackson at a safe distance in town, Mrs. Jackson delivered the hen and hatched chicks. However, the start of Ashton's flock of chickens was foiled again when a hawk dined on all of the chicks.

As winter approached, Ashton sheltered his livestock in a lean-to attached to the shack, and the animals were probably more comfortable than he. The ill-built shack was full of cracks, and there was nobody to stoke the fire when Ashton worked the Jackson's place or undertook his own chores. Winters were an endless shiver under a moth-eaten buffalo robe on loan from Uncle Ernest. Since buffalo had been decimated more than twenty years before, this robe was enriched with the accumulated grime and aromas of every one of those years. For three bitter winters, Ashton stuck it out on his patch.

He had spent his wages on four well-matched horses and, when not working, had trained them into a reliable and powerful team. Ashton loved horses and saw more potential in a good team for hire than in farming. Thus between his work at the Jackson's and the time spent with his team, there had been less time for the farm, and it was only marginally productive. Nor was carpentry, and repairs to the shack his forte.

As Alice said to Betty Lou, "Your Dad couldn't build anything."

Early in 1909, at the age of twenty-two, Ashton took a job with a crew building a bridge crossing the Souris River in Wawanesa, but it wasn't Ashton's expertise as a carpenter the foreman hired; it was his four-horse team. Ashton and his team prepared the road surfaces to the new bridge.

In Wawanesa, the Brook family took in lodgers, and Ashton, finding it more convenient to live in town, took up residence. Mr. Brook owned a harness and shoe repair business while Mrs. Brook and her daughters ran the boarding house. Here Ashton met Ethel Adelia Brook, one of two daughters still living at home and who at age twenty-four was ready for marriage. And how could she not fall for a handsome curly-haired man with a fine team of horses? Like Agnes and Robert in 1902, the courtship sped along at the pace of this other "spanking" team and a wedding date was set for early November.

Anxious for his family to attend the nuptials, Ashton sent the announcement and invitations home. Before Ethel and Ashton finalized their wedding plans, Ashton received tragic news: Clayton was dying of pneumonia. Ashton was heart-broken. His father would not live to see him married, but neither was there time for him to travel home to see Clayton one last time.

After Clayton's funeral, Emma and Alba arrived, as did John with his new wife, Beatrice, his childhood sweetheart. Ashton welcomed his remaining family to his wedding on November 8, 1909.

John Marlatt, who had tired of Manitoba farming, and/or Uncle Ernest, before Ashton, had returned with the intention of staying. Like their father, he had become a professional painter and wallpaperer, and he and Beatrice settled in the town of Wawanesa.

Because Ashton had taken up the construction job and moved into town, his homestead with the draughty shack was considered abandoned. According to the government rules on homesteading, a plot had to be continually occupied, and a certain amount of land had to be broken and planted. Therefore, Ashton lost his farm, along with his investment of about one hundred hard-earned dollars and three long winters worth of discomfort, isolation, and despair. Homesteading was risky and backbreaking, but even more so when attempted single-handedly.

1956 - 1964: Gordon River–Logging Camp Wives

Much is written of intrepid men who explored, mapped, and settled Canada. Those who ventured into the wilderness often suffered hunger, pain, disease, and isolation. They endured afflictions and a lack of material comforts to extract the resources of this land: fish, furs, wheat, minerals, and timber.

The women who accompanied them endured the same hardships, and raised their children as well; women have done far more than keep home fires burning. On the prairies, many women, and their children, worked the fields with their men, and ensured there was food to eat and clothes to wear, often under primitive conditions. Women have always worked.

In Gordon River, Mrs. Marlatt was the only single woman, and the only woman drawing a salary. Our mothers stayed home and, as children, we considered this the normal state of affairs. Their contribution to maintaining the heartbeat of the community was immeasurable, but the owners of Gordon River Camp understood their importance. 'Married quarters' were included when the camp plan was on the drawing board. The developers of this model recognized the importance of providing a family friendly atmosphere for its workers. In addition to the bunkhouses, shops, and cookhouse, the camp boasted eleven duplexes, parking garages, playground, school, and a community hall. Such amenities, in addition to the reasonable rent for a comfortable house, swayed my mother when my father took a job in Gordon River.

Although my mother spent most of her time in camp, she was a capable and confident driver. She would, as need dictated, drive the

R.Rigsby

family station wagon to attend a personal appointment or accomplish a necessary errand.

1961: Gordon River–Mum Has Gone to Town

March blows in, not as a lion, but as a thunderbird shrieking through treetops and shaking wet wings. Between fits of blowing and beating, the fowl of March tolerates intervals of sun to warm the valley in the clear-cut. With each rotation of the earth, the valley, and its speck of a logging camp, moves closer to the equinox, and the arrival of spring. The rivers, sleepy gurgles in their rocky beds, will soon wake with the melting of high mountain snow. Tight furled buds of alder and cottonwood, swelling slowly, are in no hurry to open until the March ruffian departs.

Outside, the March bully can do as it pleases, as the schoolroom is a cocoon of warmth and safety. The doors and windows are snug in their frames, lights glow, and the heater pumps ample British Thermal Units. Drawings, maps, and pictures splash colour around the room.

Mrs. Marlatt sits in the reading circle with some younger children, and, in turn, each child reads aloud. Young voices rise and fall in counterpoint to the wind buffeting the building and rain pelting the flat roof. The lesson finishes, and Mrs. Marlatt chats with each child for a few minutes before dismissal for lunch.

I sit at my desk, swinging a leg that does not reach the floor. Without too much erasing, I finish my arithmetic problems. I bend my face over the page but listen to Mrs. Marlatt's conversations with the little people, including my sister, Frances. Fran tells Mrs. Marlatt she is going to lunch at Beth's house, because our mother has gone to town. Mrs. Marlatt replies saying how nice that is, and how much fun it will be for them.

But she already knows this because I told her this morning: I will be on my own for lunch today, and I said it loud enough for my friends to hear. Mrs. Marlatt nodded and smiled, but went on helping hang coats. My friends have never been home alone, and at recess, when I mentioned this again, they bobbed their heads and mumbled.

I squirmed and whined when I learned Mum had an appointment in town and had arranged for us to have lunch with our neighbour. They have two girls the same ages as my sisters, and they are friends. There is nobody in that family my age. I told Mum that I was old enough to have lunch at home by myself. She thought for a moment, and then said all right, we would do that.

I can't wait to have the house to myself. I will eat my lunch in peace and quiet with no sisters to bug me with their squabbling, and I will play in my room until it is time to go back to school. Mum has warned me to watch the clock. She knows how I can be.

Mrs. Marlatt dismisses us for lunch. I jump from the porch, and run all the way home, leaving my friends behind. My clear plastic overshoes feel like Dad's work boots, and I kick up gravel in clumsy bursts as I leap puddles. When I reach the back porch, Paddy pops out of her house. Stubby tail a blur, she prances on her forefeet and wiggles all over. Surprised to come inside during the day, she folds up on the mat. I toss my coat on the sewing machine, and kick off the overshoes while I continue to talk to Paddy. She listens with her ears perked and tongue hanging out in a doggy smile.

The sound of my voice sends peculiar echoes around the empty house. I walk through the kitchen to the living room and peer down the hall. A growl from my stomach reminds me to look for my lunch: a sandwich under a plastic bonnet, a brownie, and an apple. I sit at the table and munch my chicken loaf sandwich, licking mustard from my fingers.

Sporadic, wind-blown gobbets of rain splatter the window above the table. The clock on the windowsill ticks, and the stove fan whirs. Paddy snuffles as she licks her paws. It is strange to hear these sounds. Sometimes Mum has the radio on, but today I hear no strains from CKWX, nor do I hear my sisters babble as they shove their chairs and clatter plates and cups. The stove is set low, so the kitchen is cool. When Mum is here, the stove is hot, and the air is full of the smell of bread, or cookies, or pie, or maybe the beginnings of stew for supper. On washdays, I smell Ivory Snow and damp sheets waiting their turn on the line.

There was no washing today. No bowls or pans soak in the sink and no flour sprinkled pastry board rests on the counter. My sandwich tastes dry; the bread sticks in my throat, so I pick out and eat the chicken loaf. I take the brownie and go to my room.

The floor creaks in an odd way I never noticed before, and the door to the linen closet is ajar, as if somebody or something might be lurking there. I shove it with my shoulder on my way past, and the bang as it slams echoes in my ears. I flinch, expecting words of reprimand.

I kneel on the floor in my room and pull my favourite toys out of their box: a play-farm with tin barn, and plastic fences and farm animals. Something is not right. The hens don't cluck as I set them into their pen, nor do the pigs snort in their sty, and worst of all, the horses refuse to nicker or prance. I hear wind swishing the branches of the fir tree. A sudden gust whacks a limb against my window.

I wander back to the kitchen where I tidy the remains of my lunch. Paddy gets a few crusts. With my apple clamped in my mouth, I yank on the plastic overshoes, grab my coat, and push the dog out the door. Maybe somebody else has finished lunch, and we can play in the schoolyard. When I come home later, Mum will be home.

1909–1916: The Family Game

After their marriage, Ethel and Ashton lived with Ethel's sister Clara and her husband Ebbott Elliott. Ashton had helped put in their crop the previous spring prompting the offer of accommodation from his new brother-in-law. In the following year, Ethel and Ashton leased a farm, known as the Godley place, in Methven. Very likely Ashton found running a farm with Ethel much easier than his previous single-handed experience, even if she was soon pregnant. Their son Albert, named for his maternal grandfather, arrived in September of 1910, to the admiration of his parents and relatives. The next month saw another celebration when Ethel's sister Hazel married Newton Elliott.

By 1915, family encircled Ashton. To his great pleasure, he had persuaded Emma and Alba to come to Wawanesa for good. They were close to him as well as to John and Beatrice, and their two children, Howard and Ethel. Alba had worked as a bookkeeper in Simcoe, and soon found a similar position in Wawanesa. With family near and happy prospects for their own family, Ashton and Ethel were living their dream–this in spite of the outbreak of World War I in 1914.

Neither Ashton nor John could leave their families to enlist, but Ethel's brother Charles joined up as soon as he turned seventeen. Compounding the fears and losses of the war years came the shocking death of John Marlatt on June 23, 1916. Only thirty years old, John died of a heart attack. Ashton mourned John, not only as a brother, but also as the friend of many shared adventures. Emma, who had already lost one child, Lulu, surely felt the agony of outliving two of her children.

Widowed, Beatrice needed to support her family, and with limited employment options in Wawanesa, she returned to her parents' home in Simcoe. There she eventually found work in a woolens mill. Ethel and Ashton were sad to lose Beatrice and the children, but with the support of family and friends, they gathered up the threads of their lives and faced the future together.

Not one to give in to loss and discouragement, Ashton continued to raise and train workhorse teams, and as a dynamic individual and a natural leader, he became involved in civic affairs. Although he may not have aspired to public office in Methven, his ascension to the lofty position of Mayor of Methven involved a well.

The well was located at the fence line on the south side of Ashton's farm. Many in the neighbourhood used it, although it belonged to Ashton. As is the case in any gathering of humankind, the unpretentious Village of Methven had its town big shot. Or, as Alice would have said, "Muckety Muck." This individual, who was also the postmaster, considered himself the Mayor, but as Methven was never a large community, and indeed no longer exists, this was not a demanding official position. One day when Ashton pumped water for his own use, this man arrived with his cattle, and with the arrogance of the self-entitled, he expected immediate access.

This was the last straw for Ashton and he said, "You have been Mayor of Methven long enough. From now on, I am Mayor."

Alice did not detail what duties Ashton performed in his new role, but his civic leadership did not prevent him from playing sports. Since joining the local baseball team in the Uncle Ernest days, he had continued playing baseball and also curled and played hockey. As an exceptional athlete, he was in demand with local teams. He also officiated, rounding out the family income with modest fees from umpiring and refereeing. His enthusiasm for sports never waned. In later years, he shared his passion and belief in fair play with his children and young players in his community. Alice, growing up under Robert's influence, had already absorbed this attitude–another life tenet shared with Ashton.

1960–1963: Gordon River–"Play Ball!"

In Gordon River, baseball became a rite of spring as soon as weather allowed, and our fervor gained momentum with the increase in evening daylight. The men's teams, as well as the boys' Little League influenced our passion for the game. My father played on the Gordon River team against teams from nearby communities including Honeymoon Bay, Mesachie Lake, Camp Six, and Lake Cowichan. In Gordon River, the games were played on the red earth field on the level below the school, but this dirt diamond was at least graced with a netted backstop and an elevated, screened platform for the scorekeepers. These were usually women. I remember one exasperated lady telling my friends and me, upon our umpteenth inquiry on the score, to just watch the game. Regardless of our apparent ineptitude as fans, we enjoyed the men's games as well as those of the two boys who joined the Little League team in Honeymoon Bay. There were no girls' teams.

Despite the lack of baseball opportunities for females on formal leagues, there was no such sexist attitude in camp. Our games included every child who could stand up and swing a bat and even then, there were only about ten or twelve people. We played softball and hardball. We placed a great deal of importance on 'fair play' and this demanded negotiation and creativity. The two Little League boys naturally had to be one to a team. We nominated two captains, and, after their selections, there would be some bargaining to achieve balance. That is, one team might have five and another six people, but the team with six would perhaps have the youngest or poorest player.

Because the school ground was gravel, and the men's diamond was too large, we played on the grassy playground of the home site. It had the only piece of playground equipment: a slide built in the Gordon River machine shop with leftover materials during a slack time. With home plate placed in front, the slide became a backstop and a handy perch for onlookers. There was no pitcher's mound. We marked out home plate and the bases with rocks, boards, sweaters, burlap bags, cardboard, or whatever other oddments came to hand. A gunnysack or a piece of matting was a prize cherished for the season.

On that wedge of grass, we learned the value of sportsmanship and fair play, reinforced with the rules of our school and Mrs. Marlatt. While we allowed smaller children four strikes instead of three, and a few feet leadoff on bases, we were fervent about winning and giving it our best. There were often hot debates on whether a hit was in or foul. Since there were no lines, this would also be a point of negotiation, and a hit might be in one time and foul the next. Whether it was allowed or not depended on the age and ability of the hitter, or the number of runs that hitter already had, or the current score of the game. Our games, with their lop-sided, short-handed teams, did not conform to regulations, but we had fun. There were arguments, but the process of sorting out differences of opinion, negotiating compensation and agreement, and adjusting standards so all could play, was a valuable learning experience.

1916–1922: The Family Band

Although his self-appointed status as Mayor of Methven was neither demanding nor prestigious, Ashton must have had some influence and connections in the Wawanesa district. His sister Alba found work as a bookkeeper for the Wawanesa Mutual Insurance Company, attaining the position of treasurer. Ashton claimed he was instrumental in this. His influence apparently also extended to that of matchmaker with the introduction of Alba to his friend Walter Leachman. Still, it is arguable that since Alba boarded at the home of Charles and Mary Leachman, meeting their son Walter was a natural consequence.

Early in 1922, the Marlatts were surprised to discover Ethel was pregnant with another child due to arrive in the fall. They were also apprehensive, as it had been twelve years since the birth of Albert, and Ethel would be thirty-seven in June. Their unease was somewhat diverted when Alba and Walter announced their engagement. At twenty-nine and thirty-six respectively, these two were by no means starry-eyed youngsters when they married on October 17, 1922. Three days later, on October 20, the family rejoiced again with the safe arrival of Ashton and Ethel's baby girl. Christened Irene, she became a special pet of big brother Albert who had enjoyed twelve years as an only child.

R.Rigsby

For more than eighteen years, Ashton and Ethel lived in the Wawanesa area. They raised their family, and had the company of friends and relatives. Ashton continued to help Uncle Ernest. Perhaps it was the stress of dealing with his uncle, but at the age of thirty-five, Ashton took up gambling and smoking, along with imbibing the occasional drink. Alice later laughed at him for indulging in these vices so late in life when he should have known better.

Such vices did not distract Ashton's interest in horses. This interest led to horse racing–specifically trotters, a hobby that was shared, and perhaps encouraged, by Ashton's friend Harry Mooney. On Harry's advice, Ashton acquired a promising trotter named Major Direct.

The Major raced in Wawanesa and neighbouring towns of Carmen, Deloraine, and Boissevain. Young Albert, then in his teens, often drove. One winter, when Albert was sixteen, they took the horse to Winnipeg to race on the frozen Red River. The Major wore cleated horseshoes for traction. Albert wore a terrified expression, but was keen to race.

Whether Major won or not was not revealed in Alice's narrative, but the love of horses was another point of connection when Alice and Ashton met. They passed this tradition to Betty Lou who also loved them, and was once part owner of a pacer named Smart Crack. Either through her stories, or through inadvertent comments, Alice bequeathed her love of horses to her children and pupils.

1961: Gordon River–Bands of Girls

The sun has shone for several weeks, and the gravel terraces, over which the camp has temporary dominion, have absorbed every ray. Each pebble radiates heat. In the long afternoons, heat-haze shimmers like melting glass. No coastal breezes bring showers, and logging is suspended. The woods are parched, and under such conditions any spark from machinery, steel caulked boots, or scraping chain, could smoulder in secret. Then with their hunger for fuel, stealthy flames could creep from their hiding place to consume felled logs, seedling trees, and standing timber alike. They could sweep outwards and upwards transitioning from peckish smudge to starving inferno.

Fires in rough bush on steep terrain are grueling to tame. They are treacherous for loggers who are called upon to fight such blazes and expensive for logging companies. Therefore, the woods, and the camp, are in shutdown mode pending rain.

There is no sign of a sea change as dusk settles over camp, and the bowl of the valley holds the lingering heat of the searing summer day. The sky is a sultry green-grey. The sun has disappeared behind Burma Mountain, but the unnamed mountain opposite flaunts a pink-orange crown where the last rays of sun strike the tuft of trees at its summit. The crown shrinks with every second, and as dusk deepens in the valley, vagrant puffs of cool air edge down the mountain slopes. The cooler air is not so much felt as smelled; the dust, oil, woodchips, and dry bracken scent of the camp is overlaid by a fresher, greener scent.

Although the mountainsides are shorn of the timber for which this camp exists, there is plenty of greenery among the stumps. Seedling trees, planted in the late forties have thrived and many are now as tall as a man. The future crop of timber slowly obscures the silver stumps. Among the crop are bracken ferns and Oregon grape, salal and fireweed, paintbrushes and tiger lilies, red current, elderberry, thimbleberry, salmonberry, blackberry, huckleberry and blueberry. Along streambeds, willow, cottonwood and alder shoot up, their growth measured in feet each season. Varying scents of vegetation, sprouting, growing, seeding, or decaying, pervade the air.

Heedless of the growth of trees, but energized by the cooling air, children play outside, taking advantage of the long days of summer.

Some of these days exist in a parallel universe of limitless prairie, where we are horses, wild and free. Of course, we are also beautiful, fast, and fearless, and tonight we canter across a windy plain, searching for fresh water and green pasture. The roads, fences, and gardens of camp have faded away, replaced with seas of waving grass, shallow sloughs, and stands of quaking aspen.

It feels fantastic to run and run, from the playground to the rink, down the hill to the empty school, and through the stumps to the river. We spent most of the day at our favourite swimming hole where some mothers sunbathed on the tiny patch of beach while toddlers waded in the shallows.

My friends and I love the river, but even though it is summer, the water numbs our fingers and toes and we can never stay in for long. Between dips, we warm on the rocks like lizards, where we listen to the *river's constant voice. The voice is a whisper in summer, but it is never silent, and although full of bubbles, the water is clear enough to see every rock on the bottom, even in the deepest pool. We cannonball into this pool from a huge slab of granite jutting out from the bank, and dive to the bottom where we pick up stones and waterlogged sticks. This year a big log washed into the pool from upstream, and has become our ocean liner. We christened her 'Canberra,' in honour of the Australian capital city.*

At the end of June, we studied countries and capitals. Our world map is immense and rolls down over the chalkboard. When Mrs. Marlatt called out a country, we took turns naming the capital city and pointing to it on the map. Unlike most capital cities, Canberra is a planned city, and I love the name. It is perfect for our great log that is big enough for at least five people to climb aboard. We will play there again tomorrow.

But tonight it is cool enough to run, and we are horses. There are four of us, all different colours, and we are Lightning, Star, Blaze, and Midnight. We have broken off branches of Scotch broom and stuck them in the back of our shorts for tails. The bent over piece stuck in my shorts scratches the small of my back, but I ignore this, as tonight I am the stallion. My band has just eluded a pack of wolves, but no sooner do we slow to rest than we see a fire in the distance. It is sweeping across the prairie toward us, and I must lead my band to safety. We gallop on.

We come to a deep gorge with jagged rocks in the bottom, and if we can jump it, we will be safe. Some mares in my band are terrified to leap, and I run behind them neighing and biting until all of them find the courage to jump. Then I follow them. I am tired from chasing the others, and I limp from a rock bruise in my hoof, but the fire threatens. My band still needs me on the other side, so I gallop to the very edge of the gorge, make a giant leap and land with room to spare. My mares neigh their happiness and we canter away.

Our headlong flight halts when we hear a mother calling from that other universe. It is time to go in. We release the horses of our imagination to roam the prairie while we jump the ditch and go home.

1922–1928: Prosperity, Pain, and Promise

Ashton's hunch that he could be successful hiring out his workhorses as opposed to being a full-time farmer proved true. The team he had trained on his homestead had enabled him to compete for other contracts in the area, and after his first successful job on the bridge, Ashton had continued to train and work reliable teams. He had also invested in threshing equipment and hired out his team, labour, and implements during the fall harvest.

After the First World War, when factories manufacturing the machines of war turned to the manufacture of machines of industry, tractors and engine driven farm equipment became more available and affordable. The demand for workhorse teams slumped. Realizing this, Ashton bought the Wawanesa International Harvester business in 1922. The boom year of 1927 saw the sale of twenty-seven binders, which the seventeen-year-old Albert helped set up. The business prospered and funded the purchase of Ethel's parents' house where they all moved, Emma included.

With every high there is often a low. The August death of Ashton's seventy-year-old mother diminished the family by one. Emma had been with Ashton and Ethel since Albert was a baby.

The following year, 1928, after six years of ownership, Ashton sold his business to one of the Jackson clan. He accepted a job with the International Harvester outlet in Brandon for which he became a blockman for the eastern sector of Saskatchewan. Recollecting his pottery-selling era, Ashton resurrected his lessons on salesmanship, and like those summer days of his childhood, he was again on the road. While he extolled the virtues of binders and tractors, Ethel and Irene stayed in Brandon with Ethel's sister, Hazel. Albert, then eighteen, went west to work in a hardware store in Eastend, Saskatchewan.

The gratification of a prosperous new career and a maturing family came to a tragic end on July 6, 1928 with the death of Ethel from the complications of a miscarriage. Before she died, Ethel stated that she wanted five-year-old Irene to live with her sister, Hazel. Ashton took Ethel's final request equally as hard as her death, but as Irene was so young, he had few options. The child needed a home and schooling, and he could not take her with him on every tour of his territory.

With his family scattered or lost, Ashton's nineteen-year chapter of family life ended. At forty-one, and now a homeless peddler of farm machinery, Ashton doubted he would ever again know the happiness of having a wife and children under his own roof.

R.Rigsby

Then the stars aligned, and in the autumn of 1929, Ashton met Alice. By the following spring, he was certain he could no longer live without this captivating woman as his wife.

Last night he had called Alice from Swift Current. She had laughed and said that any time on Sunday was fine, and yes, of course, she would love to go for a drive. She had admonished him not to drive too fast and to pay attention to the road. She would wait, and chuckled in her distinctive throaty way. Alice never giggled. He could envision the quirk she had of throwing back her head to laugh when she was particularly delighted about something. He hoped very much she was truly delighted to hear his voice, and he hoped even more she would be delighted to hear what he had to say.

If a tire hadn't blown on that poxy piece of road before Gull Lake, he would have been in Maple Creek hours ago. The only pay phone in Gull Lake had been out of order, and being Sunday, no stores were open either, so he hadn't been able to let her know he would be late.

The car bumped in and out of a rut and pitched toward the rough on the side of the road.

"Damn. Slow down Curly my boy–just as she told you. You can't get another flat."

Ashton grinned.

Sure talk to myself a lot now, he thought. It's good to have something talk about, even if the present conversation is one-sided.

He reduced pressure on the gas, engaged the clutch, and shifted down. The early evening shadows stretched, like a breath held too long, across fields awaiting the plough. Ashton had rolled down his window, as it had been unseasonably warm, and with his arm resting on the sill, he smelled the dusty furrows in the fields bordering the road. A few sparrows scratching the roadside flew up and into the willows lining a shallow slough. At the reduced speed, Ashton saw where the water had retreated from the edge leaving a whitish ring of hexagonal cracks on its shore.

A very dry spring, thought Ashton. It reminds me of that other spring, so long ago, when I first set eyes on Ethel. That we should marry seemed natural and right. We had so many good years together, and I

- 108 -

never believed we would not grow old together. The first year after I lost Ethel was awful. Poor Irene was practically an orphan, and Albert tried to be strong for all our sakes. It was a wise decision to take Irene on the road with me last summer, but finding hotels where she could get her hair done in the ringlets Hazel insisted upon was a challenge. But, the trip was fun too, and helped both of us.

In spite of everything, I can still rattle off equipment specs and features, and talk to the good folk on the farms as if I am one of them.

*"Well, Hell, I **am** one of them," he said aloud.*

He shifted up, and pressed the gas.

Sales have been very good. That stock market thing last fall kind of slowed things down, and it was a poor winter with little moisture, so farmers might be cautious, but I'm sure it will all come right. Driving about the prairies selling binders and tractors has given me lots of time to think about Ethel's death. I thought I might lose the pain out here in the 'bald-headed prairie.'

And then I met Alice. It was a lucky break when I took the west block. One thing for certain, my life started feeling right again with the first words out of her mouth. And then later, fancy her asking me to take her to the dance! What a gal! She could dance the legs off a cast iron hall tree, and talk to anybody about anything. And so funny! Her eyes could sparkle with good humour or flash brimstone when provoked.

"Whoa, watch the road and quit wool-gathering, you addlepated old fool."

The car bumped through another rut and the tiny lights of Maple Creek appeared as specks of fairy dust in the twilight. Ashton flipped on the lights and stretched his spine until something cracked. Then he stretched each arm as much as he was able within the car.

Old fool. Am I too old? I feel good. Not fat in spite of all the driving. Can still skate circles around most guys on the ice. Can still give a good run around the bases. Have a good job, good prospects, good energy . . .

Ashton's cracking spine tingled at the next thought that came into his head, swiftly followed by the uncertainty of what Alice might say . . .

R.Rigsby

Chapter Ten: The Teacher and the Traveller

1979: Leader X

Alice rolls over for the tenth time. Her eyes refuse to close, and she glares into the dark above her head.

I usually just drop right off to sleep, she thinks. Perhaps I haven't taken enough exercise today. To be sure, the day was cool and blustery, so in the afternoon I allowed Art to drive me to the post office. It was only a few blocks, but I hadn't relished the prospect of the cold wind in my face, and I have only a light jacket. Betty Lou said we would drive to Swift Current next week for winter shopping. She mentioned something about buying me that green sweater. What green sweater?

She closes her eyes, and then opens them, but not a scrap of light penetrates the blind and the drawn drapes.

"Blacker than the inside of a cow," she mumbles. The children always laughed at that expression, but I like it dark when I sleep. Except for a few months in Regina, my bedrooms have always been dark, even in Gordon River.

She closes her eyes, recalling her school apartment.

My bedroom faced west toward the river and away from camp where a few poles bore lights. One couldn't call them 'streetlights,' as the gravel roadways could hardly be dignified as such. The lights were more like beacons for lost moths than illumination for people out after dark. There was no light at all outside my bedroom. And I loved the sound of the river at night too–the soft warble of summer and the hiss of the spring thaw when there was a much stronger current . . .Swift Current?

Alice remembers when Ashton telephoned from Swift Current before he proposed. Stan took the call.

I was sitting on the couch with my book, but Stan told him I was out. She jumped around and giggled while I tried to wrest the phone out of her hand. Of course Ashton knew I was there but played along.

"Well never mind," he said, "I have lots of other girls who would be glad to see me."

Stan finally gave up the phone and took herself off downstairs, so I could have a few private words. Ashton seemed very anxious to go for a drive and have a talk, and I laughed at his anxiety. He said he would arrive around dinner.

Alice smiles, and shuts her eyes.

Stan went visiting for the afternoon and winked when she said she would be back late. I had dinner, but wandered around the apartment all Sunday afternoon–all dressed up and nowhere to go. I finally pulled out my lesson planner. I had prepared the week's lessons, but it never hurt to have another plan just in case. I tried to be annoyed for being kept waiting, but was worried that something had happened. Then I heard the car door slam, followed by a knock downstairs.
Alice drifts off to sleep.

1930: The Toughest Sales Pitch of All

Alice demurred when Ashton asked her to marry him. She told him she would have to think about it. After all, he, at forty-two was sixteen years her senior. The fact that Ashton had children, one of whom was only seven, was not an issue: she was fond of children. She enjoyed her students and had always been the caring elder sister to her younger siblings.

Yet, she loved her freedom. She earned her own money, kept her own hours, chose her own friends, and participated as she wished in the community. Would Ashton expect her to quit her job to be a homemaker? What if there were children? Did she want children? Did the age difference matter? Alice had some thinking to do.

Ashton went on the road, and a week later he called from Gull Lake. Alice "beat around the bush" on his proposal and later observed this very much set the tone for their life together–they bantered back and forth, teased one another, and joked, but somehow, they reached a profound, but implicit, level of communication.

On that evening, Alice kept up the game with Ashton until she asked if he remembered a certain girl whom he had asked to marry him.

Ashton proclaimed he did indeed, and Alice said "Well, you can have her!"

She meant herself, of course, and Ashton was at her door in an hour and a half. Their courtship was brief but the romance endured.

Ashton and Alice forewent the tradition of Ashton placing an official request of her parents for her hand in marriage. At twenty-six,

Alice was her own woman and did not need her parents' approval, saying, "You can be jolly well sure I never asked."

She must have enlightened Agnes and Robert about her prospective husband but didn't recall their response. Her parents, if they had had any concerns on the subject, would have known that, when Alice made up her mind to do something, it was as good as done. As it happened, Agnes and Robert knew this Marlatt man from his sales calls in Rocanville, before his transfer to the east block. He had turned up at dances, and they remembered him as the man who gave away cigarettes.

Alice went home in June of 1930, and a tentative wedding date was set for the following year. Ashton told his son about the impending nuptials, and Albert, pleased for Alice and his Dad, decided Irene must meet her new future mother. Borrowing Ashton's car, he went to Brandon to bring her from Aunt Hazel's, but let slip his Dad had become engaged. Aunt Hazel was not pleased.

For almost two years, Hazel had cared for Irene. In accordance with Ethel's last wish, Hazel believed that Irene would remain in her home until marriage. Albert pleaded with Hazel to let Irene go, and Hazel finally relented on the condition that she not come back. She packed Irene's belongings and wrote a long letter to Ashton. In this missive, she expressed her displeasure and pronounced that Ashton, and his new wife, must now take care of Irene. As an indication she had no expectation of seeing Irene again, Hazel enclosed Ethel's wedding ring. This was to be Irene's upon her marriage.

Ashton called Alice in Rocanville and asked if she would consider moving the wedding date up to–*now*. Alice refused to talk about it on the telephone and asked him to come to Rocanville. At the Blair farm, Ashton formally met Agnes and Robert. In the face of her assertion to marry as she pleased, Alice was relieved that her parents approved of Ashton. After a family consultation, they set the wedding date for August 30th, 1930.

Alice and Ashton had no idea of the impending hardships of the next ten years. The worldwide depression triggered by the stock market crash, combined with freakish weather on the Great Plains would affect the lives of millions of people, and those of Alice and Ashton would not be immune.

R.Rigsby

The auspicious day dawned and, like many more to come during the decade of drought, became "a hot, hot day." Under blistering sun, the modest wedding party assembled. Alice's good friend Stan could not attend, nor could Alba and Walter. Because it was the middle of harvest, not all invitees could spare the time. It was also short notice. Those who attended, including those who speculated at the short notice, celebrated, and offered traditional toasts of long life and happiness to the new couple. It was too scorching to serve hot food, so they banqueted on cold meats, salads, and "jellies of all sorts."

In the bridal suite at the hotel in Broadview, Alice and Ashton found seclusion for their wedding night. In the morning, they spent the balance of the Labour Day weekend on a leisurely drive home to Maple Creek, savouring their solitude. They were in love and married, they had work, they had prospects and plans, and they had laughter and friendship. Alice would resume teaching on Tuesday, and as they made their way across the province, they took unhurried breaks. They bought peaches. Ashton, pretending he had a pit stuck in his throat, gasped and sputtered, and then laughed at Alice's alarm. The wedding trip lasted only the width of Saskatchewan, but the honeymoon lasted all of Alice's life.

Ashton had rented a modern house with "a cobblestone fence," and Alice had shopped for furniture in Regina. Eight hundred dollars on credit later (her year's salary and a measure of her confidence), she had a chesterfield suite, a dining suite with china cabinet, and of course, a bedroom suite. With elegant rounded head and footboards, the wooden bed and its matching dresser and chiffonier were the latest design in bedroom furnishings. Setting up her first family home with such flair thrilled Alice, and although she wasn't making a fortune as a teacher, her job was secure. Ashton also had a solid job, or so they thought. The gloom of October 1929 had not yet cast its shadow across their optimism.

They moved into their home, and Irene arrived from Swift Current where she had stayed with friends. The family settled down to domestic routine. Irene went to school, Alice taught, and Ashton sold tractors. When Ashton joined Albert's hockey team in Eastend, Alice realized, in the interest of saving her sanity, she must cultivate an appreciation for sports.

On the lengthening evenings at home they talked, read, or played cards. Ashton liked reading and often read to Alice while she cooked, or folded laundry, or ironed. As opportunity, or the completion of chores, afforded, Alice and Ashton played two-handed bridge, sometimes called 'Honeymoon Bridge,' for obvious reasons. Alice said that Ashton usually won because, "he could see ahead a lot further than I could."

Moonless dark in Maple Creek, and cold has overwhelmed the feeble heat of the October afternoon. There will surely be morning frost, but inside the brick house the kitchen stove emanates a woodsy heat, while the coal furnace in the basement pumps radiant warmth throughout the other rooms.

Supper is over. Alice washes the dishes, sets them on the sideboard, and picks up her knitting. She joins Irene at the kitchen table. Between rows of knit-purl, she helps Irene with her arithmetic problems. Homework completed, Alice puts away the dishes while Irene prepares for bed. Goldie the canary, a wedding gift from a friend of Ashton, hops from swing to perch and chirps at Alice as she fills her seed and water cups.

Irene has picked out a story and Alice reads to her, but Irene, with a half-smile on her elfin face, is in the Land of Nod before the ending. Alice tucks her in and shuts the bedroom window.

Alice adores her first home. It is snug and clean, and the furniture she fell in love with in Regina looks chic and stylish in it. She plans to sew curtains and cushions, and is knitting a matching afghan for the couch. She looks forward to planting a garden in the spring and will show Irene how to space the seeds. Perhaps Irene would like a plot of her own. Alice thinks of the fresh vegetables they will have all summer and intends to have plenty to can or store for winter. The peaches she canned in September should last them through Christmas at least, and she will make more applesauce from the barrel of apples the Grahams sent as a wedding gift.

Alice packs lunches for everybody. Tomorrow Ashton will be back on the road for a few days, and she and Irene will eat their lunches at school. They have bread and cold chicken, and biscuits and jam, and apples. Alice slices raw carrots to place in Ashton's and Irene's lunches, but not in her own.

Irene has settled in at her new school, and her teacher keeps Alice informed on progress. Alice believes Irene should be further ahead, but the child has been through a lot of upheaval. Things will be better for her now, and the bedtime story is a treat for both of them.

A draught flows through the kitchen window Alice had opened to clear out the cooking smells. She pulls it closed, turns down the damper on the stove, and fills the kettle for morning. She checks the canister of oatmeal to make sure there is enough for breakfast porridge, gives the floor a final sweep, and empties the dustpan into the stove. She can relax for the hour remaining before bed.

Ashton has been re-reading a two-day-old copy of a Regina newspaper, but drops it on the floor when Alice appears in the doorway. Grinning, he reaches for the deck of cards on the side table.

Alice recently learned to play Honeymoon Bridge, and they sit on either end of the Winnipeg couch with cards laid out between them. Alice gains six tricks and can sense a big win. She jiggles a foot and grips the remaining cards in her hand. She studies her choices and with twitchy fingers lays down her next card. Ashton holds his hand close. Then he swoops in and takes all of the remaining tricks. Alice's big win is thwarted, but she is not about to take her loss without reprisal.

Crying an exasperated "Ooohhh," she reaches across the cards, and gives Ashton just the smallest of shoves. Taken by surprise, he rolls backward off the armless couch, lands against the radiator, and breaks a rib.

Alice laughed when she related this story to Betty Lou, and it is likely, regardless of, or in spite of, broken bones, Ashton laughed too. The man who could feign choking for the sake of a joke had a sense of humour matching that of Alice.

1930: The Contagion Spreads

Within three months, the comfortable, barely established routine ended when Ashton lost his job. The Depression had afflicted International Harvester, and he was let go on December 1st, 1930. Dread and fear replaced complacent optimism. They could not survive on

Alice's salary alone, and it was up to Ashton to support his family. Since age fourteen, he had never been without a job, but his employment options in Maple Creek were limited. In the depths of winter, no farmers needed hands. There were no town enterprises big enough to employ a salesman, and the dipping economy was such that the few shopkeepers had no need of help. Alice was contracted to finish the school year. Until June, they would have to manage on a reduced income, savings, and preserves.

Ashton assumed the reluctant role of chief cook and bottle washer, and although a competent cook, he wasn't charmed with his new role. This role then encompassed that of chief nurse when Irene caught measles, immediately followed by chicken pox. The doctor placed the house under quarantine and outfitted Ashton with cap and gown, but such precautions did not prevent Alice from catching chicken pox as well. She had escaped the disease as a child and in her several schools, but she would have helped Ashton with Irene, and exposure could hardly have been avoided. When infected with chicken pox, adults often suffer more than children, and Alice was out of commission for several days. Then Albert came home with an Achilles tendon ruptured while playing hockey. Ashton had his gloved hands full.

1961: Gordon River–Viral Birthday Party

An eagle hovers above the camp. He has drifted from downriver where he dined on spawning salmon floundering in the shallows. Stuffed on fish, he has allowed up-draughts to carry him here, but there is no point in going farther, as no salmon spawn so far upriver. His yellow eyes glower at the works of man built in the triangle between two rivers.

The camp poaches in the late August afternoon. Recent rain showers have raised the humidity level, and logging has resumed, as have logging repairs. In the shop yard, a welder buzzes on a log-truck propped on jacks. Blue sparks die in the gravel. A yellow pickup shudders to a halt in front of the open shop doors. Two men emerge shoving a trolley loaded with a large coil of steel cable. The driver lends a hand, and shares a joke, as they hoist the coil into the back of the pickup. He jumps in his cab and waves as the truck roars away in a cloud of beige dust. From within the shop, metallic hammering sends echoes over the ridge and its hedge of fir trees.

R.Rigsby

In the home site beyond the ridge, a woman pulls weeds in her garden and with a garden fork turns over a bushy plant. Musky earth, imported with some expense and toil, drops from yellow-brown potatoes. They will be on the supper table tonight.

Not at all interested in potatoes, the eagle banks west. With lazy flaps, he glides downriver to the labour of consuming dying fish. His vacation is over, but in camp, some continue to make the most of their own vacations.

Our summer holiday is almost over, and up until this week, it has been perfect. We have played outside after dark, swum in the river, picnicked at the lake, and picked berries in the stumps. Although we will soon go back to school, I am not bored and was looking forward to these last few weeks of August. Was.

A few days ago, Kathy and Kelly woke up with red spots on their stomachs, and later spots popped out on their brother. They have chickenpox. Since then more people have broken out, so nearly every kid in camp has spots. Except me. I had chickenpox when I was three, so I am immune.

Mrs. Marlatt told us chickenpox is a virus similar to smallpox, but not nearly as serious. Smallpox is deadly, which is why we were vaccinated. We were not vaccinated for chickenpox because it is not a threat for most healthy people with normal immunity. We discussed the meaning of immunity, and how Europeans who first came to North America brought diseases like measles, chicken pox, and smallpox, and many native people died because they lacked immunity.

We know everybody in camp will recover. Some might have a few tiny scars like the one I have on my forehead, but nobody is in serious danger. The problem is that there's a birthday coming up and we worry there might not be a party.

* * *

The word is out. There will be a birthday party after all. Since every kid in camp has been exposed, there is no point in not having a party. We are already calling it 'The Chicken Pox Birthday Party.'

1931: Trimming the Sails

Ashton's patients eventually recovered, but his anxiety level must have reached the stratosphere when Alice announced, come the following December, the family census would increase by one.

Teaching while noticeably pregnant simply was not done in 1931, so there was no possibility of teaching in the fall. Nevertheless, if Alice had not become pregnant, there was nothing for Ashton in Maple Creek. A family summit rendered a decision to move to Wawanesa where Ashton had stored his threshing equipment. Among other implements, he owned an International tractor and a separator. If they could reach Manitoba before harvest, he was confident he could hire out his labour and equipment as he had done years before. Ashton also had money owed to him from his dealership days and thought, if he could collect, this would suffice until he obtained harvest contracts. Alice finished the school year before her condition became evident, and handed in her resignation.

Unfortunately, there was not enough money to pay for their furniture. Alice regretted shipping most of it back. They found a couple who offered to buy the chesterfield suite, but who didn't have the cash on hand. Ashton and Alice needed that cash to pay for their trip to Manitoba, and consequently could not vacate their house until they were paid. In mid-July, they were still waiting.

Impatient at the delay, their Scottish landlady kept asking when they would be "oot," and began dropping by without notice. On one occasion, she walked into the house "carrying her slop pail." Alice, entertaining friends, was embarrassed at this tactless interruption of her tea party. Ashton told the overanxious landlady to "keep her nose out of their business,"–they would advise when they were ready to move.

At last, the chesterfield buyers came up with the money, and the Marlatts shipped, via train, their remaining furniture and goods to Robert and Agnes. They then packed food, baggage, Irene, and Goldie the canary into the Chevy and trailer. Setting forth to an uncertain future, Alice said goodbye to her first home as a married woman. Not for many years would she live in a home comparable to their snug house with its cobblestone wall.

They have no money for a hotel, and as dusk rises out of the eastern sky, they watch for a campsite. Alice points, and Ashton turns off the highway onto a side road between fields where shoots of green wheat poke through desiccated clods. The July rains have not arrived, and if they do not do so soon, the crop will be in trouble. The veil of green over the fields will fade to worrisome yellow and then to hopeless brown. There has been wind, but no clouds scudding ahead, and not a drop of moisture. Instead, the wind has lifted soil into the sky and what should be a twilight of cool grey is warm taupe.

Careful to stop before the first furrow, Ashton backs the car and trailer into a field entry. Earlier in the day, a dust storm overtook them, and Ashton hopes they never experience another. He shakes dust from the car blanket and spreads it on the crinkling grass.

They supper on food Alice had packed. She remembers the huge valise her mother crammed to bulging when they went to Ontario, so many years ago. Like Agnes, she has cooked chicken, boiled eggs, fruit, bread, butter, and cheese, and like Agnes, she has far more than needed for the trip. After Alice tucks Irene into bed on the Winnipeg couch, she joins Ashton on the blanket, where they lean against each other, and discuss their plans in subdued tones. They can taste the acrid air.

The sun dips below the grit-hazed horizon. A few stars pinprick the matte black sky. After the flurry of packing and finishing a hundred things before the trip, their roadside camp is an oasis of tranquility. Conversation dwindles and they stare at the sky.

There is no traffic on this track. On the distant main road, the sporadic hiss of tires on gravel alternates with yelps of dogs or coyotes and the lowing of cattle as they bed down for the night. Grasshoppers chirp in the yellowing roadside grass, amorous frogs call from shrinking sloughs, and Goldie adds a few cheeps to the ad-lib chorale. Alice breathes in the familiar scent of young wheat in earthy furrows. A warm breeze stirs invisible vortices of dust and overhead there are hoots of gliding owls and fleeting shadows of bats.

If the hot dry weather was ideal for camping, it was also ideal for dust storms, especially in the years of the dirty thirties on the prairies. Such storms could last for days, and one caught the Marlatt's–"the worst dust storm you could ever imagine"–before they reached Swift Current.

They drove with the windows rolled up tight, sweltered in the claustrophobic stuffiness, and peered through the gloom. It was a slow go, and they did not travel the distance Ashton had planned. A trip presently done in eight hours took them two nights and two days. The first night was within sight of the lights of Swift Current, and the next near Grenfell.

When they reached the Blair farm, they shook out the dust, caught up on sleep in real beds, and shared their plans. Alice had already told her parents she was pregnant and was eager to talk about the upcoming event with her mother. Agnes and Robert had become grandparents with the arrival of Laura's daughter, Kathleen, in 1929, but they were pleased with the prospect of another grandchild. No doubt they thought the timing could be better, as a December birth added an extra element of risk if the winter was more severe than usual. They hoped Alice and Ashton would settle nearby.

Again, the Marlatts considered their options, but Manitoba still held the most promise. Ashton had many contacts there, plus his sister Alba and her husband Walter. Anxious to be in Manitoba as soon as possible, Ashton wanted to collect his debts, resurrect his threshing business, and settle the family before winter. After the briefest of visits, they resumed the journey.

In Brandon, the vagabonds reached the home of Hazel and Newton Elliott. Hazel, on meeting the new, obviously fertile, Mrs. Marlatt, forgave Ashton for replacing her sister. That Alice was more than capable of standing up for herself was proven, but that she could be charming and helpful ensured Hazel's surrender. Hazel offered to keep Irene until Ashton could find his family a place to live in the Wawanesa district.

The next destination was the home of Alba and Walter Leachman outside of Wawanesa. On the Red Bridge, they saw Walter on his way to town and flagged him down. Walter, excited at the return of his brother-in-law, "flew into town" to telephone Alba and told her "to get her corsets on and her stockings rolled up" because "Curly is coming with his new wife!" While they enjoyed the Leachmans' hospitality, Ashton went house hunting.

His first choice was a property known as the Fisher Place, and Alice went to work sweeping and cleaning. Before they moved in,

Ashton found what he judged a better location in a house southeast of Wawanesa. This house already sheltered a family who had the use of the upstairs, the kitchen and the dining room. The Marlatt's took the remaining two downstairs rooms, and shared the kitchen. There were now four of them, as Hazel had brought Irene to them, and Albert had rejoined the family. Like many young men of the times, Albert had lost his job. His situation was the leading edge of what would be three in ten men out of work before 1933, but, unlike many other young single men of the times, he had the option of going home.

While in Brandon, Ashton had called on his lawyer and had retrieved the invoices for outstanding debts the lawyer had not been able to collect. This was a good decision, as crops were scant, prices were low, and everybody was poor. The lawyer could not deal with anything but cash, but Ashton could. In lieu of cash, he collected chickens and pork, flour and beans, milk and butter. It had become too late in the year for Ashton to assemble his equipment and a threshing crew, so he put that enterprise on hold until the following year. Neither were local farmers looking for hands, and as in Maple Creek, no Wawanesa businesses needed help. Nor had Alice's vision of a garden full of vegetables to preserve for winter come to pass.

In late fall, Ashton resumed his previous official capacity at the rinks, earning about three dollars per game as a referee. The bill payments in food and kind, plus the bit of cash from the rinks kept the family going while they made themselves comfortable in their shared house and awaited the birth of the baby.

One evening in late December, the Leachmans were guests for a roast pork supper and were not surprised Alice was cooking and entertaining in her rotund condition. Alice thought nothing of it. She had adjusted to the challenges of pregnancy as she had coped with all of the trials and circumstances of her life. After an evening of food and cards, the Leachmans went home, but before they could hang their coats, they received the call to come back for Irene. The baby was on its way.

The child arrived at 6:00 a.m. on December 28th, 1931. A doctor and nurse attended, and Alice was exultant to be the mother of a six and three-quarter pound baby girl. She had wanted a girl first. Ashton, who already had a son and a daughter, was simply relieved that Alice and the baby were both healthy, and the anxiety of childbirth was over. Ashton wanted to call his new daughter 'Lulu' in honour of his late sister, but Alice balked, and they compromised with 'Betty Lou.'

Betty Lou looked much like all new babies, pink and wrinkly, but she also had a birthmark on her forehead and lip. The nurse would not let Alice see her until it had faded, and Alice had rested. It may have been overcautious on the part of the nurse, because such a small passing defect did not mar Alice's love for her new daughter. She dressed her in "voiles with lots of lace all around" and laid her in a padded oval basket. Irene learned the next day she had a new baby sister, but she could not see her for several more days as she had come down with a cold. Without complaint, Irene swallowed doses of nasty medicine. Whatever concoction Alba administered was not explained, but she soon pronounced Irene well enough to go home.

In 1931, nobody dismissed a cold. Many remembered the influenza deaths of the previous decade, and Betty Lou was small and frail. Jessie, and Laura with her young daughter Kathleen, came to help in the household while Alice saved her strength for the baby.

However, Betty Lou did not thrive. After several weeks her survival looked doubtful. To help his ailing baby, Ashton spent an outlandish sum of fifteen dollars on a cow and calf so fresh milk could be had, but Alice later observed "she wasn't sure it was such a bargain." No doubt she was referring to the cow and not the survival of Betty Lou.

The fresh cow's milk did not help. At three months, Betty Lou was underweight, and Alice was frantic. She had tried every supplemental formula she could find, but Betty Lou's sensitive stomach rejected most of what went into it. Finally, an elderly neighbour heard of Betty Lou's condition and offered her own special recipe. Betty Lou was able to keep down the magic potion and gained weight.

At nine years old, Irene joined her parents' anxiety over Betty Lou, and became very protective. She was thrilled to have a baby sister.

Alice said, "I pretty nearly had to ask her permission to give Betty Lou a bath."

When Betty Lou began to improve, Alice took her out every day. She strapped her basket, well covered with blankets, onto a sled, and walked backwards to make sure baby, cradle, and all, stayed in place.

Alice was a great believer in the benefits of fresh air and exercise whenever possible.

R.Rigsby

1960: Gordon River–Weathering the Storm

Rain, rain, and more rain. This is not strange, as it often rains in the valley where the two rivers join. In winter, it rains a great deal: heavy rain, showers and sprinkles, or drizzle lasting for days. The clouds are very low this November morning: the camp is under a pile of mashed potatoes. The precipitation du jour is heavy rain.

I run to school, jumping puddles all the way. As usual, I am first, and because there are so many puddles on the playground, I find a stick and scrape ruts between the bigger pools. My friends arrive, and we launch twigs and leaves to bump along the sides of our miniature Welland canals. We leave our puddley Great Lakes when Mrs. Marlatt calls us inside.

At recess we will make more canals and enlarge the harbour; if we stayed inside every time it rained, we would never play outside at all. Mrs. Marlatt tells us fresh air clears our brains, and we will not melt in the rain.

Later in the morning, I look up from my scribbler where I finish our reading questions, and stare at the window. So does everybody else. The rain has changed. It is coming down in torrents and beats on the flat gravel roof like hundreds of shots from my Dad's rifle. One of the little kids has covered her ears, and the others, including my sister, stare at the ceiling with huge eyes. The sky outside is very dark. Mrs. Marlatt sits in the reading circle with two people but shepherds them back to their seats. She stands with her back to us and looks out the windows, hands on hips.

Her grey hair shines white against the dark sky. We jump at a sudden flash of light, immediately followed by the sound of a thousand empty oil drums rolling across the roof. Somebody squawks, and a little kid slides under her desk. I am not afraid. Thunderstorms are rare and I stare at the window, determined not to blink. Another flash, followed by another roll of oil drums. The rain does not slow down, and 'pours cats and dogs,' as we like to say. I would like to see it pour horses.

Mrs. Marlatt turns to us and chuckles, "I think you people may stay in for recess."

Anxiety switches to excitement in the whisk of an eyelash. We can do the puzzle! While we arrange ourselves in a haphazard circle on the floor beside the heater, Mrs. Marlatt hands down the big puzzle box from the top storage shelves. Nobody knows how this puzzle of the United States came to be in this school. Knowing how Canada's few provinces and territories are arranged, we feel no sense of betrayal in enjoying this puzzle so much. We also know America has fifty states, yet in this puzzle, there are only forty-eight. Because it is old, there is no Alaska or Hawaii, but each of the other states is a separate piece in a bright colour, printed with its name, capital, and state flower.

We know the rules. First, we dump the puzzle on the floor, separate the pieces, turn them right side up, and stir them around. If some pieces appear close to where we know they should be, we stir again. We chatter, laugh, and argue.

Mrs. Marlatt goes to her apartment while we work. She pokes her head out when somebody shouts. Although it is recess, we are inside, and running or shouting is for outside, as the guilty party knows. Fourteen pairs of hands re-unite the states in a way the founding fathers of the republic never imagined. While stuffing a cookie into my mouth, I sit back and admire the completed work. The puzzle is finished, and so is recess.

Mrs. Marlatt reappears, walks to the board, and begins to write arithmetic problems. We gather up the puzzle, trying not to break it too much, and I put the box on her desk. I had forgotten the storm. The sky is lighter and, although still raining, it's not 'cats and dogs' anymore, but only 'mice and rats' maybe. I peer into my desk for my social studies book.

1932: Flotsam Adrift

Early in 1932, the Marlatt family forsook their rented communal quarters for improved housing at Uncle Ernest's farm. The crotchety geezer had again persuaded Ashton to work for him, this time in exchange for lodging. Uncle Ernest alloted them the use of two upstairs rooms, which Alice re-papered. Every residence, no matter how modest or temporary, received the benefits of her talent for textiles, paint, or wallpaper. Alice completed home improvements at Uncle Ernest's in time to turn her attention outdoors, and as soon as the ground warmed, she planted a garden. Alice was adamant that this year she would have plenty of canned produce for the winter.

Unfortunately, the convenience of their quarters at Uncle Ernest's was cut short, as again Ashton's working arrangement fell apart. Uncle Ernest, who never married and, according to Alice, was monosyllabic and chronically grumpy, may not have been an easy landlord, and life under his roof became untenable for a busy family of five. Late in the fall, the Marlatts moved into downtown Wawanesa.

In the luxury of a three-room apartment over the butcher shop, Alice again indulged her inclination for decorating. Equipped with skills learned from Agnes, Alice transformed flour and sugar sacks into curtains, tea towels, aprons, and housedresses. She acquired a dining suite and a rickety buffet that apart from its condition, had potential. She painted these pieces black, trimmed with red. With the addition of curtains dyed deep blue, her family's new lodging was soon a cozy home. Alice had more time to sew and catch up on projects as there were no cows to milk or weeds to pull, and the garden produce was canned or stored for the season. In addition, and much to the family's relief, Betty Lou's precarious health was much improved.

The peace of mind lasted until December–a month fraught with anxiety and sorrow. Betty Lou, having overcome her digestive problem and rickets, contracted pneumonia and was in "rough shape." When the child of very close friends died of pneumonia, Alice and Ashton mourned with their community, while suppressing their own terrors. With mustard plasters and feverfew as the only home remedies and limited medical therapies (penicillin was not yet available), Betty Lou's survival again appeared uncertain. The family prepared themselves for another funeral, but Betty Lou responded to their care, the crisis passed, and her condition improved.

Before they could relax, Alice suffered a miscarriage. This frightened Ashton as he had lost Ethel to the complications of miscarriage, but Alice, sad and disappointed, was soon on her feet. No woman ever forgets a miscarriage and the child who did not get a chance to be. Forty-seven years later, Alice recalled the incident with regret.

1933–1934: The Only Game in Town

With her usual grit, Alice put the trauma of her miscarriage and Betty Lou's illness behind her. Wawanesa was, and continues to be, a charming town. Alice took advantage of the benefits of living in town. She could, and did, go out whenever she wished: shopping, visiting, and fresh air walks with Betty Lou. She renewed her interest in community activities, and increased her circle of friends. This included her sister-in-law, Alba. There were ten years between Alba and Alice, but as Alba had married late, her children, Mildred and Winnifred, were under eight. The two women had much in common and their families were good friends as well as relatives.

While Alice made the most of town life, Ashton and Albert played the sports of the season: baseball in summer, and hockey and curling in winter. Alice, with her newly nurtured interest in sports, attended the games as a spectator cheering on her men, and as a helper serving coffee and lunch.

Sports were not without their hazards. In a time when neither players nor referees wore hockey helmets, Ashton caught a puck in the mouth that smashed several teeth. Like Robert years before, he pulled the broken teeth himself, but dentition issues were complicated by a lingering infection. Alice persuaded Ashton to see the dentist who offered various sample drugs. There was no money for expensive treatments, so the free samples were the only option. Over time, some miscellany of medicines, or Ashton's sturdy constitution, defeated the microbes.

Ashton and Albert, always thinking of ways to survive the tough times, decided they could earn money by cutting and selling firewood. They pooled their few dollars and bought a sawing machine. Alice did not reveal if Ashton and Albert purchased logs from private woodlots, or if they had permits to obtain timber from crown lands. Regardless, the farm-boys-turned-woodsmen cut, split, and sawed, disregarding slivers and sore backs. They loaded the firewood into a wagon-box hitched to the car, and delivered it all over town for three dollars per load. Occasionally Irene and Betty Lou went along for the ride.

On one such occasion, Betty Lou, outfitted in a new blue coat and matching hat, accompanied Albert, but before he finished his round of deliveries, Betty Lou's nose started to bleed. She was susceptible to nosebleeds, but this time it was severe, and Albert panicked. Unhitching and leaving the trailer, he tore home with Betty Lou who was by then "a bloody mess." Alice, with her usual composure, dealt with the nosebleed, but Betty Lou's outfit was a disaster. Alice soaked and scrubbed until it was clean except for a piece near the hem. Therefore, this coat, like Alice's aging wine coat, became unfashionably short. Although the coat was salvaged, Albert's confidence was not and, terrified Betty Lou could die of a nosebleed, he vowed he would never take his youngest sister anywhere again.

In the winter of 1933, Ashton cadged a job unloading railcars of coal. At the age of forty-six, he was tough and wiry (and still had most of his famous hair), so unassisted and by hand, he unloaded coal for five dollars per car. By the standards of the time, this was big money. His jack of all trades employment kept the family afloat during these years of deprivation and uncertainty. Umpire and referee, threshing crew boss, farmer, sawyer, and stevedore, Ashton maximized his entrepreneurial gifts and problem-solving skills. Alice did not resume her teaching career.

As she said, "I had no notion of teaching until you people [her children] were grown up."

She believed that mothers with small children should not work outside the home, and Ashton did not encourage the idea. Alice very likely could have found a teaching position, but to do so would have cast a grave reflection on Ashton's ability to support his family. Although Ashton's employment was almost day-by-day, he did not want to stay home to mind Irene and Betty Lou, and neither Alice nor Ashton expected anybody to look after the children without payment. Because of her own beliefs, and her husband's disinclination to encourage her, Alice did not apply for a teaching position.

Notwithstanding the unpredictable income, Alice and her family were comfortable in their three rooms over the butcher shop, and while the men worked, or worked at seeking work, Alice had plenty to fill her days. Keeping five people clothed, clean, and fed without any conveniences or appliances was a full-time job.

In addition to the human family members to care for, there was Goldie the canary, and a Persian housecat. Like the cartoon characters Sylvester and Tweety, this cat's mission in life was to consume the bird, and once it almost succeeded. While Alice was out, Ashton came home to find the birdcage on the floor and the cat with its head inside the cage. He grabbed a piece of stove wood and clobbered the cat, but the bird was gone. Assuming the bird must be inside the cat, Ashton was dismayed thinking he had killed the cat and lost the bird besides. Then, after a few moments, the cat came back to life, and a few cheeps from her haven on the curtain rod proved that Goldie too, had nine lives.

Cat and bird diversions, card games, and reading were the usual family evening entertainments, as they did not yet own a radio. Ashton listened to the national hockey games at the hotel, and then recounted the play by play for Alice, with gestures and actions–the instant replay of 1934. This was when Alice first heard (via Ashton's commentary) Foster Hewitt's, "he shoots, he scores," and she joined in Ashton's enthusiasm for Hockey Night in Canada. Bolstering Alice's enthusiasm was a conviction in the imperatives of fair play and good sportsmanship.

1962: Gordon River–He Shoots, She Scores!

All of the roadways in camp are gravel: those around the duplexes, bunkhouses, shops, and offices, and all truck roads leading to the woods. The pavement of the main road stops at the trestle, and the only other paved areas are those on the 'rinks.' Never designed as such, the two rinks lay within foundations that once supported buildings. One building, the larger of the two, was a shop that burned down in 1953, and the other was the commissary that was moved to Honeymoon Bay. Filled with gravel and topped with leftover pavement, the gaps between these foundations were converted into perfect bike riding or roller skating surfaces. Since they cannot hold water, and it is rarely cold enough to freeze a sheet of water in any case, they will never see an ice skate.

However, on this Saturday afternoon in January, the smaller rink sees booted feet pounding after a skipping puck. In harmony with our camp's obsession with the National Hockey League, my friends and I play hockey. Tonight will be 'Hockey Night in Canada.'

For once, we have a puck, a Christmas gift for one of the boys. If no real puck were at hand, we would find a smooth puck-sized rock instead, but a genuine NHL puck makes the game more real. Every player today has a real hockey stick, but I don't own such a thing, and although I like hockey, I have never asked my parents for a stick.

Stickless, but not about to miss the fun, I am referee. With three people on each side, plus two goalies, nearly the entire student body is on the rink. A few little kids are spectators, and shouts and shrieks reverberate from the office building across the road. There is plenty of chasing and the puck often shoots off the boardless rink into the gravel or onto the road. As referee, it is my job to retrieve it from wherever it lands, and I laugh and puff from my last dash into the scrub willows beside the rink.

I like being referee because, for one thing, I enjoy dropping the puck, and Jeff has told me that he loves the way I do this. Unlike others, I do not dangle the puck out at arm level and drop it from my fingertips. I have watched referees on television, so, like them, I crouch down, and I scan right and left. When I decide everybody is in position, I drop the puck and leap out of the way.

As part of our passion for the game, we follow hockey scores and goal counts for the top players. Because there are only six teams in the entire league, it is simple to remember the standings. The preferred team of dads and kids in camp is the Toronto Maple Leafs. My Dad is an exception. He is a fan of the Montreal Canadiens, so I am too, in spite of the teasing regarding my choice of allegiance. I don't sit and watch a whole hockey game, but tonight when Dad watches, I will read my book and will look up when something exciting happens. I can usually tell when this is about to occur. Dad will sit forward in his chair and shout, "Yes, go, go, yes!" Mum will stop knitting for a moment to follow the action too. Dad's favourite players are Boom-Boom Geoffrion and Jean Beliveau.

In our game today, nobody is pretending to be either of these players because our game is between Toronto and Boston. Therefore, somebody is Johnny Bucyk, and somebody else is Frank Mahovlich.

Because I am referee, I have to watch for a goal and call it good. Or not. We have no nets and only rocks to mark goal posts. I must watch to make sure a supposedly scoring shot goes between the rocks from the front and not from either side. Sometimes there are arguments about this, but I am not afraid to stand up to whoever is arguing because, after all, I am the referee.

Mrs. Marlatt's car appears down the road on the curve around the big rink. She has been to town, and with her usual smile, waves to us as she drives past. We know she watches the games on television and will probably do so tonight. She tells us it is very bad manners to "boo" a team or a player, and it is very good manners to applaud or cheer when a player, no matter which team he is on, makes an excellent play. We should appreciate the skill and hard work of every good player. But she doesn't tell us which team is her favourite.

R.Rigsby

Chapter Eleven: Weathering the Depression

1979: Leader XI

The bluster of the day before continues, whipping leaves, ripping laundry from lines, slamming open doors, and tugging pedestrian's coats.

Alice, on her walk, barely rounded the block when renewed gusts pushed her this way and that like a lone stalk of wheat in a mowed field. Gritting her teeth, she leaned into the wind and pushed on for home and dinner.

Betty Lou wipes her hands on her apron and sits down at the table across from Alice. The recorder rests on the table between them, and Betty Lou rewinds the tape to before their last session ended. They listen for a minute, and Betty Lou hits 'Pause.'

"Ready to work?"

"Yes, slave driver, I am ready." Alice laughs. "That was a very good dinner. I haven't had johnnycake for ages and to think we used to eat so much of it. Do you remember the time–it was a Sunday–and a hot day so nobody was hungry and all you people wanted to eat was johnnycake and syrup? Then our neighbour–I can't remember her name–stopped in and she went away thinking cornmeal was all we had in the house to eat!"

"No I don't remember because I was too young, but I remember you telling the story often enough. You were mortified. So many families would have been happy to have johnnycake, but I don't remember ever being hungry."

"No, we didn't have a lot, but we always had enough to eat, even though by the end of winter we were tired of beans. Nothing was fancy, but we had all we needed."

When they stop for the day, Betty Lou goes to her desk to make some telephone calls. Outside the breeze tapers off, and leaves settle into new nooks.

Alice thinks about the Methven farm, where her family thrived on homegrown food, homemade fun, and family love. The thirties were tough years, but eventually the everlasting winds died down and harvests improved.

At no time did she ever think the winds of her life would blow her away from the prairies and what seemed certain, anchored, and unchangeable. But then, life always changes, and the winds of life are neither constant nor predictable.

1934: Down on the Farm, and on the Farm, and on the Farm …

The relative luxury of the butcher shop apartment ended in 1934 when new owners decided they wanted it for themselves. Ashton moved the family to a "little house by the railroad tracks" and then to another shack down by the river. The one room shack had no cook stove, so Ashton dug a fire pit outside and covered it with a sheet of steel. That fall, on this rude stove, Alice "cooked and canned, made soap, and heated wash water." This hovel was only temporary as Ashton had found a farm to rent outside of Methven, but it was not available until November 1st. Before they moved, Alice confirmed she was pregnant, and everybody hailed the good news.

Worry followed excitement when Betty Lou came down with whooping cough. Alice evicted Albert to the granary, and reclaimed the long serving Winnipeg couch as a makeshift sick bed. Out in the gloom of the granary, Albert listened to night noises he had never noticed from within the house. Chirps, squeaks, and rustlings close by, accompanied by yaps, barks, and shrieks farther away kept him sleepless until Betty Lou recovered.

Betty Lou, who then continued her career of proclivity to calamity, fell against the heater and burned her arm. No sooner was this healed than she tried to drown herself in a pail of milk. She liked to watch Albert going about his milking chores and "she would stand and sway in time to his movements" while he separated the milk. She was still small, so when she stepped backwards and fell bottom first into a pail of fresh milk, only her feet and head stuck out. The subsequent spray nearly emptied the pail. Poor Albert thought he had some kind of jinxing effect on his youngest sister, if such a mundane act as milking a cow could cause a commotion.

Commotion was something Beauty brought to the family upon her arrival from the farm in Rocanville. By this time, Robert Blair's herd of Holsteins was flourishing and that year he presented each of his children with a young cow and calf. Beauty "was a wonderful milker," but she missed her former cow friends and, in compensation, developed a strong attachment to Ashton. If not within sight, she plodded around the shack bawling until he appeared. Fed up with the silliness, Ashton fashioned a scarecrow out of his clothes. Cows are not renowned for their intellect, so this worked very well, and Beauty "was totally comforted." She still had preferences, and only Alice could milk her, perhaps because Alice led her down to the good grass along the tracks, or for some reason known only to Beauty.

Once during a rare occasion when Alice was unwell, possibly due to a bout of morning sickness, Albert took over the job of milking Beauty. To prevent her from punting him across the barn, he tied her fore and aft. The bawling and carry-on woke Alice who went to the barn to find Beauty, fighting her tethers, and "kicking to beat the band." She released her, and "milked her right through while Albert peeked around the corner, afraid to upset the cow some more." Poor neurotic Beauty did not make the trip to the Methven farm when the Marlatts moved in November. Ashton sold her to a neighbour for the very good price of one hundred fifty dollars and replaced her with three good, less opinionated, cows.

Only in size was the Methven farmhouse an improvement over the previous two shacks. It had three rooms. Before they moved in, Alice and Ashton discovered, to their disgust, the whole place infested with bed bugs. The specks they thought were fly dirt were bugs. Everywhere. Alice decreed she would win this round of war on bedbugs. Ashton brought in several quarts of turpentine and squirted this into all of the cracks and along the baseboards. In an iron kettle, he boiled up a noxious potion of "formaldehyde and sulfur" until not a bug remained in the house. Then they painted.

In this house, Alice unpacked the wedding china she had not been able to use since Maple Creek. Ashton presented her with a bookcase bought at a sale in Nesbitt, which Alice painted black with red trim like the rest of her kitchen furniture. Then "pleased as punch," she set out her china. The house may not have been the height of elegance, or even much of an improvement over the previous two shacks, but she soon made it a home.

Ashton had assembled his equipment and had gone threshing that fall of 1934. At that time harvesting still required a large amount of manpower, and most farmers could not afford to employ so many men year around. Ashton's crew travelled from farm to farm throughout the harvest, as Robert had done in 1904.

With his threshing money, Ashton bought more livestock. There was "a lovely cow called Freckles" who was red with round white spots. She came with her calf and a few head of other, less namely, cattle. Alice bought chickens and cooped them in a box stall in the barn pending construction of a proper chicken house.

Ashton also indulged his passion for horses. At another sale, he bought a black mare for five dollars, and they named her 'Dolly' in honour of the Dolly of Alice's childhood. This mare, a former racing trotter, was a reasonable price because she had foundered and walked with a stiff legged limp. She had been bred to another racehorse and her bay filly, Babe, was part of the package. Alice suspected Ashton's "itchy fingers" for racing were behind the deal and he was entertaining notions of getting back into the business. Then Babe, the would-be racehorse, slashed her leg on a piece of wire or metal, and not only was the nearest veterinary far away in Brandon, but the fee for his services was beyond Ashton's means. Ashton's home remedies were not enough. Babe died from infection, and so too died Ashton's hopes for a winning racehorse.

Although the farmhouse, or shack as Alice labelled it, was de-bugged and painted, none of the cosmetic enhancements improved its insulation, and winters were merciless. Continuous stoking of the cook stove and its companion Quebec heater failed to produce enough heat to warm the kitchen, let alone the other two rooms, and most heat escaped through cracks and gaps. Any water left in the teakettle or reservoir overnight froze before morning. Winter mornings were heralded by Ashton stoking the stoves and smashing ice for reservoir and kettle.

By the harsh winter of 1934, the Depression was firmly entrenched in the Canadian economy, but the family "managed just fine" on the Methven farm. Cream, and any other farm commodity, did not have a high price, but the depressed values did not depress the spirits of Alice and Ashton. They had enough food, even if the selection of winter fare was limited. Alice recalls having only one dozen eggs to last the winter, and no money to buy more. By the next winter, she made sure she had more chickens, and stored eggs in waterglass or buried them in wheat to keep as long as possible.

The tedious diet did not inhibit friendships. Alice recalled many an evening when they entertained friends: the Dunks, the Rogers, or the

Briercliffes, or Alba and Walter. A company dinner was usually a big crock of baked beans, perhaps with bacon, followed by a dessert of johnnycake with Beehive syrup.

"Nobody slighted beans," when they could play cards, laugh, and listen to Foster Hewitt announce the play by play of the Saturday night hockey game on the radio. Unable to cheer on the Toronto Maple Leafs from his seat at the hotel, Ashton had purchased this entertainment extravagance upon their move from Wawanesa. Set on a high shelf out of reach of Betty Lou, the radio broadcasts were not only a source of enjoyment but connected the family to the world beyond the farm.

Connecting to the world, or even to their neighbours, became problematic when the winter storms of 1934 delivered an overload of snow. Visits to town or friends and family were slotted between blizzards, but no convenient break in the weather occurred on Christmas Day, and Alice's housebound family missed dinner with the Leachmans. While the blizzard raged, they sat down to one of Alice's chicken dinners. She was five months pregnant but had not yet seen the doctor. The Christmas whiteout was the beginning of a spell of wretched weather keeping Alice home for the next six weeks.

The farm was isolated and during the winter it was downright inaccessible. The Marlatts did not own a motor vehicle capable of making way on unploughed roads, and horse drawn conveyances, while reliable, were slow. Wawanesa was over eleven kilometers away. Compare eleven kilometers in the relative comfort of a car at a brisk fifty km/hr to an unheated sleigh at maybe five km/hr–ten minutes to two hours. Although Methven was closer, it was a tiny hamlet with limited services, and the Marlatts' nearest neighbour was almost two kilometers away.

Alice could drive the cutter, but the horses were slow workhorses, not driving horses. Besides, she didn't dare take Betty Lou out in the cold, and she couldn't leave her alone while Irene was in school and the men worked. They did not have a telephone, and since Alice had been used to living in town–in Leader, Maple Creek and then in Wawanesa–where she could go out any time she liked, she found the confinement wearisome and her usual good temper tested. Pregnant and irritable, she snapped at Ashton and the children.

Occasionally, when somebody was home to keep the fires burning and mind Betty Lou, Alice dealt with her exasperation in her own way. Donning her fur coat (the ancient wine number had long since been recycled into other projects), she mushed the snowy drive "to clear the air." She found the exercise of a good walk improved her mood.

When not cooking, cleaning, and caring for her children, or walking the drive, Alice knitted woolens and continued to turn flour sacks into useful items and clothing. She favoured green for herself and would dye the sacking to match her own taste and décor. While an excellent seamstress, Alice lamented her lack of knitting skill in that she "never learned to turn the heel on a pair of socks" and always needed help. She later observed she shouldn't have bothered putting in heels because now there are heel-less sport socks. Ashton solved the problem of lumpy mends on his heels by wearing the socks heel-side up. He would have appreciated the sport sock innovation.

When breaks in the storms became more frequent, the weather reprieves offered opportunities to relieve the tedium. Ashton drove Alice, with Betty Lou, to sewing get-togethers with her sister-in-law and friends.

1956–1964: Gordon River–In Stitches

Mrs. Marlatt sewed dresses for her grandchildren, as my mother made outfits for my sisters and me. Dresses, skirts, pants, blouses, shorts, and even a tent, emerged under the flashing needle of Mum's treadle Singer machine. 'Clunka, clunka, clunka' would emanate from the utility room on evenings when either passion or a looming deadline urged her on.

Other ladies in camp also sewed, and this was the incentive compelling Mrs. Marlatt and my mother to found the Ladies Sewing Circle. A few evenings each month, the ladies gathered and worked on their projects, sharing expertise and conversation. The mandate of this club was for the members to help each other with sewing or needlework, and to provide the ladies with an evening 'out,' without leaving camp. They met roughly once per week, taking turns as hostess, and coffee and dessert wound up the evening's production.

One year the ladies decided to produce a skit for the Christmas Concert.

1959: Gordon River–Sew Risqué

Laughter and the clash of moving chairs fill my ears when I open the big front doors of the community hall. My family is behind me, but I press forward through the throng in the foyer to look for my friends. I weave through people talking as they hang coats and shake hands. I smell coffee, and over the counter running the length of the foyer, I see one of the mothers peeling wieners and another making a jug of Freshie. After the concert, we will have hot dogs and treats, and Santa Claus will arrive with a pack of toys–something for every child. Everybody in camp will be here. I burst through the throng where the bright lights, including those on the huge Christmas tree, make me blink, and the roar of organized mayhem washes over me; sporadic laughter erupts over the general hubbub of many conversations, the calls of men setting up tables, and the thunder of little kids' running feet.

As always, the wonder of the hall in party-mode sets my innards aflutter. We play badminton here every Monday evening, but tonight the glittering tree, red and green streamers, echoing voices, and waiting stage uplift the space from gymnasium to concert hall.

The stage at the far end, erected earlier in the week, and the chairs in prim rows dominate the now exotic space. The stage has curtains on either side and across the back, sealing off the backstage deeds from the audience. The shiny curtains shimmer in the draughts from the opening doors.

From its home at the back of the hall, the men rolled out the upright piano and heaved it onto the stage. It now has a new pride-of-place location in front of the curtains on the right. The radio-record player from the school, out of sight but just as vital, is behind the curtains on the left. Soon, our school will perform our presentation, which will include a play, a nativity scene, and plenty of singing.

But, first, there will be skits by the Ladies Sewing Circle and the Volunteer Firemen, of which my Dad is one. Mum has been very secretive about the ladies' skit, and has refused to share even one detail with me. I caught her writing some lines, but she covered her work and then put it away in her bedroom. Dad is just as in the dark, and my friends' mothers have been equally close-mouthed.

This evening's master of ceremonies stands on the stage and invites everybody to sit. The ladies are ready to entertain us.

The curtains quiver with the movements of people behind them and somebody peeps through a gap. Finally, the ladies walk on stage, one by one. The laughter begins with a few snickers when the first lady enters and swells to a full-blown chorus of hilarity as they all make an appearance. Each one is dressed in her husband's work clothes. My mother wears Dad's long johns and his rain-test pants with the suspenders. She has his lunch bucket tucked under her arm and his tin hat on her head. On her feet, thick wool socks bunch up over the tops of his caulked boots, and she clumps across the stage like one of the seven dwarfs. My Dad is nearly falling off his chair, and I have tears in my eyes.

The ladies form a semi-circle on the stage and each, in turn, steps forward and recites a rhyme about her husband's work. We reward each with loud laughter and louder applause. Then it is my mother's turn. With one hand holding Dad's tin hat on her head, she steps forward. Her voice quavers but then strengthens, and the entire room is caught up in the rhythm of her verse:

> *I'm Rigger Reid from the high country,*
> *When they want a tree rigged, they call on me.*
> *With my rope and my spurs and ki-yippee-yee,*
> *I jump in the passline, and ride that tree.*

1935: Sibling Revelry

Alice's few outings and driveway forays for exercise, and to exorcise cabin fever demons, plus her many household tasks helped her deal with her snowbound winter. But spring was still a long way off. Toward the end of February, Agnes wrote Alice that she was making a trip to Winnipeg for chiropractic treatments for her arthritis, and wished to visit afterwards. Alice was ecstatic.

Ashton fetched Agnes from the rail station, but upon greeting her daughter, Agnes was shocked to learn Alice, at over six months pregnant, had yet to see the doctor. Agnes wasted no time in packing her off to Wawanesa. After February, the weather improved and Alice was able to go to town, and to her appointments, regularly.

With the arrival of spring and new life in field and fold, the Marlatt household prepared for the arrival of the baby. Jessie, at twenty-two years, came to help. Of Alice's three sisters, Jessie was the live-wire, still making the most of her unattached freedom. She never missed a dance, yet she always had time to help when needed. She arrived intending to be on hand for the delivery, but while on a mission to the cellar, Jessie discovered Albert's cache of chokecherry wine. She decided it should be quality tested.

Alice went into labour, and despite his Aunt's unhelpful state, Jack Ashton was born April 30, 1935. He revenged his Aunt Jessie's malingering at his birth by shooting her in the eye with his first out of the womb pee.

Young Jack Ashton Marlatt, at a chunky seven and one-half pounds, had dark curly hair and was plump and lusty. The family was enthralled. He was named for Ashton's brother John, but Alba was disappointed that Jack would not be called 'Johnny.' Alice rolled her eyes and was grateful Jack thrived from the beginning. She had no trouble feeding him, and if he didn't seem full, she relied on the trusty recipe. Still suffering pangs of guilt for "starving" Betty Lou, Alice, like many young mothers, regretted her lack of experience with the first baby. Although Jack did not have Betty Lou's digestive ailments, he was barely less accident-prone. When he was a toddler, he crashed his head against the three-cornered radio shelf. The doctor, summoned to the farm, stayed throughout the night to make sure there were no serious consequences.

Nor was Betty Lou done with her chain of calamities. One year's crop of pale-faced calves had outgrown the corral, and Ashton decided they should have more space. For the fencing project, he purchased wire and fence posts, and stacked them in the yard, but they were not out of range of the inquisitive Betty Lou. She managed to trip over some of it, whack her leg, and bump her forehead. The despairing Albert found her and carried her in. When Ashton came home in the car, they turned around and took Betty Lou to the doctor who diagnosed a fracture in a leg-bone. She had to stay still for two or three weeks but Alice kept her busy minding Jack while she tended her house and garden.

Betty Lou was as attentive to her new brother as Irene and Albert were to her. It was expected. From the time Alice and Laura could offer their own baby brother a rattle, minding younger siblings was ingrained in Alice's upbringing. She expected older children to look out for those younger, and she instilled this mindset in her children and pupils.

1962: Gordon River-My Sister's Keeper

A few days into November, the murky puddles of the school ground reflect a pallid sun. Pale clouds stretch vaporous arms between the encircling mountaintops. Below these embracing limbs, the alders along the river are a dull grey-brown, like the winter coat on a deer, and sepia bracken subsides between silver stumps. Among the stumps, emerald soldiers siege the camp. Planted over twelve years past, the baby fir trees have shot up and with teenage impudence, every year reclaim more of the realm of their ancestors. The camp will one day be gone, surrendering to the brigade of green. Even now, this young forest encroaches upon trails the camp children cannot trample often enough to repel intrusion. Some trails are forever lost in the battleground among the stumps.

Yet, those paths near the school ground are well-trodden during recess and lunch-break games. Today recess and lunch have come and gone, and the playground and its puddles are empty. As usual, the schoolroom is warm and bright, but within, all is not well.

Mrs. Marlatt is worried. And because she is worried about my six-year-old sister, Jo-Anne, I too am worried. Although my sisters bicker with each other, they don't often bother me. Being so much older, I have my own friends, but I usually know where they are and watch in case they get in trouble. I help if, rarely, somebody picks on them, or they fall down and cry.

Today at recess, while playing with her friends, Jo ate some peanuts from her Hallowe'en stash. A piece went down the wrong way and when she coughed and sputtered, I left my friends and went to help. I thumped her back and made her blow her nose. After a few more minutes of snorting and blowing, she seemed better. In class, she began coughing again. At home for lunch, Fran and I told Mum about Jo's peanut. She looked in Jo's throat and asked her some questions, but Jo said she had a bit of a tickle but was feeling better. We ate and went back to school.

A few minutes ago, Jo started coughing again, and Mrs. Marlatt took her to the back of the room. I watch from my desk as she listens to Jo breathe. I hear Jo's whistling wheeze, and I don't like the look on Mrs. Marlatt's face. She dismisses us and says I must tell my mother to come down to use her telephone, as she believes Jo needs to see a doctor. I tear home leaving friends and Fran behind.

* * *

It was a close thing. Mum called the doctor and as soon as Dad came home, we drove to Lake Cowichan. The doctor sent Jo right on to the hospital in Victoria where they operated to remove the peanut stuck in her windpipe. Then she got pneumonia, and remained in hospital for over a week.

Home at last, Jo is well, and I am glad to hear her nattering Fran, and me, again.

1935: New Shoots on the Family Tree

Come springtime, a young man's fancy may turn to love, but if he is a prairie farmer, he has no time to indulge his yearnings. At least not during spring planting and not during the harvest. Albert, at twenty-five years, may have had courting in mind in the spring of 1935, but did not propose to Thelma Cory until early fall.

She accepted, but both families were poor, thus there was no immediate date set for the wedding. Thinking ahead, and apparently also possessing a gene for being pro-active, Albert decided he should have new pajamas for his wedding night, whenever it occurred. He asked Alice if she would make them. She was happy to do so, but her aging sewing machine would not cooperate, and frustrated her efforts to fix whatever ailed it.

Not being handy with sewing machines, Ashton solved the problem by taking Alice, her projects, and the younger children to Rocanville where Alice sewed to her heart's content on her mother's less cantankerous machine. Jessie offered to assist with the final hand sewing, and Alice should have been suspicious.

In mid-October, Albert and Thelma decided they would elope to Brandon and marry, so Albert asked Ashton for the loan of the '29 Chevrolet. Mindful of priorities, Ashton agreed, if Albert would first escort a cow to its date with a neighbour's bull. Afterwards, Albert

- 143 -

packed his fiancée, and new pajamas, and set out for Brandon, but the trip of only forty kilometers became a test of endurance when they ran into an early blizzard. With no heater in the car, and consequently no defrost, Albert drove with his head out the window. Freezing cold, the newlyweds spent their wedding night thawing out and picking out Jessie's handiwork on Albert's pajamas. She had stitched together all of the openings.

Upon their return, Albert and Thelma rented a house in Methven and Albert commuted, via shank's mare, to work on the farm. By springtime, he was "sick, sore, and tired" of tramping back and forth. Weekdays he lived with Alice and Ashton and walked home for the weekend. While he worked on the farm, Thelma worked on a project of her own. With minimal delay, she had become pregnant and delivered Ethel in the summer of 1936. Ethel was Ashton and Alice's first grandchild. They were captivated, but, as many young couples do, Albert and Thelma decided they must move to greener pastures. The farm could not support two families.

Albert bought an elderly Ford for nineteen dollars. With a remaining eighteen dollars to invest in their new life together, he and Thelma packed their daughter and their few belongings, said goodbye to their families, and drove to Swan River. Albert envisioned his future as a salesman of Rawleigh's home care products. The exhilaration of setting out on his own was tempered with sadness, as he and Ashton were more like brothers than father and son. Over the next years, Albert prospered, turning his hand to a number of enterprises. Albert maintained close contact with Ashton and Alice, and, when she was older, Betty Lou often visited. In 1945, Thelma and Albert welcomed a second daughter they named Glenda. At that time, Albert drove a cream truck for a Swan River company, and shortly thereafter decided to start his own fleet. In 1954, he sold this enterprise and bought a partnership in an auto dealership when everybody was buying cars. He then had a gas station, a taxi business, and an ambulance service. The jack of all trade lessons of his father, and those of life in the dirty thirties, were not wasted.

However, Albert was still in Methven in December 1935 and was on hand to witness the 'Great Race.' Renowned as a sportsman and especially as a speedy skater, Ashton's reputation came up during a fall visit to Brandon, and sparked an argument. A man from Treesbank bragged that he was the fastest skater in the area, and, as Alice said, "when you get in a beer parlour, you argue," so the debate was on. A match race being the only possible means to resolve the dispute, it was booked to occur as soon as ice was ready on the Wawanesa rink. Ashton bet ten non-existent dollars he would win and then had to break the news to Alice. She was appalled. Ashton was confident. With no ice forming anywhere yet, there was no way he could practice so, to get in shape, he ran. He herded the cattle to water and then ran all the way back. One day he asked Alice if she noticed anything different about him.

She looked and asked, "What am I supposed to notice?"

"Oh, you don't see anything?"

"No, I don't."

To improve his wind, Ashton had quit smoking. He was forty-eight years old.

As the temperature drops, the icemakers craft ice in the Wawanesa rink. With no date yet set for the race, everybody inquires daily to hear if the match is on. Some say it may be cancelled because the ice will not be ready in time, but at the last minute, the icemakers deem the sheet perfect and the race is announced.

Housewives, wearing aprons under wool coats, scurry to join the excited crowd of men and children. Gabbling voices and steamy exhalations fill the air. Youngsters dash back and forth shouting, and jump up on the boards vying for the best view. Fathers lift those too short to see. Money changes hands.

Albert, with his arm around Thelma, stands beside his uncle, Charlie Brook. Alice watches with Betty Lou and clutches Jack. He squirms and she releases her grip. She knows Ashton can skate and is especially good in the corners, but he is not a young man.

Barrels mark the course, and in each barrel a man is ready to watch for fouls and shout encouragement to his favourite. The racers line up. On the count, they shoot around the rink. In the corners shaved ice sprays from their skates. Each man tries to gain an advantage by skating as close to the inside edge as possible.

When the two racers bump in a corner, Alice sees the other fellow, with a quick yank on Ashton's sweater, pull Ashton back. He then takes the lead. The pocket of Ashton's sweater dangles, but none of the other watchers, hypnotized by the flashing skates, notice. Alice knows Ashton will not retaliate in kind. Besides, he cannot risk a foul and lose the ten dollars. For nine more laps, Ashton chases his opponent around the rink. On the last lap, with a burst of speed, Ashton takes the lead and wins the race.

1935-1938: The Race of Life Continues

The race winnings helped make Christmas merrier that year. Apart from the beer parlour shenanigans preceding the duel of skates, Alice was proud of her husband, not because he had won, but because of the integrity he had displayed.

She told Betty Lou, "he was fair-minded, your Dad, and would not cheat."

The usual Marlatt Christmas of the thirties was a low-key affair celebrated with a church service, a family get-together, and a special meal. Gifts were practical items that were usually handmade: wooden spool toys, socks and mittens, scarves and toques, flour sack aprons and dresses. Alice managed gifts for her children, and "always sent things home."

One year Agnes and Robert gave Alice a black silk skirt and a sweater decorated with tatted daises. Alice cherished her marvelous outfit and wore it for many years. With the deprivations of the thirties, she was grateful to have one smart ensemble, which she had not made herself, for special occasions. Alice did not recall any gifts she and Ashton may have exchanged. She said sometimes, upon his return from a town errand, he would present her with toffee candies, but they did not have money to spend on trinkets for each other.

In the fall of 1937, Betty Lou began school, and Ashton said she was "too short on one end" to walk all the way. It was an easy march for fifteen-year-old Irene but a bit much for Betty Lou who was four months shy of her sixth birthday. None of the workhorses was suitable for the inexperienced or timorous to drive, so Ashton bought Dick, an elderly chestnut gelding, and a buggy to serve as the Marlatt household school bus. Irene was "not much of a driver," and grasped the reins so tightly that Dick, misunderstanding the signal, backed up. Ashton claimed Irene was so fond of Dick she wanted him in the buggy with her.

Although quiet and reliable, Dick was single-minded when it was time to go home. He would trot forward as soon as Irene hooked the last tug. If she did not board with an agile hop, she was left chasing the buggy down the road. With the coming of snow, Irene and Betty Lou caught a lift in the Briercliffe's cutter, and Irene was spared the stress of dealing with Dick's eccentricities.

With Irene in school and with the loss of Albert's help on the farm, Ashton and Alice were short-handed, but there was no money to hire a man, or even a girl to help in the house. The decade of desperate unemployment was harsh on both prospective employers and on the jobless. Competition for the few available jobs was a struggle for the young and able-bodied, but for the elderly or handicapped, employment was almost impossible.

Short and slight, Herbert Brindle turned a frail sixty-five in 1937. He hailed from England, and how he came to be in Manitoba remains unknown. Perhaps the posters for prairie land had seduced him, but Canada had proved to be a fickle mistress. He may have been one of many who left England during the depression following the Boer War. Possibly, he was a 'remittance man,' one of many young men with no prospects in Britain whose families paid them to leave the 'old sod,' presumably so there would be more reapings of said sod for those left behind.

Regardless of his adventures, or misadventures, Bert, in his twilight years, was penniless in a time of economic hopelessness for men like him. He could have died of starvation but for a short time had found a refuge. Responding to the tribulations of the times, the government had enacted a farm placement program offering five dollars per month to any farmer who would take on a man, so Bert worked for the Briercliffe's under this arrangement. With lack of government foresight, this program ended with each harvest and, in the fall of 1937, the Briercliffes said they could not keep Bert, claiming he was not strong enough to be truly useful.

Ashton thought otherwise. He decided the oldster could be helpful and offered Bert a proposal. There was no money for pay, but Bert could work for his room and board by milking, splitting wood, feeding stock, and fulfilling other household chores, as deemed by Alice. This included driving the turkeys from pasture to barn each evening, as Alice feared the predations of wolves. Bert's options were limited. He had a brother in Souris, but would not burden him, and because of his age, no other farmers in the area were interested. Bert accepted the proposal.

At first, Alice wasn't sure Bert had all of his faculties because "he did a lot of foolish things. He was a great guy for burning up little bits of things and they would flame up . . . he always had his eyebrows burned off and bits of his hair." This was because Bert, when he thought nobody would catch him, used gasoline instead of kindling to get the stove going in a hurry. Regardless of his impatience for combustibility and penchant for pyrotechnics, Bert worshipped the Marlatt children and had enormous respect for "Mr. Curly."

Occasionally they urged Bert to vacation with his brother in Souris for a week or longer when he wished. Bert would only stay a day or two, then catch the train to Methven, and be back with the cows for the next milking. Because Ashton's fingers were semi-crippled from baseball injuries, Bert took over the bulk of the milking duties. Bert also peeled potatoes. Alice's occasional bouts of eczema worsened with potato peeling, so with irrepressible cheerfulness, Bert peeled Alice's potatoes for the next seventeen years.

Bert joined the family's joy when Alice and Ashton announced another child was due in January 1938. As if aware of another impending winter baby, 'Old Man Winter,' with his entourage of storms and deep snow did his best to inconvenience and frighten the Marlatt household. Ashton took the safe course. At the first sunny break, he bundled Alice off to Wawanesa well ahead of her due date. Not risking the treacherous roads, Ashton gassed up the tractor and, with Alice jouncing on the hayrack, travelled cross-country to Reid's siding, where he loaded her onto the train. To cover all bases, they had engaged a local girl to come each day to cook, clean, and mind Betty Lou and Jack. At the Mitchell's in Wawanesa, Alice settled in to await the arrival of the baby.

Dr. Mathers delivered Ernest on January 11, 1938, without complications. 'Ernest' was not Alice's choice of name, because she feared it would be reduced to 'Ernie,' a name she loathed and thought ridiculous for a full-grown man. Ashton insisted his newest son bear the name of dear old Uncle Ernest Evans who still accepted his nephew's goodwill. Unlike his irascible namesake, baby Ernest was placid and good-natured; he was easy to feed and slept soundly in his wheeled crib. He was "as blond as blond," and Bert doted on the fair-haired chap.

June breezes on this sunny Sunday flutter curtains, whisk dead leaves, and riffle the slough. Creamy cumulus clouds shape-shift their way east, and tender shoots of young wheat are a green haze over dark fields. On the Marlatt's farm, all is as it should be on a fine late spring day. Or is it?

Baby Ernest has had his noon feeding and snoozes in his crib. His family has been to church, and the Leachmans have come for dinner. Along with their own girls, Mildred and Winnifred, ages thirteen and eleven, Alba and Walter have brought a young relative and her baby. About the same age as Ernest, but not at all sleepy, this child reposes on Alba's lap. Almost everybody has gathered in the kitchen-cum-sitting room of the three-room house. A pair of chickens sizzle in the oven, and Alice makes tea while Irene picks through the remainder of last fall's potatoes. The open door lets in air.

It is cozy in the kitchen, and made even cozier with the collection of bodies tucked into every nook. From his stool in his favourite place by the stove, Bert rarely voices a comment. Between nods and smiles, he directs watchful glances out the window where Betty Lou and Jack play with Winnifred who, unlike her sister, is not above childish fun. They have scratched some lines in the dirt and have invented a game using sticks and pebbles. On a bed in the next room, Mildred sits with a book in her lap, but more often looks out the window to watch the younger children giggle and screech as they win or lose their game.

Alba cuddles her relative's baby, and praises his virtues and gifts. He is seemingly the most beautiful child ever created. Ashton sits at the table and nods politely, but his face darkens. Bert glares at Alba. He sits up straight on his stool. One hand clutches a protuberant knee while the other kneads a fold in his Sunday best pants. He opens his mouth, but closes it again. On cue, the baby on Alba's lap burbles happy baby noises and this is apparently an example of his goodness and charm.

"See that? He is always sooo gooood. Just a darling, isn't he?"

Alice clamps the lid on the teapot and Ashton clamps his lips.

Bert hears snuffles from the other room. The slumbering Ernest burps and passes gas in his sleep. Bert abandons his post by the stove and tiptoes to the bedroom. Everybody turns at the sound of the wheeled crib rumbling across wooden floorboards.

*With a flourish of spindly arms, Bert says, "Now do you want to see a **good** baby?"*

After that, Alice decided Bert wasn't so foolish after all. Alba never forgot Bert's devotion, and how the old fellow put her in her place that day.

1938: Irene and Friends

Irene completed her chores around the house with few reminders and fewer complaints. Mature and reliable, she often minded the younger children when Ashton and Alice went on visiting or shopping trips that did not include the family. Yet, in many ways she was a typical teenager. Because everybody had to get up early, it was expected Irene and her charges would be abed and asleep soon after dark. On at least one occasion, Irene, being a typical teenager, stayed up late, literally burning the midnight oil. As soon as headlights shone on the drive, Irene dowsed the glim, replaced the warm lamp with a cool one, and hopped into bed. And, like a typical teenager, she thought her parents never figured this out.

When not in school or helping at home, Irene liked the company of other young folk of the district, including school chum Edna, and Edna's brother Dave. Ashton had concerns about some of Irene's friends and was not comfortable with the new pastime of the local teens. Cars were very common now, and most farm boys learned to drive as soon as their feet reached the pedals. Consequently, it was the 'in thing' for a gang of young people to ride around in a car, visiting friends or going to dances. When a group of boys called for Irene, Ashton had reservations.

It is early evening of another scorching summer day, not that many summer days in this harsh decade have been anything other than scorching.

All morning Irene and Alice canned fruit, starting early in order to process as many jars as possible before the heat became unbearable. The kitchen felt like the anteroom to Hell, and the sealed jars of fruit were set to cool in rows on the back porch. After the fruit, and since the stove was going full blast, Irene peeled and boiled potatoes for dinner. This was Bert's job, but Bert had gone to visit his brother in Souris. Alice mixed a johnnycake and slid it into the oven. She neither looked at the recipe nor looked where she reached. With brisk moves, she grasped every ingredient, then measured and stirred, while Ernest, propped in his cot, watched the proceedings.

With the completion of supper, and all bodies sufficiently nourished for the day, Alice is free to leave the kitchen. At close to thirty-five, she is strong and energetic. She picks up young Mr. Ernest, and goes out to the cooler air of the garden. She calls Betty Lou and Jack to walk with her to the slough. Ashton goes to the barn to tinker with something in preparation for harvest.

Irene finishes the supper dishes, sweeps the floor, and feeds the slops of peels and cores to the pigs. She too, is free for the evening. She lugs a pitcher of warm water to the privacy of one of the other rooms, and pours it into the ceramic basin. She washes and slips on her good dress, clean socks, and shoes. There is a dance in town. Dave has his Dad's car and he, Edna, and the others should be on their way to pick her up.

Out in the garden, as she trickles the used water around the tomato plants, Irene sees dust flowing behind a black 1927 Ford coming down the road. The car slows at the driveway, grinds through the turn, and jolts up the drive. Irene carries the basin to the porch and shades her eyes. Like white potato sprouts, arms wave from the car, and with a roar, it halts in the yard. Rough shouts and laughter accompany Dave and the three boys who leap out. One of them holds the door, and with a gallant bow and a grin, invites Irene to enter. Edna is not with them.

Sensing Irene's hesitation, Dave says, "Edna has to help Mum. We'll pick her up next."

Irene nods, but before she can step into the car, Ashton emerges from the barn.

"Whoa, there. What's going on?" He strides across the yard.

Irene's mouth goes dry. She knows this does not look good, and her stomach lurches at the expression on her Dad's face. Drat Edna.

Before she can open her mouth, one of the boys says, "Come on Irene, say goodbye to gramps and let's get out of here."

Ashton is past fifty years old, but his grey hair is thick and full. Irene knows it is almost standing on end now. Ashton's face goes very still.

"I don't think Irene is going anywhere tonight."

Irene bites her lip and wills the boy to shut up. He doesn't.

"Aww, it's okay gramps, we'll take good care of her."

The combination of idiotic leer and belligerent stance guarantees his doom. With three strides, Ashton reaches him, and the boy's leer becomes one of shock and fear as he feels his shirt collar and seat of his pants grasped in two powerful hands. He becomes airborne. The upholstery of the back seat stifles his squawk of surprise. The rest of the boys get the hint and waste no time in climbing aboard and reversing down the drive.

Irene knew her Dad did not approve of her gallivanting about the country, unchaperoned, so she quit going. Alice "couldn't see there was anything wrong with going out with a bunch of boys." Younger than Ashton, she had experienced the growing liberty of 20th century women. Although more in tune with changing times, she would not contradict Ashton who was still a product of his Victorian upbringing.

Irene did not become an old maid. In 1950, she married Charles Strong, they had four children, and in 2012, although widowed, she was still a bright and active great grandmother, who, even with some health challenges, crocheted with relentless determination. She died in the late spring of 2013 at the age of ninety.

1938: An Aptitude for Skipping

When Albert and his family moved to Swan River in 1936, Betty Lou had been the most dejected five-year-old in Manitoba. She yearned for her big brother. He had often joined her games, and, regardless of his apprehension for her capacity to invite disaster, he had often taken Betty Lou on his trips to town and on errands about the farm.

Once in school, Betty Lou had learned to print, and she had sent letters to Albert, Thelma, and Ethel. Both printing and reading had come easily to her, and she had been able to read the funny papers by Christmas. Her first teacher, Marian Green, had encouraged Betty Lou's progress and condensed her first two years into one. In June of 1938, Ms. Green 'accelerated' Betty Lou to grade three, thereby 'skipping' grade two.

Alice did not say how she felt about Betty Lou's promotion, but, like most parents, she and Ashton would have been proud of their child's accomplishment. Alice did not comment on if, or how, she may have influenced Betty Lou's advancement. From her own teaching experience, or from the experience of Betty Lou, Alice challenged able students and helped them capitalize on their gifts.

1959: Gordon River–Skipping Times Two

It is late morning on a school day in early February and rain, driven by a north wind, falls in sheets, filling puddles and pouring in mini-rivers down roads and paths.

As always, the schoolroom is a warm bubble. Within all are sheltered from the drops that splat against the windows and stream a bleary backdrop to the bright row of gloxinias in their pots on the ledge.

From across the room where I sit with other people in grade two, I stare at the windows and Mrs. Marlatt's plants. Since I have completed the spelling work on the board, I have time to admire the plants and the watery designs on the glass. I could pull out my book to read, but I prop my chin on my hand and continue to stare at the windows. In a few more days, I will be eight years old.

I don't know what I will receive for my birthday, but I have a feeling it will be something big. Eight years will make me one of the eldest girls in school. Only Penny is older than I am, and she is in grade three. Besides me, there are three others in grade two: Jeff, Kathy, and Kelly. Lately, Mrs. Marlatt has taken Jeff and me to the back of the room for extra work. We have read forward in our reader, 'Streets and Roads,' and are much further ahead than the twins. I love reading. I enjoy spelling too, and every day Jeff and I work through a list of new vocabulary words Mrs. Marlatt prints on the blackboard.

* * *

R.Rigsby

It is the last day of school and ages since my birthday. As I expected, my present from Mum and Dad was big: a two-wheeler bike. It is a 'Glider' and I can now ride through the twisted trails in the stumps with only a few crashes.

But that first morning Dad huffed up and down the road behind me, holding the seat. Too worried about falling over, I didn't catch on right away. After a while, Dad, puffing, asked if I could practice by myself for a while and went in. I did try but kept falling from one side to the other. I always had a leg out and never crashed to the ground, but I barely went one turn of the pedals before tipping over. I was tired, but not ready to give up.

Then, the best idea. Between two of the duplexes is a narrow alley about four feet wide and running about thirty feet. If I rode in the alley, I could catch my falls by pushing off the fences and so keep going. I thumped and bumped from one side to the other and was about to give up when Ray, the biggest boy in school, appeared at the other end of the lane.

He shook his head. "No, no, you will never learn to ride that way!"

We went back out to the road and he ran behind me, shouted orders, and told me not to be a sissy.

"Falling is nothing," he said.

Miracle of miracles, before the day was over I rode my bike.

Now I don't even think about falling. I have, of course, and so have my friends, who also received bikes on their birthdays. If we crash, we get up and carry on.

This afternoon my bike leans against the steps of the school in the best position on the right. Being an early bird, I usually have that spot, where I can jump on and be the first on the path to home. For the next few months none of this will matter. It is the last day of school, and we wait for dismissal.

The side door is open to a muggy, overcast sky that may, or may not send down rain. We hardly care. Mrs. Marlatt is about to hand out report cards, and then we will be on summer vacation. She laughs and talks with the big boys; Ray, my cycling teacher, and his brother Randy will not be back next year, as Ray has finished grade six. There is no grade seven in our school, and there are no other high schoolers. The

- 154 -

school district will not send a bus for one boy. The family is leaving camp.

Mrs. Marlatt picks up the bundle of report cards from her desk. Each card is in a construction paper folder. Last fall we spatter painted the folders over designs of leaves, and then stapled the folders to our report cards.

While I think about a new design for next year's report, Mrs. Marlatt steps to the front of the room and wishes us all a good summer. Her glasses flash as she turns her head to smile at all of us, and then she hands out the reports. With a wave we are dismissed and we rush out the door. Instead of leaping on our bikes, my friends and I stop on the steps to look at our reports. I open mine and glance at the grades, and then I look at the final comment.

"Very good returns on her Grade III work. Congratulations and the best of luck on a successful year next term in Grade IV."

What grade three work? Grade four? Is there a mistake? Jeff looks confused. He has the same comment.

Tires spitting gravel all the way, I pedal home, and show my report card to Mum. Not surprised, she assures me, yes, I have skipped grade three.

1938: December Tidings

As Alice and Ashton placed a great deal of emphasis on the value of education, they were pleased with Betty Lou's development. Although it was early in Betty Lou's academic career, and she was still only looking forward to her seventh birthday, Alice was confident that Betty Lou would continue to do well in grade three and beyond.

Before Alice and Ashton could celebrate Betty Lou's birthday, they received tragic news from Agnes and Robert: Laura had died on December 27, after complications following the birth of her third child earlier in the month. She had turned thirty-four in November and left three young children for a grieving husband to bring up alone. Alice and Laura had been close sisters. They had always corresponded and visited whenever possible, but Alice could not leave her household for long to help the family cope with their loss. Again, Jessie stepped into the breach, assisting the family until they were able to manage on their own.

Mourning Laura, Alice may have also considered all of the things one wished one had said to a dear sister whose loss is sudden and unexpected. No doubt Ashton was reminded of John, whose death was also sudden and unexpected.

Chapter Twelve: Methven–Safe Harbour

1979: Leader XII

When Alice opened her eyes this morning, the remnants of a dream clung to her wakefulness. She had felt light and transported, but when her feet found her slippers, the dream sank beneath her consciousness, as dreams do.

Today, after a walk, morning chores, and dinner, she dictated more of the story, and the memories came easily for a satisfactory day's work.

After supper, Betty Lou went to a bridge game. She had invited Alice to come and watch the plays, but Alice had declined saying it would be too much for one day. Besides, she was looking forward to a quiet read in her room.

Alice sits in her armchair, open book in lap, and mulls over the dream that re-surfaced in her mind as soon as she sat down. The dream had something to do with travelling or moving or leaving. At one point, near a precipice, like the Trans Canada in the Rockies, she was driving her car and she felt uplifted and free. This, despite the dream highway becoming a one-way dirt track and she was no longer driving a car but riding a child's wagon. She was not afraid because she was eager to reach whatever was ahead, around the corner. She thinks this is where she woke up, but, along with the odd details, the sensation of freedom and movement remained.

Maybe I felt no fear in the dream, Alice ponders, because I drove that stretch of Trans Canada Highway so many times. It became as ordinary as driving to Lake Cowichan for groceries or to Victoria to visit Stan. I wonder which direction I was supposed to be going in the dream: 'home' to Rocanville and then to the cottage on Kenosee Lake, or 'home' to Gordon River after the summer.

Alice thinks about Kenosee Lake and the cottage she adored. She had always wanted a cottage on a lake, and when she found the perfect lot, she bought it. In early 1963, Ernest and Jack salvaged lumber from the derelict Sceptre skating rink and moved it all the way to the lake. They began work on the cottage, and named it: 'Alice in Wonderland, in the House that Jack Built.'

I was careful with personal details shared with pupils, Alice thinks, but I couldn't resist sharing this bit of happy news, and the children all laughed at the clever name.

1939: The Fall of Broken Promises

The spring and summer of 1939 passed much like other years with seeding and planting followed by the frenzy of the harvest. Weather conditions had improved somewhat over the past few years, as had the economy, and although the Marlatt family was not rich, they were getting by on their rented farm.

The returns from produce, harvests, and custom threshing were adequate to ensure a decent, if precarious, standard of living. Most of their food was homegrown: potatoes and beans, eggs, milk, fowl, beef, and pork. Any cash profits from the farm and Ashton's threshing enterprises they invested in machinery, fuel and oil, replacement stock, as well as food, clothing, and household goods. The Marlatt family economy was improving, and they would have felt more optimistic about their future if it were not for a cloud of worry on their rosy horizon.

Although southern Manitoba was a long way from the sabre-rattling in Europe, Ashton and Alice were well aware of developments taking place there. They shared the shock of their fellow Canadians when Germany, in spite of its promises otherwise, invaded Poland in September. With Canada and other countries declaring war on Germany, Alice and Ashton hoped the fighting would be brief and would not initiate another appalling episode like the previous world war. They well remembered the anxieties of family and neighbours, the sorrows of those who lost relatives, and the melancholia of those who returned forever changed.

At fifty-two, Ashton was too old to enlist, Albert had a family, and the other children were too young. Alice and Ashton realized if there was no swift end to the hostilities, it would not be long before young men and women, friends and relatives, would be joining up and shipping out. They would then pray with other families for the safe return of all.

1939: Going to the Dogs. And Fair.

The crisis in Europe did not prevent everyday life for the Marlatt children to continue as usual. Neither Alice nor Ashton burdened the younger children with their worries, and Ernest, Jack, and Betty Lou, wrapped in the cotton wool of a happy childhood, played their games with the oblivion of youth. Unconcerned with events beyond their farmyard, Jack and Betty Lou had a more immediate problem. Ernest was too young to be included in his siblings' assertion that their family was missing an essential element: a dog.

Jack and Betty Lou kept asking for a dog. They plagued their parents until Ashton and Alice relented, and then found a pooch that would arrive for Christmas. Agnes and Robert, aware of the plot for the children's dog, consulted that oracle of rural retail, their Eaton's Catalogue, and for Christmas, they sent Jack a dog harness. As planned, the new dog, named Pat, was part of the Christmas morning excitement. Jack was anxious to start training Pat to pull a wagon or a sled, but although Pat was a "stocky dog with a short tail," he wasn't stocky enough and the harness was "miles too big."

As was expected of a farm dog, Pat took up residence in the barn because, as Alice said, they had a three-room house and "there just didn't seem to be a place for a dog." Pat did not integrate well with his barn-mates. Not discriminating between cattle and horses, he nipped heels, harassed the chickens, and really was a dog in the manger. It was clear Pat did not possess the correct farm dog attitude and had to go to a new home.

Agnes read the bad news from Alice. She would hunt for another dog for Jack–one big enough to wear the harness and wise enough to be useful on the farm. After inquiries around the neighbourhood, Agnes found a likely candidate at the Brownlee's. She claimed her choice and let Alice and Ashton know the dog would be ready for them at Easter.

On Easter weekend, Alice and the children took the train to Rocanville. Jack, aware there was a new dog, took his treasured harness. With it tucked under his arm, he marched off the train primed to start dog-training. Aunt Jessie's laughter stopped him in mid-march. Jack knew there was a dog waiting, and he couldn't wait to see him, but was mystified by Jessie's mirth. 'He' turned out to be a 'she,' and she was a puppy, a collie mix, and way too small for the harness. Happily, children and puppies are an unbeatable combination, and while Jack and Betty Lou made friends with their new pet, Alice helped her mother kill and clean chickens for Easter dinner.

Ashton later arrived in the Whippet, their current car, and joined the family fuss over the new pet, now christened 'Pal.' After dinner, the Marlatts, plus the pup, made ready for the journey home. Ashton laid papers on the floor of the car for Pal who seemed well rounded, even for a plump puppy. They rocked down the lane with the usual goodbye waves, but on the main road they travelled only a short distance–"as far as the slaughterhouse"–when "there was the most terrible smell" in the car.

While everybody else had dined on chicken roasted, Pal had discovered, and dined on, chicken entrails. Pal's Easter feast had not sat well, and the unfamiliar motion of a car on a bumpy prairie road had not helped. Pal's innards had rejected the misgotten meal.

Everybody bailed out of the car, and then Alice and the children stood by holding their noses while Ashton cleaned up the mess. Pal managed the rest of the trip without further upheavals.

Over the summer, Pal grew and became an exemplary farm dog; she did not worry the stock and lived up to her name by being a companion to Jack and Betty Lou. She lived in the barn and had no interest at all in making her bed in the manger. The only bad habit she acquired was chasing cars. There wasn't a great deal of traffic on the road past the farm, and it didn't travel at high speeds, but whenever a vehicle appeared Pal pelted after it barking in mad pursuit to the borders of her territory. As winter approached, Pal continued to grow, but the harness was still too large. Jack ignored it throughout the winter.

The following spring, with Jack's birthday coming up at the end of April, Ashton suggested to Alice they buy him a wagon, if there was something affordable. Alice said perhaps Mr. Peters, proprietor of the store in town, would sell them a wagon, costing about eight dollars, on charge. Ashton inquired, and, Mr. Peters, knowing he would be paid as always, did not hesitate. The wagon was theirs.

The wagon had a tongue, so it needed some refinements in order to be converted to dog power. Alice studied the problem and it occurred to her she might have a solution. She had a washstand that had originally arrived with a towel rack. Because she had no use for the towel rack, she had dismantled it, and the pieces now leaned against a wall in the back shed. The supports for the towel bar were two curved sides.

Ashton took the wagon and the rack pieces to Joe Ferris, a local handyman, because, as Alice reiterated, Ashton's carpentry skills were deficient if not completely absent. Joe fashioned two elegant curved shafts from the sides of the towel rack and attached rings to hook the harness. On his birthday morning, Jack awoke to discover the revamped wagon. He was astounded. He unearthed his harness, called the unsuspecting Pal, and strapped her in. Because Pal had grown over the winter, the harness was a perfect fit. Hitching her to the wagon, Jack climbed aboard and urged Pal to do the expected. Not understanding the game plan, Pal sat on her haunches. This was not what Jack had envisioned.

Alice never knew what inspired Betty Lou, but, with a piece of bread on a string, she enticed Pal to follow her, and pull the wagon. Before long, Pal understood. She was soon hauling the delighted Jack full tilt around the yard, and with more drilling, she learned to change direction when Jack pulled the lines attached to her harness. From then on, dog power drives around the farm were a daily highlight.

One afternoon, the Marlatts hosted a small party comprising Alba and Walter, plus the Evendons and their young daughter, Sylvia. Jack and Betty Lou took charge of their guest and decided Sylvia should have a wagon ride. They had no sooner plopped her in the wagon and hitched up Pal when a car appeared on the road. Pal knew her duty. She bolted across the yard after the trespassing car, and with demented barks, dashed through the fields. Betty Lou and Jack dashed too, shouting and calling in her wake. The "hue and cry" brought forth the adults in time to see the wagon careening from side to side, "one, two, three, four, sharp turns" before she stopped on a grade with a slough on both sides. When Sylvia's alarmed parents reached the panting Pal and the wagon, Sylvia was upright and grinning.

Aside from her bad attitude toward motor vehicles, Pal was a smart dog and one that fulfilled most expectations. These expectations may not have included the seventeen puppies Pal presented to the bemused family one year.

The purchase of the wagon was one indication of improvement in the family economy in this waning decade of the 'hungry thirties.' Many agricultural departments of prairie universities had been developing new strains of wheat that were more drought tolerant and rust resistant, and by the end of the decade Alice and Ashton, in addition to the custom threshing business, were growing Thatcher wheat for seed.

They had never gone hungry through these dreadful times, but neither had they many luxuries. Life was a year around grind of continuous hard work. From everyday chores like milking and cooking, to the seasonal gardening, butchering, planting, and threshing, to the ongoing equipment maintenance and repair, there were no days where there were no tasks. Any farm duties neglected had a cumulative and negative effect on the family livelihood.

The strain of scratching out a living on their rented farm was not without relief as the family visited relatives and friends, with whom they shared food, games, and gossip. Most of their neighbours shared the same circumstances, although the Leachmans may have been slightly more affluent. Betty Lou recalled she loved to visit her cousins Winnifred and Mildred, as their house was graced with an icebox, a piano, and most amazing of all: indoor plumbing. This luxury resided in an upstairs bathroom that actually contained a bathtub. Moreover, in the bathroom was a towel roller magically dispensing a fresh piece of towel with every pull. Although the child Betty Lou was impressed with these advantages, Alice did not mention them in her narration, nor did she imply that she resented the hard work, the lack of conveniences, or the desperation of the long decade.

Few in the Methven and Wawanesa area were in better straits than the Marlatts, but the struggle and toil of the community was relieved by seasonal low-cost entertainments including Friday night dances at the Methven School, picnics in the Reid's pasture by the creek, and corn roasts in the Rogers' or Elliott's yards. The admission for the dances was twenty-five cents, and every woman in the neighbourhood contributed food for the midnight lunch. Field days, occurring in late summer and autumn, in Methven and sister hamlets, showcased "platform events:" drills, folk-dancing, and music. There were also games for children and adults (potato races, sack races, or spoon and egg races) and no field day was complete without a ball game. The Marlatts never missed an occasion in their district.

As their finances improved, the family had made more expeditions away from the farm, usually to Brandon for major shopping.

Brandon was also home to the annual fall fair. The Marlatt's could not afford to go every year, and when they did, it was just for the day.

Betty Lou had been going on four when she attended her first fair and Irene had stayed home with Jack. On that trip, Alice and Ashton had been prepared to pay for Betty Lou's admission to all of the rides, but to their surprise, and relief, Betty Lou had been more interested in the horse barns, the cow barns, and the pig barns–she "was a cheap one!"

In a later year, Bert had joined the expedition. To his joy, he had been permitted to take Betty Lou and show her the wonders of the fair while Alice and Ashton strolled about on their own. Ashton had given the car keys to Bert, so he could take Betty Lou back to the car when she tired. Alice and Ashton had tired before Betty Lou and had to wait at the car for some time before Bert and his ward arrived. Alice had been cross at being kept waiting, but Betty Lou had had a fantastic time.

When Jack was older, he joined the family's annual trip to the fair. Like Betty Lou, he wasn't interested in the rides, and joined her enthusiasm for the barns, and the horse races. Once, when they got home, Jack and Betty Lou draped a towel over Pal and walked her round and round, like a racehorse at the fair. The good-natured Pal went along with their game, but probably wondered what she was supposed to do.

Fairs in any season are thrilling events especially for children. Alice and her family attended as often as finances allowed and few who have ever attended can forget the aromas of hot dogs, onions, popcorn, and cotton candy. Some might not recall the livestock aromas quite so fondly, but may have better memories of carousel music, hawkers on the midway, roller coaster screams, and even cries of lost or disappointed children. And over all, soundless and invisible, but tangible for all that, pervading joy.

1962: Gordon River–A Fair Achievement

The sun slips toward the western mountain, and on the rough plain of gravel behind the community hall, a tiny metal toy winks back at the setting sun. Dropped from a toddler's chubby hand, it is all that remains of the afternoon festivities. For a short time, the grounds had the aura of a fair, and while there was no food, no music, and no decoration, the camp residents brought their enthusiasm for games and spectacle. With a generous input of good humour, they celebrated May Day.

A parade and a fair, what could be better? If a few children propose an idea involving fun and display, they won't be short of willing participants. The day was a success and the adults are amazed at the children's imagination and industry. That night, everybody recalls the merriment wrought out of an otherwise humdrum Sunday.

I am so tired, but I lie awake with images of this day popping up and down in my mind like flashcards. The palms of my hands have blisters but every sting reminds me how our day turned out even better than we had hoped.

Several weeks ago, Mrs. Marlatt taught the little people in grade two about the Queen celebrating her birthday on May 24th–there is even a rhyme about it:

> *The 24th of May is the Queen's Birthday*
> *And if we don't get a holiday*
> *We will all run away!*

This was old news for my friends and me, but it prompted some thinking about the month of May. May 1st would be May Day. Last year, Mum and Dad took my sisters and me to Nanaimo to see the parade, and later we watched some kids dancing around a May Pole. They wove ribbons in and out, and were able to undo the weaving. I was mesmerized. There was a fair too, which was not as big as the Pacific National Exhibition in Vancouver where there are farm animals as well as rides and games.

My friends and I decided we should have a May Day parade and a fair, and a May Queen too. We elected Beth, who weighs the least, to be Queen and Mrs. Emerson loaned us a genuine sceptre for her to hold. In the parade, we carried Beth on a float that the boys had built: a seat between two poles. We took turns, but since Doug and Ian wore their Little League uniforms and wanted to play catch as we walked, Kathy and I did most of the carrying. My sister Fran was upset she wasn't Queen, but we named her First Princess and she wore a long dress. Other people dressed up too. All of the camp dogs were rounded up and leashed, although some of them seemed to wonder why this was necessary. My sister Jo led our dog, and little Tommy walked in front with a white piece of cloth on a stick for a flag.

We paraded through camp and then to the flat piece of ground beyond Kelly's Hill, (which was not named for my friend Kelly), and among some crumbling shacks, we had our fair. I was in charge of the fishpond. For a nickel, a little kid could hang a fishing pole inside the boarded up door of the shack, and we hooked a toy onto it. I had dug in the bottom of our toy box for outgrown toys and others had done the same.

Some of our mothers followed us to the 'fair ground,' and then other dads, men, and wives, came up too. Mrs. Marlatt was away. Everybody laughed and had fun and said what a good job we did.

No wonder I am tired, but with my brain flashing scenes and echoing with happy noise, it will be a long time before I sleep.

***

It is Monday, and as soon as we finish the Lord's Prayer and sing O' Canada, we tell Mrs. Marlatt about our fair. We show her the jar of money. We made almost six dollars, so Mrs. Marlatt suggests we donate it to U.N.I.C.E.F.

1940: Turkey Trot and Other Fowl Stories

Shortly after the move to the Methven farm, Alice had bought some young turkeys, and had raised a substantial flock of these ornery birds. Each fall she sold her butchered turkeys and used some of the money for Christmas. In the fall of 1940, the turkeys destined for market were thriving and fat, and prices were good. After catching, beheading, plucking, cleaning, and selling the birds, Alice pocketed twenty-seven dollars. She wrote her Christmas list. This included necessities for everybody plus a few Christmas treats, but still, there was no room on the list for toys. Never purchased, toys were homemade out of cardboard boxes, wooden spools, string, wool, fabric, and twigs. On the designated shopping day, Ashton and Alice drove to Brandon where they intended to fulfill their Christmas list and indulge in a rare treat of a restaurant dinner.

With her list in her hand, and hard-earned cash in her purse, Alice surveyed her retail targets on the main shopping street. While Ashton busied himself elsewhere, Alice trekked from store to store. She bought overshoes, socks, yarn, fabric, fruit, candy, nuts, and anything else she thought would round out their Christmas celebrations. Arms overflowing with parcels, she lugged her booty to the restaurant, as she didn't have a key to lock the car.

In fact, there had been no key for the Whippet since the family had attended a summer field day in the Village of Carol. Alice, with Ernest on her hip and one hand holding the car keys, had tripped in a gopher hole. Pitching forward, but not falling, she had lost her grip on the keys in order to maintain her grip on Ernest. They had gone spinning out of her hand never to be seen again. The family had searched, but with no sign of the charmed keys, Ashton had decided they had disappeared in another gopher hole.

Henceforward, the Whippet was 'unlockable' and only 'startable' via two crucial wires connected with a clothespin. When Ashton saw Alice struggling with her parcels, he asked why she hadn't left them in the car, and she replied that she feared their theft.

Ashton said, "Oh, they won't be stolen."

Ashton placed the parcels on the back seat of the car and took his wife to supper. On their return to the Whippet, "all that was left on the back seat of that car was twenty-five cents worth of apples." Alice was distraught. She had not spent all of her turkey money, but the shops had closed and there was nothing left to do but go home.

It didn't take long for the news of their misfortune to spread around the neighbourhood. With her remaining money, Alice went to Wawanesa to buy at least the much-needed overshoes. Mr. Harrison, the proprietor, had heard of their bad luck, and insisted Alice take the overshoes at his cost. Alice then had enough money to buy fabric at his store. Ashton encountered similar generosity, and brought home candy and oranges given to him by friends and neighbours.

Alice said, "We had never had two boxes of Japanese oranges before."

Although raising turkeys and chickens brought Alice extra cash from meat and eggs, it was not without risks. Once, when Ernest was toddling about, a cranky rooster attacked him. Armed with knife-edge spurs, the territorial fowl inflicted a few nasty scratches before Betty Lou beat him off. This rooster once tried the same tactic with Irene, but she carried a pail of water and watched him out of the corner of her eye. Just as he flew at her, she dowsed him with the water. Alice did not say if this had a lasting remedial effect on the rooster.

Nor did Alice escape the ire of crabby poultry. When she peeked into the nest of a sitting turkey hen to see if the eggs had hatched, she found indeed they had, but the hen, filled with maternal outrage, flew at Alice, and landed on her back.

Alice said, "I tell you, I did run with her wings flapping about my head."

Alice did not say how she dealt with the intractable turkey, but non-conforming farm critters were soon on the menu.

When Irene was able to manage her own turkey flock, Alice gave her a hen, and before long, Irene too was in the turkey business. Irene then raised, butchered, and sold her own turkeys. She saved her turkey money, but unlike most girls, did not buy fashions and trinkets. Instead, she paid to have her tonsils taken out. They had bothered her off and on for years, and she always had a cold. The tonsils should have been removed after the first few bouts of inflammation, but Ashton had the notion that Irene could bleed to death, and feared the operation. Aware of her father's anxiety, Irene did not want him to feel responsible if anything happened. On her own, she went to the doctor, and then to Souris for the operation. All went well, and Irene survived to raise more turkeys.

R.Rigsby

Chapter Thirteen: Rocanville–Home Port at Last

Leader XIII

Alice waits at the kitchen table with her cup of hot water warming her palms. The water reflects the sun slanting through the window, and she stares at the liquid mirror with lips parted and a crease between her brows. On the windowsill, Betty Lou's plants, including a patience plant, bask in the heat of the September afternoon. Alice looks up from the depths of her cup, winces at the sight of the patience plant, and instead looks around the sunny kitchen.

I have seen many kitchens, she thinks. Many girls hardly left their farms; they lived with their parents until they married, and then they lived with their husbands and families. But I became a teacher, and I lived in many places. Then there was Ashton and our family, and the places we lived before going home to Rocanville. And after that...

My apartment kitchen in Gordon River. Such good years there, and such good friends: the Wylies, the Miles . . . as well as Stan and Reg Toole in Victoria. It was such a coincidence that Stan married Reg Toole from Normal School. The Tooles, after various prairie postings, moved to Victoria, where I often visited on weekends. I can't recall Stan coming to see me in Gordon River, but my place was so tiny.

But then, Betty Lou, Art, and the children came out to visit– twice. The first time they stayed two weeks, and the next year for over three months. It was tight, but we made it work. Art, Betty Lou, and the children made friends with people in camp and joined in everything.

The Brant hunting expedition with the Stephens family comes to Alice's mind.

On a weekend in March, Alice had the loan of a beach cabin in Parksville. The women brought food, blankets, and warm clothes. The men brought shotguns. Although it was March, the weather was mild, and the outgoing tide left acres of wet sand where the children, in boots, built castles, dug holes, searched for crabs, and ran and ran. When the tide turned, the children were far out on the sand, and Betty Lou worried that they would be cut-off from shore.

We teased Betty Lou, Alice remembers, because the water was barely six inches deep, and even if it surrounded the children, the only danger was a bit of water in their boots. The Stephens girls knew all about incoming tides, and led the others in a dance of shrieking and skipping as they ran back and forth ahead of the waves. The men had fun, but the hunting trip was a bust–nary a goose did they see.

Soon after, I was sad to see Betty Lou and her family go home. I think that was 1962, and the school closed in June of '64. After Gordon River, I accepted a position at the Youbou School where I had a bungalow and another tiny kitchen.

Youbou's school had several rooms. It was difficult to work with other teachers, and a principal, after so many years of doing things my way, but I made some new friends, and kept in touch with Gordon River friends. The camp was winding down, but many people had only moved as far as Lake Cowichan, and we saw each other often. The next four years went by in a flash, and then I retired.

Betty Lou comes in with a pan of greens from the garden. She sets them in the sink and rejoins her mother at the table. Alice resumes her story and after an hour, Betty Lou stops the tape.

"Well that is enough work for us for one day, Mother. Why don't you rest on the couch while I make supper?"

Betty Lou rises and looks in the oven, but Alice doesn't go to the couch. She pours the remains of her water into a plant, sets the table, and washes the greens.

1941: Re-Mapping the Plan

In the spring of 1941, Agnes and Robert were sixty-two and seventy-one years of age. Despite an inauspicious beginning, they had fared well on their prairie farm; they had survived the appalling winters of those early years, had made some gains over the next twenty years, and had hung on through the depression. Their tenacity in the face of climatic hardships, pestilences, diseases, economic unpredictability, and the harsh realities of making a living off the land, was typical of many of those who had anchored their lives to an island in the prairie sea.

The Blairs had in fact bought more land and had enlarged their herd of Holsteins. They had taken risks, but the ventures had proved worthwhile.

Nevertheless, Agnes and Robert knew they could not farm forever. They were healthy, but the aches in their bones and declining strengths reminded them every day that they should retire. After considering their options, they invited Alice and her family to come for Mother's Day. Alice and Ashton, short on cash to cover the gas, replied they couldn't make it that year. Agnes and Robert insisted; they would pay for the gas.

The Marlatts were barely settled in the kitchen for tea, when Agnes and Robert "broached the subject about buying the farm." The Blairs wanted $3,500. This was to be paid in yearly installments of $350, no interest. Although Alice and Ashton were flabbergasted, they didn't need time to think it over. They took the offer. All parties agreed a moving date in late September after the harvest would be best, but it would be a tight deadline.

Driving home, Alice and Ashton discussed their unexpected opportunity, and once the euphoria wore off, they realized how much work lay ahead in order to wrap up their lives in Manitoba and transfer those lives, and those of their children, to Saskatchewan.

Agnes and Robert also had deadlines to meet. They found a house to rent, but there was much to do before enjoying their rocking chairs and the attractions of downtown Rocanville. Over the next few months, they arranged for a sale to dispose of their goods and stock, while Alice and Ashton made plans for the sale or shipment of their own.

Ashton compared prices of train and truck transport. He chose the stock and equipment to keep, and decided which to sell. The threshing equipment would be on board, as Ashton intended to continue hiring out for the harvest as he had done in the Wawanesa and Methven area for years.

Although the Marlatts considered Bert a member of the family, and not just a hired man, he was sixty-nine years old, and Ashton suggested he might retire at his brother's place in Souris. Bert, devastated at the thought of losing his family, "cried and cried." Ashton and Alice couldn't stand it, nor could they "deny him the right to come," so Bert, too, packed his bag.

Betty Lou's teacher and classmates, knowing she would not be back in the fall, threw a party for her on the last day of school. One of her gifts was a patience plant, and she bore this home to Alice, coming in the door, "large as life, and twice as natural." Alice detested patience plants. There was something about their watery, transparent stems that gave her the creeps, and she didn't want it in the house. Ashton over-ruled her objections, saying if "the child wants something, let her have it." Betty Lou left her plant in her mother's care while she got on with summer fun. Alice grit her teeth every time she watered the thing.

R.Rigsby

Alice may have hated patience plants, but she loved other houseplants, for example her Boston fern, and later, gloxinias.

1962: Gordon River–Botanical Mapmaking

High, square-paned windows span most of the length of the schoolroom's east wall. They are useless for students to gaze outside while 'thinking,' unless they find sky inspirational. Even standing, the view rarely varies: the rocky hill with wispy willows and grey-green broom, the graded road, and the square brown office. Traffic is minimal, confined to an occasional yellow pick-up truck pulling up in front of the office, or the meanderings of a black and white springer spaniel on some doggy business of his own. Beyond this dull scene, there are the mountains with shorn sides and a fringe of trees on top.

Mrs. Marlatt is tall enough to see out while standing, but the students are still "too short on one end," and must stretch necks or stand on tiptoe. Apart from letting in light, the windows are perfect for Mrs. Marlatt's gloxinias. Velvety trumpet-shaped flowers in pink, purple, deep red, and white, wreathed with fuzzy dark green leaves, overflow their pots and make a row of continual colour against the usual grey backdrop of mist and rain.

Today, Mrs. Marlatt waters her plants and snips away yellowing leaves and finished flowers while her charges tumble in from recess. While they hang coats, take their seats, and pull out texts and scribblers for the next subject, she continues snipping.

I glance at the plants on the window ledge, but I am impatient to work on my map of Gordon River. A few days ago, Mrs. Marlatt taught us not only how to read maps, but how to draw them.

Standing in front of us, she shaded her eyes with one hand, and then narrowing her eyes as if squinting into the distance she said, "Imagine you are standing on Kelly's Hill."

We often play on Kelly's Hill and the view of the camp immediately sprang into my mind's eye. She told us the big mountain in the distance is north, and north is always at the top of a map. We will draw the camp, the rivers, the roads, and the mountains as if we were looking down from even higher than Kelly's Hill.

The thrill in my stomach was better than seeing a horse. When my family travels, Mum is the map-reader and she often shows me where we are on the map, and how the rivers, roads, and towns are all marked. I never realized I could draw my own map, and this is by far the best lesson we have had in Social Studies this year.

Mrs. Marlatt finishes pruning her plants. My mother has houseplants too, but none are as stunning, or as bountiful, as Mrs. Marlatt's gloxinias. I look at them and at the colours on my map. They are both brilliant, and I wish I could make a plant last as long as a map. Once–birthday, or last day of school–Mrs. Marlatt gave me a small plant as a gift, but it did not survive. Our duplex has an east-facing window over the sink in the kitchen, but I chose to keep my plant in my room, which is cool and shaded by evergreens. It may not have had enough heat and light, or I killed it with love and then with neglect. If I ever have another plant, I will not water it every day for a week, and then forget it for a month.

1941: A Move to Patience

Before the school year had finished in June, Alice had decided Betty Lou should go to Rocanville ahead of the family. She was to start the new school year there, from the beginning, rather than attend only one month in Methven.

Before September, with the harvest underway, Alice drove nine-year-old Betty Lou to Brandon, where she caught the train to Rocanville. Jessie, who had married Hugh Dauncy a few years before, met her at the station. For the month of September, Betty Lou stayed with Jessie and Hugh during the school week. On weekends, she visited her grandparents, and when not helping Agnes and Robert with chores, she spent every spare minute with Robert's horses.

Perhaps the Brandon fairs influenced her judgment that Sandy and Prince needed extra grooming. She took it upon herself to even up their, in her mind, untidy tails. Several applications of the shears later, the horses' tails barely reached their hocks. When Robert noticed, he said nothing, but he hitched the two geriatric equines to the democrat and took Betty Lou for a drive. All she could see were those ugly tails. Fortunately fly season was over and there was time for Sandy and Prince to regrow their tails before the return of summer pests. Betty Lou never forgot her shame.

While Betty Lou learned grooming lessons in Rocanville, the Methven neighbourhood prepared to say goodbye to her family. In accordance with a long-standing tradition of prairie generosity, the Marlatt's could not leave without a proper going away party. The neighbours collected donations for a gift, and organized a dance at the school. Alice, who was undergoing dental work, discovered her last appointment, also in accordance with a long-standing tradition called Murphy's Law, was the same day as the dance. She had seventeen teeth extracted and new dentures fitted.

Because of the pain and leftover effects of the anesthetic, she was woozy in the evening and "couldn't eat lunch or do much dancing." By this she probably meant she did not dance the legs off of Ashton, and any other partners up to the challenge, as it is hard to imagine Alice missing an opportunity to dance, woozy or not. Submerging her discomfort, she smiled all evening, and her good manners ensured her graceful acceptance of "a red chair" as a going away gift. Although the sluggish economy of the depression was giving way to the brisker economy of the war, expenditures on furniture and household goods, especially new items, were still very close to the bottom of the priority list. Alice said she kept that chair for a long time.

The day after the dance, Alice still "wasn't feeling very spry" and whether this was due to the after-effects of the dental work, or because of the evening's festivities, she did not say.

However, the moving process had already begun and could not be re-scheduled. The implements and stock, loaded in trucks and trailers, had already departed with Bert in charge, and all that was left was luggage, some household effects, and Irene, Jack, Ernest, Pal, and Patchie the cat, to be loaded into the car and trailer.

The last minute packing would have been less complicated if Jack also hadn't woken up feeling unwell. The evening before, Alice had cooked up a three-gallon pail of mushrooms to accompany their last supper at the dance. Perhaps Jack overindulged or perhaps they just did not sit right, but either way, on moving day, Jack was "green about the gills" and vomiting. The removal of the last items of furniture and baggage took place around the invalid, and around Patchie who had taken refuge under the stove. The stove was one of the last items dismantled and removed, but Patchie, who wasn't pleased at having his refuge disturbed, slashed a helping hand. Incensed by the assault, the man retaliated with a swift kick, and Patchie shot out the door to the safety of the fields. Deaf to Alice's entreaties, he remained hidden and did not make the move to Rocanville. Neither was Goldie the canary on the passenger list, as she had passed on to canary heaven some years before.

Of all goods and bodies to be stowed aboard, Jack was the last. He stayed in bed until it was taken to the trailer, then he too was stuffed into the car with Ernest, Irene, Pal, and Alice's Boston fern. It was magnificent. The fronds trailed three feet and it was two feet across. Alice purposely put the patience plant behind the pantry door where it would 'accidentally' be left behind. She hadn't counted on Ashton's thoroughness, born of his years on the road, when a brush or shirt left in a hotel was not easily replaced. With the family waiting for the signal to cast off, he went back into the house for one last look. When he reappeared, he carried the patience plant.

While Alice and Ashton were loading the furniture, kids, and plants, Bert was with the cavalcade lumbering its way northwest. Cattle, horses, hogs, tools, seed, and machinery loaded in trucks, and on top, chickens and turkeys in crates. The bawling cattle, squawking poultry, and rattling trucks announced to all en route that the Marlatts were on the move. Yet, even on moving day, cows need milking. Bert squeezed in among the cattle in the truck, and handed out free milk to anybody who brought a lard pail. Alice was amazed Bert was not squashed or trampled, but then, Bert was a survivor.

In 1941, distances were in imperial measure, so from Methven to Rocanville was about 210 miles. Today this trip can easily be done in under four hours, but then, over mostly unpaved roads with an average speed of forty miles per hour, it took over twelve hours, including stops to milk cows and change twelve flat tires—one for every hour of travel. Arriving in Rocanville after dark, there was still work to do. Crates of turkeys and chickens were handed down, milking cows were unloaded, horses were fed, and furniture was piled in an empty granary. Alice, Ashton, and the children joined Agnes and Robert in the house.

Robert had advertised his sale for the next day, September 30th. When prairie farmers sell or leave their land, it is customary to have a sale. Farm implements, machinery, tools, household goods, cattle, horses and even the farm dog, can be on offer. Sometimes the event is conducted as an auction, with a neighbour or hired expert officiating, or it may be like an urban garage sale with tagged items, over which prospective buyers bargain and haggle. Agnes and Robert needed the proceeds of their sale to relocate to town, and to use as a reserve until Alice and Ashton paid the first yearly installment.

On the day of the sale, the grand plan became muddled when Ashton's cattle mixed with Robert's. The cattle-sorting went from one of irritation to one of immense entertainment when it was time to unload a truckload of calves. By September, calves are a good size, and as they had been cooped in the truck for two days, they were frisky. The plan was for each man to rope a calf and lead it to the barn, but nobody explained this to the calves. The roping went well, but when they lowered the ramp, the calves, en masse, bolted for the wide-open spaces. Robert and others not engaged in the unloading, convulsed with hilarity when the calves "flew all around the pasture" each dragging a man holding on tight. Robert, usually dignified, "laughed so hard, he could hardly contain himself."

The sale, and the circus, concluded. With the departure of livestock, tools, machinery, and surplus household goods, Robert and Agnes faced their new reality. They were leaving forever their land and home of almost thirty-five years. Agnes well remembered her dismay upon her first sight of the crude log cabin adrift in acres of windswept snow. Beginning with that wild December of 1906, the Blairs domesticated those acres and transformed their bleak homestead into a productive farm.

Like other homesteaders, they netted the land with fences and planted alfalfa, oats, barley, and wheat where native bluestems, buffalo grass, forbs, and grama grasses once held sway. Where buffalo, the first victims of European exploitation, once wandered, placid Holsteins grazed. The house, granaries, barn, and outbuildings represented many years of hard won achievement in a never-ending campaign against the natural character of the prairies. Although they likely never thought of it in such terms, Agnes and Robert had raised a flag over their island in the prairie sea, and they were ready to pass that flag to the next generation.

The metaphorical flag passing was enacted over the next few weeks. As Agnes and Robert moved their furniture and other belongings out of the farmhouse, Alice and Ashton moved theirs in. Then Alice went to work refurbishing her home to suit herself.

Alice enlisted her father to help her cut new blinds to fit the windows. She first removed the plants, including the patience plant, from the windowsill to the kitchen table. Standing on a chair, Alice wielded a yardstick to measure the windows while Robert prepared to cut the blind accordingly. Catching sight of the patience plant, Alice felt the last straw snap.

She said, "I just reached over and I just clipped her off at the top."

Robert gasped. Then he started to laugh. He had not heard the plant story, but he knew his daughter well enough to recognize her irritation. Alice possessed incredible patience. Up to a point.

1962: Gordon River–The Yardstick, A Measure of Patience

In the corner by the fire door leans the school yardstick. In addition to being an instrument for actually measuring things, it serves as a pointer, a straight edge for chalking lines on the blackboard, and a compass for marking circles on the floor for dancing. Once shiny with varnish, faithful service has eroded its finish to a drab brown, and the numbers and lines once bold black are faded or worn off altogether. Its assortment of nicks and dents testifies to its long residence in the school, but is still straight and strong. When not in use, few pay it little mind, but soon it will be the center of attention on this dreary November afternoon.

The oil heater chugs, the room smells of wet wool, and a mizzly humidity rises from damp coats hanging on the rail. The thrumming oil burner, rasping pencils, rustling papers, foot-shufflings, and subdued murmurs and coughs, combine to make a sleepy drone rising and falling like the wind at night.

Mrs. Marlatt, at the board, erases the grade fours' spelling words, replaces the eraser on the chalk ledge, and retrieves the yardstick from its corner. Pressing the ruler against the board with four outspread fingers, she commences to draw some lines. The grade ones and twos work on their arithmetic, using chestnuts for counters, and the click clack of chestnuts mingles with the grate of Mrs. Marlatt's chalk. When finished their arithmetic, the little people will use the lines on the board to practice printing. The two boys in grade four are supposed to be working on their own arithmetic problems, and my friends in grade six are supposed to be writing a paragraph about the story they read this morning.

I yawn. My lunch of soup and grilled cheese gurgles in my stomach. I should be memorizing a poem from my grade seven reader, 'Beckoning Trails.' This reader has a terrific name, but disappointing contents. With my chin propped on one hand, I turn to 'The Daffodils' by William Wordsworth and again read the four verses. The poem rhymes, which is a relief, but I find the 'jocund company' annoying and dull. I flip back to one of the few stories I like very much. It is called 'One Minute Longer,' about a collie named 'Wolf,' and is written by one of my favourite authors: Albert Payson Terhune. I have read all of Mr. Terhune's books in the town library, and all are magic. I re-read a favourite paragraph, but instead of returning to the poem, I answer a question from a friend.

We are not the only people talking. Not loudly, not altogether, just chit-chat, especially the two boys in grade four. I glance at Mrs. Marlatt. Intent on her lines, she gives no clue she notices the rising level of noise, like the buzz of a wasp's nest as you step closer, or poke it with a stick. I give up on my memorization. I watch Mrs. Marlatt making her steady lines, and look at the two boys in grade four who are snickering and jabbing each other. My friends look at one another's paragraphs and giggle. I sense tension in the room and again look at Mrs. Marlatt's straight back and even straighter lines. Although she seems unaware of the growing buzz in the room, I see the tautness in her stance, like an elastic band stretched to its limit. She has been my teacher for a long time. Nobody else seems to detect this aura of imminent trouble, so I turn back to my reader and flip forward a few pages to see if the pieces up ahead are more interesting than 'The Daffodils.'

Wham!

The crack of wood on wood fills our ears. We flinch, jerk, and jump. The grade four boy in the front desk jumps highest because his desk received the smack of the yardstick. He had turned to fool with his friend behind him. Now both boys sit straighter than the yardstick and gawp, open-mouthed and pop-eyed, at Mrs. Marlatt. The rest of us only goggle a second, and I find 'The Daffodils' positively riveting.

1941–1942: Rhythm in Heaven

Within weeks, the Marlatts resumed the rhythm of rural prairie life on their new farm. Compared to the draughty three-room shack in Methven, Robert's well-built house was a palace. The roomy kitchen accommodated everybody at the table, there was the separate living room for those who had time to relax there, and up the staircase were the four bedrooms. In addition, there was the summer kitchen–that cool spacious area ideal for summer cooking and canning, or for winter storage.

The space, comforts, and convenience of the house were a relief to Alice, but this was secondary to her euphoria and the contentment of having her own home. The rented Methven farm where she and Ashton lived for almost seven years, was never truly 'home.' But this land was theirs: a blessed place for the younger children to grow up close to their grandparents. The family would miss Alba and Walter and their children, as well as their other friends, but as they had often journeyed between Methven and Rocanville, there was no reason why they would not continue to do so. They would stay in touch with relatives and friends left behind.

Except for, perhaps, Uncle Ernest. Alice and Ashton had been sorely disappointed when, with typical perversity, he had sold his property to a neighbour, rather than to them. Assuming ownership of the Rocanville farm far exceeded anything they could have expected from Ashton's volatile uncle.

In the autumn of 1941, Betty Lou had entered grade six, and, once the family was settled, Jack entered grade one. Ernest, going on four, spent his time toddling everywhere after Ashton or Bert. Robert did not sell Sandy or Prince at the sale. Both retirees stayed on the farm, and Sandy's solid form was Ernest's refuge when his dad herded the cows from pasture to barn. When Ashton yelled at Ernest that he was opening the gate and the cows were coming, Ernest ran and stood with his back to Sandy's tail, elbows on hocks. Apart from swishing his tail over Ernest's ears, the docile horse didn't budge.

With much to do after the move, winter came quickly, and so did a succession of trials to test the Marlatts' patience and resilience. First Ashton came down with lumbago. Before he was again operating on the vertical, a severe spring snowstorm caught their small herd of cows outside. All were chilled and several came down with pneumonia. Sick cows that lie down must roll over every three hours in order to keep breathing properly and thus fight off infection. Alice, Ashton, Bert, and even Betty Lou did their best, and the local veterinarian, Dr. Sharp, also attended. Every vet visit required re-shoveling the lane, but the best efforts of the family and Dr. Sharp could not save three good milkers. Alice was relieved to see the last of the snow and the coming of summer.

The arrival of summer brought the school year to a close. While Betty Lou had excelled in all subjects, as she had done in Methven, Jack had struggled. At the end of his first year in Rocanville School, Alice was appalled to find he still couldn't read. She was in turmoil. Should she hire a girl and teach him herself? She was a great believer in phonics and didn't understand why Jack hadn't been taught by this method. In the end, she let Jack return to Rocanville School, believing it was best for him to be with other children. Later she questioned her decision, but in the 1940's home-schooling was only a last resort if no school was within range.

Although farm chores were never-ending, Alice also taught Sunday School and joined the Women's Missionary Society. To help raise funds, Agnes and Alice embellished pillowcases to sell at church sales. Alice embroidered the designs and Agnes crocheted a decorative edging. The completed goods sold for two dollars per pair. Participating in church and church activities was not new to Alice, as she had always joined the church congregations in her communities.

1962: Gordon River–Divine Guidance

The lonely patch of ground beyond Kelly's Hill is sometimes an unsanctioned play area for the camp children, and indeed, in one corner, it contains a 'graveyard.' Here, in eternal repose, lie a few small animals and pets: birds, rodents, a bat picked out of the grill of a car, a kitten, and some bullheads that didn't survive life in a dishpan. Markers of sticks and rocks indicate creature interments in ground consecrated only by the blessings of the children who buried them there.

Rain, nature's holy water, sprinkled the graveyard overnight, but this March morning has dawned with just a slight haze of cloud already dissolving and lifting away over the mountains. Robins hunt on the lawns, and around the ponds pussy-willow buds flaunt silver coats. Among the stumps, the young firs sprout another year's growth, with bright green needles erupting from scaly buds. In the home site, blue smoke rises from a few chimneys as morning coffee pots are set to perk. Another Sunday in camp and most inhabitants are easing into the morning. Nevertheless, in front of the school, the teacher's Pontiac is ready to roll and spews grey exhaust as its engine warms.

My bare legs stick to the cool vinyl seat in Mrs. Marlatt's car. She is taking six of us, including my sister Frances, to the United Church in Lake Cowichan where we will go to Sunday School. Because I went to Sunday School when we lived in Chemainus, I bring my sister and friends up to speed on what to expect. Mrs. Marlatt smiles at me in the rear-view mirror.

I wear my best dress, and my shoes are polished. I have a pink barrette in my hair, a white hankie in my pocket, and a shiny dime for the collection plate. Mrs. Marlatt wears a blue suit I have never seen before, but otherwise she looks just the same. Her silver hair flows back from her face in waves, and her glasses reflect our shiny cheeks.

She adjusts her rear-view mirror and then explains: when we are in church, we will listen to the first part of the service. We must be quiet and patient, but she knows we will enjoy singing the hymns.

We sing every day in school and we love it even if all we have time for is 'O' Canada.' Sometimes we sing rounds, like 'Row, Row, Row Your Boat, and, until we get it right, we often have rounds of laughter. Mrs. Marlatt laughs too, and waves her hands at us to stop. Singing is fun, especially when we get the words and the rhythm right. Today, after some prayers and singing, we will go to Sunday School during the sermon, and Mrs. Marlatt will find us afterwards.

Mrs. Marlatt puts both hands on the wheel and steers across the trestle out of camp. With a single lane and no guardrail, she drives this slowly. Once we are on the pavement, the car picks up speed. We will be there in no time.

* * *

Now, after our pilgrimage to Church, Mrs. Marlatt's car again crosses the trestle. Everything was exactly as she explained. The people we met outside greeted Mrs. Marlatt and patted our heads, as they chatted and shook hands. We went in and took seats on the left, close to the front from where we had a good view. The church has stunning arched wood beams, and wood paneling on walls and ceiling. The pews are wood, as is the choir stall and pulpit. Light from the tall stained glass windows fell in multi-hued bands. Awed by the wonder of the space, I could not say a word.

I did breathe though, and sniffed a pleasant blend of wax, warm wood, carpet, flowers, and hymnbooks. Dressed in a purple and white robe, the minister, from his high pulpit, led the congregation in prayers and hymns, often spreading his arms as if to hug all of us.

When the minister invited the children in the congregation to Sunday School, we rose as one and marched with the others to the basement. Painted pale green, it was a close-ceilinged space with a kitchen at one end, and several small rooms along one side. We didn't know where to go, but a chirpy lady soon had us distributed among the rooms with other people our ages.

Our teacher read a Bible story about Jesus' parents losing Him in Jerusalem. He had gone to the temple, and was surprised they did not think to look for Him there. We talked about the story, and although I didn't say so, I thought it inconsiderate of Jesus to worry his parents. The lesson ended with the Lord's Prayer, which we recite every morning, and we then joined the other children in the big room for cookies and juice. Voices accompanying tramping feet on the stairs announced the service was over, and Mrs. Marlatt appeared. She smiled and talked, and then she gathered us close to her and we left. I think I like going to church.

Gordon River School closed at the end of June 1964. My family then moved to Lake Cowichan where I rejoined them after living with my grandmother in Chemainus for the year I attended grade eight.

From the fall of 1964, the United Church was part of my life in Lake Cowichan. As a member of C.G.I.T. (Canadian Girls in Training), of which my mother became a leader, I was there every week for our meetings in the basement where we used the same Sunday School rooms we had visited as children. The walls sported the same shade of green paint. Our C.G.I.T. group often participated in church services, and I probably spent more time admiring the wood finishing, the graceful windows, and the elegant design, than paying attention to the service.

I saw much of this church until my graduation in 1968, and then I was married there in 1969. Sadly, this beautiful building, with its magnificent wood interior, burned to the ground in April of 1990. A modest building was erected in its place, but attendance dwindled to the point that, by 2013, there was no longer a congregation or a minister.

1940's: Singing and Writing

Although Alice regularly attended church, Ashton was not much of a church go-er. He didn't mind his family going to church, and usually took himself off to the 'poker shack' joining the other male abstainers for the duration of the services. Alice did not nag, and went about her church pursuits on her own. She was a loving wife and mother, but an independent woman who followed her own interests. Also, as she had had a driver's license for years, she drove herself to visit family, or attend whatever community or church event she wished. Having learned to drive on the straight and empty roads of the prairies, Alice drove fast, probably singing all the way.

Alice loved to sing and if not singing while she worked, she hummed or whistled. There was much to sing about now that she and Ashton owned the farm. Although happy to be home in Rocanville, Alice did not forsake friends and relatives left behind. She added those in Methven to her list of correspondents that included Annie Graham, Albert and Ethel, Stan Toole, Elsie Plummer, Belle Dobbs, and many others. Alice regularly wrote letters, and she considered letter writing and penmanship a fine art.

1960: Gordon River–In Praise of the Pen

Several times per week, mail arrives at the office, from where camp residents must collect it themselves. Up front steps pockmarked by scores of caulked boots, they enter a room barricaded by a long counter. Interposed by a swinging gate, and bearing a notice advising 'No Caulk Boots,' the counter makes a clear distinction between those who wear caulked boots (loggers), and those who do not (management). The mechanics of the gate is of endless fascination to the children who sometimes collect the family mail.

While they wait to be noticed, they push the gate and peer at hinges that seem to come away from their pivots depending on which way the gate swings. Sometimes the squeaking gate alerts the keepers of the inner sanctum that a supplicant awaits their pleasure.

A thump of a coffee mug, a squeal from a chair, and a man from one of the offices beyond the barricade clumps to the doorway. A pall of cigarette smoke mingles with that of musty ledgers, wool, wood, and other aromas associated with working men. Without question, the office is the domain of men. Nervous camp wives may visit the office to use the telephone for urgent calls, but no women or children, like caulk-booted men, venture past the long counter.

Upon inquiries for mail, the guardian checks the labeled boxes on the right hand wall above the end of the counter. The boxes are within reach of those standing on the other side, but nobody has the temerity to reach into their box themselves. This is the sole responsibility of the man in attendance. Clutching their letters, the mail recipients exit with appropriate thanks.

Most mail is simply addressed with the name of the resident followed by 'Gordon River Camp, Via Honeymoon Bay, B.C.' There is no postal code. Mail may comprise bills from the oil company servicing the camp (for those who did not pay cash), mail order catalogues, greeting cards, and letters. Yes, people do receive, and write, letters.

Letters advise grandparents on the well-being of their grandchildren, request documents, appeal bill adjustments on Eaton's accounts, or update friends on life in camp. With few telephones, the primary means of communication with friends, relatives, and agencies is by letter, and unless a person has access to a typewriter, legible handwriting is imperative. All schools in British Columbia acknowledge this with the inclusion of 'Writing' in the curriculum, with an approved guide.

The MacLean Method of Writing. We have our books spread open and set at a slight angle. The page is clean, white, with pale blue lines. I have filled my fountain pen, and my recently washed hands hold the page where the letter 'R' in both capitals and small letters adorns the top left corner. I must fill the page with more elegant 'R's, just like the samples.

Mrs. Marlatt writes the letters on the blackboard and on a sheet of ruled paper that she holds in front of her. She tells us beautiful writing takes much practice, but each of us is capable of handwriting as perfect as in the book.

And as perfect as hers, I think.

Her handwriting is a marvel. She often shows us how she does it: she sits up straight at her desk, places both feet squarely on the floor, and turns the page so it slants just so. She lightly grips her fountain pen, and her hand flows across the page.

"Your hand must move to form the letters, not your fingers."

Her hand certainly does flow over the page, and lines of fluid script appear.

I scrunch my face over my page, and grip my pen. Too tight. I release some pressure and the pen makes the wobbliest letter 'R' I have ever seen. This shouldn't be so hard, as I draw something every day— usually horses, but I can draw a reasonable image of almost anything, and after all, my name begins with 'R.' I should manage at least one letter of the alphabet that does not look like something scribbled in grade two. I keep at it. By the end of the page, some of the letters look better, but I know my grip is too tight. This is because my fingers are now sweaty, and my nice Sheaffer's fountain pen slithers like a piece of wet licorice. I become aware my feet are no longer planted on the floor under my desk. My legs are crossed and one ankle twines about the other and the foot on the end of it twitches up and down. Nor are my shoulders back and my page slanted at the right angle.

I sit up straight, unravel my legs, and finish the lesson with a sentence of my own, using as many letters 'R' and 'r' as possible: 'Rosemary rides a roan horse through Gordon River.'

The exercise done, I sigh. I know it isn't perfect, but it's getting better. I think.

A notation in my final report of grade five reads, "Try and improve your writing. You can do much better than your marks indicate."

My marks were a dismal 'C-, C, C' with a final mark of 'C-.' I knew my writing was terrible, but with the beckoning bliss of summer vacation, I submerged my shame. Upon return to class, I found a miracle had not occurred over the summer, and my handwriting was just as awful in September as it had been in June. Remedial action was unavoidable, so, although I don't recall how I arrived at this resolution, I decided that, if I went back to the beginning and printed everything, I could re-learn to do nice writing. So, I printed.

I wasn't sure if Mrs. Marlatt would approve, or agree with my logic. Although the look she gave me was speculative, she said nothing. I was surprised at this, but as I had opened my mouth, I persevered. Either this strategy worked, or I had matured enough to take the care and focus needed to achieve the comment on my first report card of grade six, "I am so pleased with her improvement in writing it is almost fantastic. All of Rosemary's work is done with great care."

Mrs. Marlatt placed a great deal of emphasis on legible printing and writing, and equally neat legible work in all of our subjects. Grubby eraser marks or fingerprints on the page were as unacceptable as misspellings and poor grammar. Writing, both the formation of letters, and phrasing of sentences and paragraphs was an important part of our schooling.

We learned the fundamentals of letter writing–where to place the date, the salutation, the body, and the signature. We learned the correct way to sign letters and documents, although we hardly knew what kind of 'document' we would ever sign.

Mrs. Marlatt explained the correct signature for a married woman (with husband still living), was to use her husband's name, as in 'Mrs. John Doe.' As children, we should sign our letters as 'Miss Jane Doe,' or 'Master John Doe.' We had great fun with this, calling each other 'Miss' or 'Master.' 'Master' struck us as particularly hilarious, and I almost wished I had a brother to torture with this designation.

Mrs. Marlatt grinned at our silliness, but finished the lesson that day with the information that, because she was a widow, she now signed as 'Mrs. Alice M. Marlatt.' We wondered about that. Although we knew about Jack and Ernest, and Betty Lou and her family, Mrs. Marlatt never mentioned anything about Mr. Marlatt.

1942–1945: Prejudice on the Home Front

Betty Lou and her brothers made new friends at school, but at home they were each other's playmates. Alice claimed their childhood on the Rocanville Farm was a "wonderful spell" in their lives. Alice and Ashton's pride in their farm and the security of ownership spilled over to influence their children.

They imitated their parents by playing 'farm.' Like Alice and her siblings years before, Betty Lou and her brothers hitched Sandy to the stone boat and went into the fields to collect rocks and sticks, and play at stooking. They picked berries, caught gophers, played in the sloughs, and built forts. As they grew, they developed hobbies: Ernest discovered gardening.

"He always had a garden of his own, with popcorn and pumpkins," said Alice.

One year he planted pumpkin plants in tomato cans and put them on the window ledge in his bedroom. They thrived, and "there were great big pumpkin vines growing every way–then we couldn't get the pumpkin out of the tomato can."

The Marlatt children, like their uncle and aunts, also had chores, but there was still time for sports: curling, hockey, and baseball, according to the season.

From the first winter, Ashton joined the local sports scene and was soon a fixture at the rinks, playing, refereeing, and coaching. He coached the boys' hockey team who made it to the finals one year. At one of the big games, some fathers complained that the boys on the other team were too big for their ages, and the Rocanville boys were not likely to win. It took the heart out of the boys. Exasperated, Ashton kicked the dads out of the dressing room, then told the boys "not to get down in the dumps" because they really could beat that team. Such was his 'can-do' attitude to all impediments.

With summer, came the turn to baseball. Again, Ashton coached and, when they were older, Jack and Ernest were catcher and pitcher. The three Marlatt men took the game very seriously–"it was a real tight business–you didn't make a fool of yourself out there." Ernest pitched anything at any opportunity. Once, Alice had Bert toss some mouldy potatoes into the yard for the chickens, and when she came out soon

R.Rigsby

after, the potatoes had disappeared. Puzzled by this, but hot on the trail of a missing hen, she found a pile of potatoes in the middle of the pigpen. The pigpen was the original log cabin that had so disheartened Agnes in 1906. By the '40s, the chinking *had* fallen out, and the former family home had become a "nice place for the pigs to go on hot days." Ernest had pitched the potatoes through the gaps between the logs, and as if the challenge of this wasn't enough, he pitched balls through a pear shaped opening on the feed door in the barn.

Irene was nineteen when Alice and Ashton moved the family to Rocanville. Shortly afterward, she took a job in the printing office, and continued to work this and other jobs in both Rocanville and Moosomin. In the fall of 1943, she went to Brandon to visit Aunt Hazel. Alice and Ashton had given her money to buy a new winter coat, but the next thing they heard was, instead of a coat, she had bought a ticket to Ontario. The war was on, and industries were calling for all hands. Irene took a job in a rubber factory, and Alice's sister Bobbie found work in a plant manufacturing shells–an original 'Bomb Girl.'

Except for the participation of Irene and Bobbie, the years of World War II passed with minimal effect on the Marlatts' everyday lives. As did the Blairs in the years of World War I, Alice and her family read newspapers and letters. They also had radio broadcasts to keep them updated on the dreadful events overseas. Betty Lou had a teacher whose fiancé fought on one of the fronts, and as she too followed the news, she offered her own prayers for his safe return. There was a certain amount of rationing, but again most of their food was homegrown.

'Marlatt' was an unusual name in a region mostly settled by people from Great Britain or of French descent, but Ashton and Alice never denied the name possibly had German roots. Alice dismissed whatever static the family endured as just foolish talk, and a product of the fear and anxiety of those families who had men in the battlefields.

Whether due to this experience or from some point of view passed on from Agnes and Robert, or from some experience of her own, Alice despised prejudicial attitudes or actions.

1962: Gordon River–If We Could Take A Bus

Spring steals up the valleys, searching out snow tucked in sheltered pockets. Giving in to the inevitable, water trickles downhill. The trickles become creeks, the creeks become rivers, and all streams in this watershed find their way to Cowichan Lake. The lake tops the weir at its foot by several feet, and fills the river. The river seeks release in the Strait of Georgia but unable to contain the volume, it nudges up its banks and menaces the village.

Oblivious to the threat not fifty meters away, I wait in our station wagon in the Co-Op parking lot in Lake Cowichan. My family is in the store, but I would much rather sort through my lapful of books, recently checked out from the library. My sisters and I went there with Dad while Mum started shopping, and now they have gone to join her.

I look up from my books to see whirlpools on the Cowichan River. Between eddies, the surface is smooth and reflects the blue sky. I realize the high water could flood onto the road and into buildings as it did last year. I know this wasn't pleasant for the people who were flooded, but still the sheer volume of water flowing out of the lake fascinates me. Our rivers at home are high too, but lie deep between their banks, and camp is never in danger.

Accepting the river is not about to do anything exciting in the next few minutes, I hold with two hands 'The Black Stallion and Flame' by Walter Farley. I hunt for Mr. Farley's books on every library visit, and this is a brand new book. It deserves my undivided attention. As soon as supper is over, I will go to my room and read in my bed until Mum tells me to put out the light.

I start reading another book, but my focus falters. It is a busy Saturday and there are many people coming and going. An East Indian family pulls up in the next parking spot and everybody chatters as they open doors and get out. There are two ladies dressed in bright pants and tops, and each has a shimmering shawl around her head and shoulders. The man driving the car is tall and made even taller by his bright blue turban. A couple of little kids start running for the entrance to the Co-Op, but the man calls them back until everybody is out of the car. Giggling and holding hands, they jump up and down as they wait.

There are many people from India and Pakistan in Lake Cowichan. Mrs. Marlatt explained how some have been here since this area was first logged and settled. Many men went to work in the mills. I have heard East Indian people called 'Hindus,' but Mrs. Marlatt tells us that 'Hindu' is not only rude, but incorrect, as most of these people are followers of the Sikh religion. We should never call anybody by his or her religion, nor should we call anybody names like 'Injun' or 'Chink' or 'Nigger.'

Mrs. Marlatt once visited her Uncle Dalton in the United States where Negro people ride in the back of buses, have separate toilets, and cannot go into 'white only' restaurants. This 'racial segregation' is wrong and shameful, but many people, both Negro and white, are protesting and marching to abolish these rules.

* * *

According to plan, I came to my room to start my book as soon as my sisters and I finished the supper dishes. It has been bliss. Now late evening, my sisters are asleep, the television is off, and Mum and Dad are having their evening cup of instant coffee. The scent of coffee, my parents' low-toned conversation, and the nighttime sounds beyond my window exist outside the bubble of my mind's eye world.

Mum pokes her head into my bubble. Ten minutes more.

I return to a tropical island with two incredible horses—one raven black and the other bright chestnut. They are rivals, but at the same time they must work together to rid the island of a terrible rabid bat. Two colours, one goal.

1945–1949: Horsing Around

Nobody knew from where the original Marlatt immigrants had hailed, but Ashton believed the name originated in the Lowlands of Holland or Belgium. Ashton stated 'Irish' descent on some census returns including that of 1916 completed in Wawanesa. Alice declared he claimed a different nationality with every count.

Perhaps the 'Irish' heritage manifested itself in the family's love of horses. When Betty Lou wanted a horse of her own, she began her first business. From scraps of wool felt, she crafted small flower bouquets to adorn ladies coats. She saved her profits, but at thirty-five cents per bouquet, it was clear it would take a long time to amass enough capital to buy a horse.

Ashton, who didn't need much of an excuse to go horse shopping, heard of a sale at a neighbouring village. There, he spotted Flash. She was a splendid bay mare with one white sock and a white star on her forehead, but she was also young and spirited. Concerned that she might be too much horse for Betty Lou, Ashton spoke to Flash's owner. She assured him that yes, the mare was fast and willing, but she was also sensible and well mannered. Therefore, for the grand bid of thirty-nine dollars, Betty Lou became a horse owner. Ashton teased her saying her contribution had bought her the tail.

With the arrival of Flash, Sandy enjoyed full retirement, and Betty Lou and her brothers drove at a speed that Sandy in his best years had never attained. Riding and driving this lively mare became one of Betty Lou's passions.

Although Jack and Ernest were good boys, they were still boys who found their share of mischief and made questionable decisions. Shortly after the move to the Rocanville farm, probably on a dull afternoon when nothing appealed, they deduced that if horses could be ridden, then why not pigs? The pigs were not agreeable to this, and although the boys managed to hang on for a few bumpy yards, their mounts soon ejected them. The landing site was naturally not grass or the dust of the yard, but the very muckiest part of the pigpen. Alice was not amused.

On another occasion, when Ernest was older, he was out in the fields fooling around with his friends, and they accidentally set the grass on fire. Alice did not say what she suspected they were doing, but a few possibilities come to mind. A grass fire is never a good thing in a dry country where sources of water are limited, or non-existent, and a fire out of control can destroy not only crops and woodlots, but homesteads and towns as well. Out on the tractor, Jack witnessed his brother and friends leaping about as they stamped on the flames. Rather than join them in what was surely a futile attempt to stop the fire, Jack trundled home to call the volunteer firefighters. The tractor at top speed was far too slow for his liking, so upon reaching the lane, he hopped off and ran ahead of it. He placed the call for help, reclaimed the tractor that had by then reached the yard, and returned to the field to build a fireguard to contain the blaze. Meanwhile, the volunteers, confused as to the location of the fire charged full tilt into the farmyard only to find it deserted.

When they spotted the smoke, they joined the boys. Disaster was averted. Alice and Ashton, who were away in Wawanesa visiting Alba and Walter, missed the excitement. What consequences were bestowed upon Ernest, Alice did not say.

Chapter Fourteen: A Distant Bell

1979: Leader XIV

White puffs rise from the mouths of walkers and from the tailpipes of passing cars. Alice nods to people walking dogs, a few going to jobs in town, and others, like her, out for exercise. Watchful for slippery patches, Alice picks up her pace, notes the ice melting in sunny spots and thinks that Jack Frost still does not have the upper hand.

This morning they will make an early start on the story, as Betty Lou and Art have business in town. Betty Lou had asked her if she wanted to do the story early, or later after she and Art returned. Alice had chosen early. I'm always up anyway, she had reasoned, and I feel my best first thing in the morning.

There are always so many choices in life, she thinks. Everyday choices: what to have for breakfast, what to wear, what letters to write— usually easy choices made without much thought, but occasionally bigger choices in need of more consideration. Such was the case during my last year at Youbou School.

I knew I would leave B.C. and all of my friends there, but the question was where to live when I returned to Saskatchewan.

Instead of the fall morning with its crispy grass and sparkling rooftops, Alice sees the Trans Canada Highway in July of 1968 as she drives home to Saskatchewan for the last time.

* * *

The highway stretches ahead in an undulating strip of dark grey that, with every undulation, becomes thinner and thinner as it disappears into the horizon. On either side of the highway, young wheat, stirred by the breeze, swirls in rooted eddies.

Driving at top speed on this empty stretch, Alice keeps a clear eye on the road ahead and thinks the remaining years of her life will be like this highway–ups and downs that will also become thinner and thinner with each passing year. She will miss teaching, but then Betty Lou is a teacher, and maybe one of her grandchildren will carry on the tradition.

She has had long talks with Betty Lou and Bobbie about her future, but she has decided that, after summer at the cottage, she will live in Rocanville. She and Bobbie have agreed to buy a trailer and live there together. Jessie also lives in Rocanville, and Alice looks forward to seeing more of her. She wishes her mother was still alive to welcome her home, but Agnes died five years ago.

R.Rigsby

Alice recalls that after the funeral, instead of going immediately back to Regina Airport, she chose to take a detour to Kenosee Lake to check on the building progress of the cottage. That was a mistake and she missed her plane.

Alice slows to allow a tractor to cross the highway, and returns the farmer's wave as she sails past. She thinks her life is like a ship on a highway of waves, battered by the occasional storm of sorrows, but with beacons of love, friendship, and many delights marking the way.

* * *

Alice pauses in her walk. The time Bobbie and I lived in that trailer were good for the first few years, she thinks. Later Bobbie became the big sister, or a mother, as I found myself becoming more easily confused with each passing year. I was difficult at times, and I know I still have lapses.

Bobbie and Jessie weren't happy to see me go to Leader, but Betty Lou insisted it was best. That was another hard decision, but I sometimes wonder how much choice one really has in selecting a path.

Turning the last corner on her chilly outing, Alice walks home.

1949–1953: Hidden Shoals

By the fall of 1949, Alice and Ashton had celebrated nineteen years of marriage and were enjoying the fruits of their many years of toil. Life was good. Betty Lou had graduated in the spring of 1948, and had then worked a term as a supervisor at a school in Kipling. Choosing to be a teacher, she then began her studies at the University of Saskatchewan. The boys, at ages eleven and fourteen, were in school, and when not curling, or playing baseball and hockey, they helped on the farm. Bert, with a reduced chore-list in keeping with his age, still peeled potatoes. Family and farm prospered.

Alice was comfortable in her father's house, and was active in her community. Ashton, when not working the land, worked teams of young baseball and hockey players, and curled. All was well. Then Ashton started to have some trouble.

Alice said, "He kept passing out and we didn't know what was wrong."

They took him to the hospital in Moosomin, but the doctors, unable to find the source of the trouble, discharged him before Christmas.

Producing a bottle of wine for Christmas dinner, Ashton prepared to do the honours. To his dismay, he was unable to pull the cork. In February, Alice persuaded him to go to the hospital in Esterhazy and the doctor there immediately made a diagnosis. Ashton had serious heart disease. The doctor estimated he had from four to ten years to live. The beginning of the new decade, a decade of prosperity for Canada, of high hopes and optimism for most Canadians, was one of apprehension for Alice, Ashton, and their children.

The doctor had a grim discussion with Ashton and had a separate similar conversation with Alice, but Alice and Ashton never spoke to each other about the ramifications of the disease, or the ghastly prognosis. Ashton resumed curling and the doctor told Alice she must not fuss, "that [she] wasn't to worry, [she] wasn't to stop him from doing this or that," so in keeping with the doctor's advice, they "never talked about it," and carried on.

With unstated acknowledgement of Ashton's condition, the family made adjustments. Ashton couldn't work the farm, but the boys were strong and willing. After school each day, they worked until dark: milking, ploughing, planting, feeding stock, fixing machinery, and whatever else was necessary. Alice gave Jack a white hat to wear when out on the tractor. When she checked periodically, the white hat bobbing along assured her Jack was under it, and safe. Ashton often drove out to the fields. Waiting by the car, he watched the boys cultivate and sow.

Ashton never discussed his condition with Alice and his children, but he talked to Jessie. Laura was gone, and Jessie, the fun-loving girl, was now a respectable married matron of thirty-seven. She was a good listener, but that was all she could do. Occasionally, over the next few years, Ashton suffered bouts of phlebitis and weakness, possibly anemia, which put him back in the hospital for one or two days where he received shots of vitamin B12.

Although Alice and Ashton never discussed his disease, Ashton knew the family would have a difficult time on the farm with only the boys to work it. He urged Alice to resume her teaching career. He pointed out a job opening in Maryfield. Jack was out of school and worked in a garage in Rocanville, and Ashton suggested he could do the same there. Ashton insisted they sell the farm and move to Maryfield, or to any place where Alice could get work. Alice refused. She said she was stubborn and didn't want to leave him alone while she went to work. She went everywhere Ashton went. This was the doctor's advice and Ashton must have been aware, because he never forbade Alice from joining him. Instead, they had a tacit understanding that if the worst should happen, she would sell the farm.

Punctuating the years of foreboding were times of anxiety, sorrow, and celebration. Irene married Charles Strong in 1950, and the new couple began their life together in Moosomin. The following year of 1951 Jack suffered through a bout of appendicitis but with the resilience of youth soon recovered. That same year Robert died at the age of eighty-one. He and Agnes would have been married for forty-nine years come the fall, and Alice and her family mourned his passing along with the close-knit community who respected this quiet, resolute man. Agnes kept her grief to herself, and did not share her despair with Alice or her other children. At seventy-two, Agnes was still hale and involved in her community and ever present in the lives of her family.

1953: Beachhead Revisited

In the spring of 1953, Alice and Ashton planned a summer excursion to visit their respective friends and relatives, and their childhood homes, in Ontario. Local friends, Olive and Bill Street, wanted to visit family in Toronto, so the foursome agreed to travel together in the Marlatts' car. Realizing such a long drive would be impossible for Ashton, they drafted Betty Lou as chauffeur.

They mailed letters, laid out maps, selected routes, and on a Thursday in July, Alice, Ashton, and the Streets travelled to Moosomin, the first stop on the itinerary. At the train station, they met Betty Lou, who, at twenty-two, was a confident young woman with a newly launched teaching career in Estuary, a hamlet north of Leader. After an overnight stay with Irene and Charles, and with Betty Lou at the wheel, the voyagers began their adventure.

They had packed most of their own food. The example of Agnes never being without provisions for the family had been well-learned, and they planned to stay in motels with kitchenettes. At Winnipeg, they turned south and climbed the Red River Valley to the town of Grand Forks where on the first night, a whole seven dollars bought them exactly what they wanted. The next night, Saturday, they stayed on the outskirts of Ashland, Minnesota, where for five dollars they enjoyed a cabin overlooking Lake Superior. By then they had established their travel routine wherein Betty Lou cooked breakfast and prepared the day's picnic lunch, while Alice and Olive showered and packed.

Alice did not relate the men's responsibilities, but presumably they were in charge of the car. Gas, oil, tire pressure, and water would have had to be monitored to make sure their loaded vehicle, like a prairie schooner full of settlers, was up to the expedition. Although not following the same route (via CPR) both Alice and Ashton had travelled in 1906, they were surely going back. Back to the land of their births and roots, to see relatives, friends, and sights for the last time. Alice and Ashton may have felt an unspoken sense of urgency in response to the steady knell of a warning bell in their mutual sub conscience: make the trip *now*.

Regardless of the states of mind prompting the trip, the travellers were cheerful. Their schedule was leisurely, as the journey was rarely resumed before 10 a.m., and by late afternoon, they were cozy in the evening accommodation. On Sunday night, for the bargain rate of six dollars, they snuggled into a perfect three-room log cabin on a pinnacle overlooking the joining of Lakes Michigan and Huron at the Mackinaw Straits. Exhilarated by the expanse of lake and the moist breeze, they opened all windows to hear the crashing waves. Although it was summer, the breeze was brisk, necessitating lighting the oil heater–a holiday extravagance for sure, perhaps produced by the hypnotic roar of the lake dashing itself on the rocks all night long.

On day four, the quintet crossed back into Canada at Sarnia and settled for the night at cabins just east of the city for another great price of five dollars. Alice noted the cost of every motel and was impressed with the comfort and quality of all lodging. However, having tolerated bedbugs and in cramped quarters most of her life, Alice would have made the best of any accommodation. A bed of nails in a roofless hut might have elicited a complaint.

Each morning the group rose ready to continue the adventure, and Tuesday found them en route to Toronto where they planned to stay overnight with the Street's relatives, the Brownlees. Their Sarnia departure had been later than intended, and Betty Lou drove the approach to Toronto via Lakeshore Drive in mid rush hour. With her usual composure, the prairie farm girl piloted their vehicle through traffic, lights, and lane changes to a safe arrival at the home of the Brownlees.

The Brownlees had acquired one of the new contraptions called a television. The evening's programs were much enjoyed regardless of Mr. Brownlee's pronouncements that television was "old stuff" by now and "he was tired and fed up with it." Mr. Brownlee also considered himself in a position to offer marital advice to Betty Lou. On finding that no, she "had not caught a man yet" he intoned she "should hurry up and get someone, oh anyone, as marriage is a great institution." At Betty Lou's expression, Alice trembled for fear she would "slap his simple face." Alice knew Betty Lou had never been a fan of Mr. Brownlee, but Alice said of Betty Lou "she behaved admirably and I wasn't shamed."

The next day, Alice, Ashton, and Betty Lou parted company with the Streets and Mr. Brownlee's helpful observations. They pushed north to Simcoe to the home of Ashton's sister-in-law Beatrice. After John's death, Beatrice, with her children Howard and Ethel, had moved back to Simcoe to be close to her parents, and although Ashton had kept in touch with her, he was thrilled to see her in person. As for Beatrice, she was beside herself with joy. Together they visited Howard and his wife, and then daughter Ethel and her husband who owned a tobacco farm. Both Alice and Ashton were intrigued with the "racket" of growing tobacco where fourteen teaspoons of seed would sow thirty-seven acres. Harvesting was another matter, and they learned that this cost $175 per day. Ashton also went to visit his eighty-six-year-old Aunt Nellie from his mother's side of the family. On this trip, he was determined to reconnect with as many of his relations as possible.

One unexpected reconnection occurred in the Simcoe Farmer's Market. Alice and Ashton joined Beatrice on this jaunt, and while Ashton wandered elsewhere, Beatrice met a black man whom she introduced to Alice as Joe. This was the very man who had been Ashton's friend when Beatrice, John, and Ashton were schoolchildren. Alice searched out Ashton. Overwhelmed by this unexpected meeting with Joe, Ashton accompanied him home where the two friends caught up on all that had happened since they played, and fought, in their Simcoe neighbourhood. On his return to Beatrice's house, Ashton did not say if they had discussed mutual health conditions, but they shared the same fate. Joe died of heart failure in 1954.

After saying goodbye to Beatrice in Simcoe, the trio traveled to Markdale to the home of Alice's cousin, Annie (Graham). Many years had passed since Alice and Laura, as children, had buried their apple-loved-ones in the Graham orchard. Annie was ecstatic to see her cousin again and introduced Alice, Ashton, and Betty Lou to Doug and Keith, two of her sons at home. The young men, who were about Betty Lou's age, were on their way out for the evening. Ashton walked them to their car.

In the living room, Betty Lou, perched on a chair, listened to her mother and Annie launch into conversation about friends, relatives, and ancient days. Before her eyes glazed over, Doug returned and asked her if she would like to join them.

"I would LOVE to go!" Betty Lou sprang from her chair.

Alice said it was like a volcano erupting, and the young folk vanished until the next morning.

The following days were a whirlwind of visiting, picnics, ball games and sightseeing. Annie's husband, Russell, returned as did their other son Hugh, and the whole clan visited Annie's brothers, Howard and Wilfrid, and their families. Ashton was amazed at how much Wilfrid resembled Alice's father, Robert. They remarked on how Wilfrid's hand movements and the manner in which he crossed his legs and swung his foot were like Robert's. On top of finding unexpected physical family resemblances, Ashton was unexpectedly cheered to find the male members of Alice's relations, especially Russell and Howard, shared his zeal for sports. They had interminable discussions on baseball and hockey.

During their visit with Alice's cousins, Ashton reminded Alice of a conversation they had had as they planned their trip that spring. He had then told Alice "all of these years together I have been with your relations," but on this trip, he wanted to spend time with *his*.

Now he told Alice if he had known what remarkable people they were, he would have been more enthusiastic to see them sooner. Alice said Ashton had not realized how much he enjoyed sharing favourite sports stories with people with similar passions.

"For once Ashton found a whole gang who could see funny things in ball and tell them in such an entertaining manner."

He wished they had more time.

On a sunny afternoon they toured the former Blair homes–that of Robert's father and the home Robert and Agnes had left to go west. Trees drooped with ripening fruit, gardens overflowed with vegetables, and fields bore fine crops of wheat. Looking at the abundance and the green rich land, Ashton was amazed Robert and Agnes had left it all to go west. The present owner of Robert's farm, an Irishman named Pat Sweeney, welcomed them to look around, and as Alice said, "he must have licked the Blarney Stone" because he looked at her, pointed at his farm, and remarked how "one so fair could be born there!"

Alice also visited the mother of her friend, Elsie Plummer, from the Leader days. Elsie's mum, although elderly, was still spry, and cared for an even older lady. Alice's spring letter writing had produced a wealth of reconnections and no day went by they did not call on a friend or a relative.

Alice's cousins brought her up to date on other long-time friends and neighbours of her parents. This included Minnie Graham who had been, before he fell for Agnes, Robert's former flame. Howard and Wilfrid recalled how, when Robert was babysitting them, Miss Graham came to the house, and as Robert and Minnie were "spooning" on the couch, up jumped little Wilfrid saying, "Uncle Wobbo, I want to dobbo," somewhat interrupting the moment. This produced hoots of laughter tempered with the sad acknowledgement that Minnie Graham was now very elderly and ill, and not expected to live much longer.

Betty Lou, escorted by her cousins, went swimming, bowling, picnicking, and sightseeing, but the visit could not conclude without the families having a baseball game. Betty Lou astounded her cousins with the power of her throws, and Ashton participated too, with discretion. As always, Alice was the sole spectator.

Ultimately the spate of visiting came to an end, and, after damp goodbyes, the Marlatts retraced their route to Toronto. They topped off their Ontario tour with the special treat of a baseball game between the professional teams of Toronto and Syracuse. The next day they found the Streets and embarked on the first leg of their journey home.

Due to a later than expected start, the first evening found them only as far as North Bay where they stayed in cabins overlooking Lake Nipissing. From there they followed a route through Sudbury, crossed into the United States at Sault Ste. Marie, and thence through Marquette, Ashland, Duluth, Bemedji and Grand Forks, before again turning north for the border. They spent three nights on the road for the return trip, and Alice knew the tour would have been impossible without Betty Lou. As soon as they relaxed after the excursion of their lives, Alice wrote to Agnes, who was visiting Bobbie in British Columbia, and described every detail of the trip in nineteen pages of correspondence.

R.Rigsby

Chapter Fifteen: Three Endings

1979: Leader XV

Dawn revealed platinum clad rooftops and diamonds glinting in the grass. In the gutters, miniature silver rinks suspended leaves and twigs in freeze-frame parodies of the national sport. Those leaves still clinging to trees, waiting to be drafted, wore their own frosted jerseys. As the day wore on, the sun withdrew behind pewter clouds, and the silver rinks did not thaw.

An early and murky dusk descends over Leader. Alice would not be surprised to see a few flakes in the air before full dark. From her bedroom window, she looks over the street where a few boys, in denial of the lowering gloom, play hockey. Shouts and laughter follow grating sticks and the puck clunking over the pavement. Alice smiles and fancies a ghostly shape waving arms and shouting silent instructions. The boys, but not the ghost, exhale vapours in the cold air.

Alice holds the edge of the curtain, but finds it hard to stop watching the boys and their imaginary coach. She thinks about the day Ashton died and how her world pitched into a trough of despair.

She rose from that, as she knew she must, because Ashton would not have wanted her to wallow, and because there were still the children.

In the summers of '54 and '55, she upgraded her teaching qualifications with courses in Regina where she again lived in a boarding house. The landlady was a Mrs. Crabtree, and Alice had a very strange sense of déjà vu. Much had changed since 1922 but not as much as she had expected. Her room, the food, the walk to school, and her courses transported her back thirty years. At the college, she met several people who were also upgrading, but unlike before, she felt comfortable with everybody. She did not "flash around" though (she laughs aloud at that thought), because her heart was not in it.

It was good to be away from the farm and Rocanville where she daily expected Ashton to wave at her from the barn, come out of Murray's Barber Shop, or be waiting outside of church.

When she accepted an offer for the farm, the next step was a sale. A young couple bid on Jack's childhood wagon and Alice was not expecting the pang she felt when they loaded it into their rusty truck. She watched them drive away and could not take her eyes off the wagon's two curved shafts bumping up and down on the tailgate as if waving goodbye. Later that day, she too left the farm that would never again be her home.

They finished the story this afternoon and Alice thought she would be thankful, but instead she is gripped with melancholy. She held her breath when she watched Betty Lou label the last tape and place it in the box with the others. This last session was the hardest but, in a way, the easiest too.

Those last memories are so clear and close, she thinks. I hardly have to think about what happened, probably because the memory of Ashton is always with me. Even with my travels and all of the years since he died, he is always close to me, and the memory of his smile, his humour, his form and touch are part of all of my years alone. I am only seventy-six, so there is a good chance I will be around for a while yet, and the story is not completely over.

I wonder who will ever listen to all of those silly tapes.

1953–1954: Sailing On

Ashton had held up well during the trip and once home was relieved to find the farm had survived their absence under the management of Jack and Ernest. The boys had put a new roof on the milk house where the center beam, which had cracked years before, looked as though it was about to give way. They had removed the offending timber and most of the roof when their Aunt Jessie came by to pick up some cream. Jessie, the family jokester, received a shock when she opened the milk house door only to see blue sky above. They replaced the roof and covered it in sod in the traditional manner.

The fall of i953 produced a crop of wheat that, although tainted with some rust, was marketable, as were good crops of barley and oats. However, before the hot weather passed, Ernest sickened with what Alice prayed was only 'summer flu.' Polio was recurring in the area, and Alice and Ashton dreaded this, as they had six neighbours who had contracted the disease. Of these, one had died, and the others had lasting damage in the form of "twisted faces" and limps. To everybody's relief, Ernest's illness was not polio, and he was soon well.

Like all of the years before, the year wound up with Christmas and New Year's celebrations, and prayers their lives would go on as happy and prosperous as ever. It was not to be. Ashton's lurking heart condition ignored their prayers.

Alice was not with him at the end. On February 13, 1954, Ashton played in a brier at the Rocanville arena, and after curling, he borrowed Jack's skates for a few turns around the rink. Twice around, and he decided it was enough, as he had fallen several times. On the bench, he removed one skate . . . and was gone. Distressed onlookers called Alice. With the support of friends, Alice and Jack dealt with the immediacy of death, as Ernest was in Regina with his own curling team, and Betty Lou was working in Estuary.

Alice thought she was prepared for this inevitable event, but nonetheless, it was a shock. She recalled she and Ashton had bantered that day, "just talked a lot of tomfoolery–he called me an old hen and I called him an old rooster."

They had had only twenty-three years together: years of hard work and heartbreak, but years of laughter and joy. Ashton had worried about the future of his family, but probably took comfort in the knowledge that not only were his children strong and healthy with good prospects, but Alice too was energetic, independent, and above all, resourceful.

The loss of Ashton forced Alice to chart a new course for her life. She needed an income. They had paid off the farm long since, but grain-growing is ever a risk. She could teach, and provide for herself and the boys, and a teaching job would guarantee an income. Again, she faced some hard choices. Could she and the boys farm the land without Ashton? But Ashton had made her promise to sell the farm. Ernest was only fifteen and Jack not yet nineteen. Was it in their best interest to keep them tied to the land when they could do better if they learned a trade? Could the farm support two families if the boys married? How should it be divided? And what about Betty Lou? She had become engaged to Art Heeg, but they might need some help too.

If farming did not work out, would there be time for Alice to update her certificate, find a job, and provide for her old age? She was past fifty years old–an age when most women looked forward to slowing down and enjoying grandchildren. Women with the security of pensions, healthy bank accounts, or working husbands, that is. Alice had her land, her energy, her intelligence, and her gumption. She made the hard choice. She would sell the farm, and she would teach.

Alice was sure she would find buyers for the farm eventually, but until that happened, and until she upgraded her teacher credentials, the land could not be left idle. Jack put in the crop that spring and told her he kept looking for his Dad waiting by the car.

As the year progressed, life went on. Bert, age eighty-two, still peeled Alice's potatoes. He attended the December 1954 wedding of Art and Betty Lou, but it was hard not having Ashton to walk his daughter down the aisle. It was a bittersweet wedding and a subdued Christmas season. The next season, she rented the farm, and she and the boys moved in with her mother. She found a place for Bert at St. Hubert's in Rocanville, and promised to visit often.

She had enrolled in courses the first summer, and the upgrading enabled her to accept a teaching position at Perth. After more courses the following summer, her new certification qualified her to work in other provinces.

In early 1956, she found buyers for the farm in the persons of Don and Lois Bell, a very young couple who had little money and little hope of having a farm of their own. No doubt some of Alice's family, and her banker, considered it ill-advised, but she sold her farm to Don and Lois on time–essentially the same arrangement her parents had offered her and Ashton fifteen years before.

Before the Bell's assumed ownership, Alice scheduled a sale, but a late snow not only covered the machinery and equipment, but also blocked the roads and limited the access of prospective buyers. The sale could not be cancelled. Many items were underbid, and the sale did not generate as much cash as Alice had hoped.

Despite the disappointment of the sale, and the painful parting from the farm that had been the home of her heart since 1906, Alice straightened her spine and looked forward.

The edge of the newspaper riffles in a breeze from the open window. The scent of printer's ink and newsprint blends with that of fresh turned soil in the fields outside of Rocanville. Except for the riffling paper, it is quiet in the kitchen and Alice is alone. Agnes is at Jessie's, Jack is at work, and Ernest in school. There was a time when Alice would have cherished a few moments of peace and quiet, but now she would give much to hear the children squabbling in the yard, and Ashton hollering from the barn.

Alice shopped this morning, and a box of groceries waits on the floor. The Quaker Oats man looks surprised at this state of affairs as if he knows, not so long ago, Alice would never have postponed a chore like this.

She tossed the newspaper in last, but it was the first thing she opened when she got in the door. It is yesterday's edition of a national paper, and she sits on the edge of the chair with the classified section spread out on the table. One hand keeps the edge clamped down while a finger of the other goes down the column under the heading 'Employment–Teachers.' The house breathes around her and creaks its prairie bones. Suddenly her finger stops. Somebody needs a teacher. Urgently. A small school, ten to twenty pupils, an isolated area, and duties include janitorial. But good pay and accommodation on school premises. Where? The School District of Lake Cowichan. On Vancouver Island, British Columbia.

Alice knows where Vancouver Island is located, but she pulls down her dusty Collier's World Atlas from the shelf in the living room. She polishes her glasses and locates a pinpoint designated as Lake Cowichan. The school is not even in this town–it is in a logging camp some distance away. Alice knows little about logging, but she knows much about small communities.

Would they have her? The ad said urgent. And they advertised in a national paper, so they must be desperate. If there are so few children in the school, then it must be a tiny community, and they would all know one another. She would be an outsider. Would they accept a teacher from Saskatchewan? Could she fit in? Could she become part of the community and give these children an education that would make a difference in their lives? Give them tools of learning to last a lifetime? Would a complete change of scene keep her from seeing phantoms and ease the ache in her heart?

Alice drums her fingers on the paper and looks out the window. She has looked at that prairie view for so many years. Of course, she would miss it. Then again, she would come back in the summer. As if caught in a spell, Alice rises and opens the box where she keeps her letter paper. In her graceful hand, she writes . . .

Summer 1963: Prairie Voyage–and Farewell to Gordon River

All logging camps are temporary. In Gordon River, rarely more than a dozen families have occupied the modest duplexes at any one time. Closed for several years now, the bunkhouses and cookhouse are showing their years of abandonment. Their paint peels, and their windows are grimy. Blackberry vines send sneaking shoots across lonely porches, and insidious broom plants grow in the gravel wasteland where caulked boots once tramped.

Before tarmac replaced the railroad, the bunkhouses were full of loggers and echoed with talk, laughter, and heavy boots hitting the floor. In the cookhouse soups bubbled, meat sizzled, pies baked, and cooks shouted orders to galloping flunkies bearing coffee pots. Once the road was in, many men found it more convenient to commute daily, rather than live in camp. The bunkhouses emptied, and the cookhouse closed.

In the home site, there have been no new families for several years. Many duplexes are empty, and they too show the years of neglect, but the school looks much as it ever has. Its roof has new tar and gravel, its paint is fresh, and its windows are clean. Still, weeds have invaded the patch of lawn, and the fence, once an intricate shape of fanned pickets, is fallen and entombed by grass. A few stained pickets, once painted bright white, stick out of the desolation like bones, and the cottonwood sapling by the fire door is now a sturdy tree.

Where no longer tamed by residents, grass and trees have overrun yards. Like those in the stumps, the camp evergreens (once planted as garden ornamentals) have grown bigger with every season, thrusting fences aside and looming over rooftops.

The camp is nearing the end of its life, and so is the school. No preschoolers will begin grade one in the fall. The school will close after this term, and families with school age children will move away. The camp will slowly dwindle until no residents remain. The houses, and the school, will be sold and dragged away.

For the present, the children living here have no conception their sheltered lives will soon be open to the broader influences of town living, mass media, more classmates, more friends, and more risks. It will be a bigger world, a global community, with an insurgence of technology in a world of challenging choices and swift changes, the realities of life in the remainder of the 20th century and beyond.

None of this enters their heads, and as it is summer, they are making the most of their freedom in camp, and some vacation afar with their families.

* * *

"Well, it's not all flat, is it?" I say.

We are in Leader, Saskatchewan, and Dad and I have walked out of town along a dirt road heading off to nowhere in sight. From where we stand in the early evening light, our shadows stretch to fields of alternating gold and black. We are on a holiday, and it is the first time in my twelve years I have been east of the Rockies. I am on the prairies at last, and I want to see it all. It is amazing.

Our dog thinks so too. Nose to ground she trots up and down in the clumps of weeds and small bushes beside the road, stubby tail in constant wag. So far, the only birds she has flushed are some lazy little brown things flying only a few yards and landing on the road in puffballs of dust. Paddy, not at all discouraged, makes the most of her snuffling freedom after being cooped in the station wagon for most of our trip out here.

A few days ago, we left Banff. From my place in the back seat behind Dad, I looked in the side mirror, and watched that comforting line of mountains recede as the land around us slowly flattened and expanded, and the horizon became, well, a horizon. This is something I have rarely seen, except from the beaches of the west coast. My first view of the prairies was unlike anything at home, and most of British Columbia is like home to me. Each summer holiday since my youngest sister was a baby, Mum and Dad packed us into the station wagon and, with homemade trailer in tow, we camped our way around the province: The Fraser Canyon, the Okanagan, the Kootenays, Barkerville, Kamloops, and Manning Park, as well as treks to Jasper and Banff, in Alberta. Forested or not, there were always mountains.

I love mountains, but I was keen to see the prairies. Mrs. Marlatt often described Saskatchewan to us, and I have seen many pictures, but words and pictures are nothing like being here. I feel like I want to get under a tree, but at the same time I want to get up high where I can see it all. I don't want to miss a thing.

R.Rigsby

"Kind of feel like an ant on a tabletop," Dad says.

I know he doesn't like it much. The air is too dry for his asthma, and he is wheezing more than usual. It is hot for sure and doesn't cool at night like at home. It cools a bit, but it isn't fresh. There is a constant smell of dust, or something like pollen, or maybe it is simply the prairie-ness of it all. Not a sniff of water or damp, although I have seen ponds of water surrounded by whitish rims, and some with lumpy dykes to keep them from leaking away. I heard somebody call them sloughs.

I look over the fields toward the horizon. It is just as Mrs. Marlatt described–if it weren't for the town behind us, it would be a perfect circle. It is a circle with a wavering pattern of green, gold, and black, depending on the angle of the light, the direction of the breeze, and the ripples of the land. It is odd to have this much open-ness and so much space to see at once. I am used to seeing scenery within the boundaries of mountain walls; used to seeing the sky as wedges between mountains, not as an inverted bowl over my head.

Today it was a blue, blue bowl, painted with random blobs of white. Under this bowl, we stay with Art and Betty Lou Heeg, and their kids. Our families have become good friends, but Mrs. Marlatt is at her cottage at Kenosee Lake. I had forgotten she goes there for the summer, and was disappointed to find the cottage is on the far side of Saskatchewan. We will not travel so far. My sisters don't mind, but then they are young, and since they are about the same ages as the Heeg's oldest girls, they are having a great time.

There is nobody my age here, but I am not lonely and yesterday I joined Dad when Art invited him on a tour of the Heeg farm. We drove along several roads, all crossing at exact right angles, and going straight for miles and miles. Miles and miles of dust also. I hoped the farm might have a horse or two, or at least a cow. Mrs. Marlatt's farm always had horses and other farm animals, but no, this farm just grows wheat. Tons of it. Inside a granary, where yellow dust glowed in the light from the door, I stared at a huge pile of grain. Art's brother, Bud, gave me a paper bag of wheat to take home. I chewed a few grains until they became gummy, but Dad warned me not to overdo it and get a bellyache.

"The breadbasket of Canada," is how Mrs. Marlatt described the prairies. With the amount of wheat I saw on one farm, I am sure the prairies have more wheat than the whole world could ever eat.

We amble back to town with the low sun in our eyes, and I think about how much this trip to Saskatchewan has been a dream come true. I wish we could travel farther, but this is not to be–tomorrow we must start the return trip. Soon it will be September.

I realize this is the last summer vacation of my elementary school years. This fall I will begin grade eight in high school. I will live with my grandmother and go to school in Chemainus, because there is no school bus from camp to the high school in Lake Cowichan. They won't send a bus for only me. I look forward to staying with my grandmother, because we do such fun things together. It will be like a long visit.

I am reminded of my last visit with Mrs. Marlatt. On the last day of school, she handed out report cards as usual. I rushed home to change into play clothes, and start summer holidays. At supper, Mum told me Mrs. Marlatt was leaving in the morning, and she wanted to see me before she left.

The next morning after breakfast, I went down the hill to the school, and around to the door to Mrs. Marlatt's apartment. Her car was parked at the foot of the steps, and a big suitcase sat on the back seat. I paused before knocking, but before the first rap Mrs. Marlatt opened the door and invited me inside.

Except for the time I was beaned on the head with a rock, I had never been in her apartment. That time I was just a kid and too busy blubbering to pay much attention to the space around me. Sometimes during class, when I went to one of the toilets, I would peek in if she had left the door open but could never see very much.

Barely alighting on the edge of the single bed she used for a couch, I gawked around. A corner cabinet held some ornaments and a side table held a lamp and a book. There was an oil stove like the one in our kitchen, a refrigerator, and a short counter with cupboards above. The door to her bedroom was open, but with no sun shining on that side of the school, it was dim. Instead, the sun shone through the square window over the sink and reflected from the top of the kitchen table, making me blink. Mrs. Marlatt sat on one of her kitchen chairs, but I was so busy looking around I didn't pay attention when she began to speak.

Mrs. Marlatt said she had very much enjoyed having me for a pupil all of these years, and she hoped she had taught me everything I needed in order to do well in high school. Something in her voice I had never heard before caught my full attention. I looked at her face and nodded, but couldn't think of anything to say. Then she said she hoped, as I grew up and met "challenges" and "temptations," I had learned enough to make the right choices. She hoped I would keep my chin up and not give in to "just going with the crowd because it was easier" and "to wear bobby socks all through high school."

I jerked my head up and down to all of this and managed to find my voice to say, "Yes, I will!"

I am still not sure what she meant, but I do know I want her to be pleased with whatever I do. I know I might not see her again for a long while.

Epilogue

Alice, as an attractive and independent widow, may have drawn interested suitors, but she never remarried. In 1979, while telling her story, she told Betty Lou that she had by then been a widow for over twenty-five years: longer than she had been a wife. In all of the hours of tape recorded narrative, this one of the few instances where Alice speaks with regret of one of the sorrows of her life. There was only one Ashton.

Ashton's memory, if not his ghost, accompanied her to Gordon River, where she made a new life, and shaped young minds, including mine.

Before Alice's retirement in June of 1968, she was a guest at my high school graduation, and at the end of the term, she retired and returned to Saskatchewan. As planned, she and Bobbie lived together in Rocanville and enjoyed summers at Alice's cherished cottage on Kenosee Lake. In the summer of 1975, they travelled west to visit friends on Vancouver Island during which time Alice attended my sister's wedding. In 1976 my parents picked her up in Rocanville and drove her to Kathy's wedding in Manitoba. Here she offered the toast to the bride, and joined our parents in happy reminiscences of their years in Gordon River. Alice and Bobbie again visited Vancouver Island in the summer of 1981.

My parents had continued their close friendship with the Heegs, and with Alice, often visiting during summer vacations and after my father's retirement. It seemed as though Alice would always be a part of our lives.

I was not expecting my mother's telephone call in January 1989. She told me she had some sad news: Mrs. Marlatt died on January 18. Caught up on the merry-go-round of career and family, I could not go to her funeral, nor did I know how she had spent her last years.

I knew she had had some health problems, as expected of the elderly, but eighty-five years seemed like a fine achievement. Almost fifteen years later, when I began writing Alice's story, I learned that she had had Alzheimer's. Betty Lou had suspected that her mother was in the early stages before she moved her to Leader in 1979, after which she knew her mother was leaving her. Alice's disease progressed and, before her death, she was already lost to those who loved her.

How do you rate the legacy a person leaves to the world? Alice did not achieve celebrity or notoriety. She simply worked hard, coped with hardship and loss, and did not allow the burdens of life to crush her humour and optimism. She laughed much, but didn't tolerate bad manners, cheating, or selfish behaviour. She led by example. Her ethics, attitudes, and moral code continue in the world views of many of those she taught, loved, and disciplined, and through them to future generations. This is Alice's legacy.

All that I learned from Alice Marlatt in that one-room school is part of my life, and indirectly, the lives of my children and grandchildren. Therefore, I hope that when Alice returned to Saskatchewan after the years she gave to us in Gordon River, both she and Ashton's ghost found peace.

Acknowledgements

This work began as a short project–a simple transcription of Betty Lou's tapes, and then it became a living thing: one that developed a thirst for words and more words. As the words flowed, I realized that the pump would need help. Without the guidance, support, and pump-handling of many people, the well might have dribbled and dried.

No writer works alone, and I am indebted to, first of all, my husband, Grant, who never stopped believing, although I am sure he never expected the finished product to take ten years. Thank you, my dear, for your patience and for your conviction–you gave me strength to plumb deeper.

I also thank my family, who read, corrected, suggested, and listened. Hopefully, I listened to you too. My parents' recollections filled in many blanks, and revealed that there never is just one story, or one stream of words.

My friends have been a source of encouragement and information. Some of you have become friends through advising, reading and editing, in whole and in parts, and I thank you for your red pens, blue pencils, and bottles of wine.

And of course, there is Alice's family, especially Betty Lou. Without hesitation, you gave me everything I needed to write Alice's story. Because of the person you are, you deserve much better than my attempt to characterize a woman who, in differing ways, made us both the people we are.

R.Rigsby

1903.
Alice Mary Blair.
Already smiling.

1904.
Robert,
Agnes, and
Alice Mary
Blair.

R.Rigsby

1905
Alice and
Laura.

1906.
Alice, Laura,
Agnes, and
Raymond.

1919.
Blair family,
prior to birth of
Roberta. Alice
center, back.

GRADE. 6. 1929.

1929.
Above. Alice
and her class.

Right. Alice and
best friend,
'Stan.'

R.Rigsby

Late 1920s.
Alice, young and single
in good times.

August 30, 1930. Left.
Alice and Ashton's wedding day,
with Albert behind them.

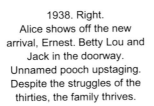

1938. Right.
Alice shows off the new
arrival, Ernest. Betty Lou and
Jack in the doorway.
Unnamed pooch upstaging.
Despite the struggles of the
thirties, the family thrives.

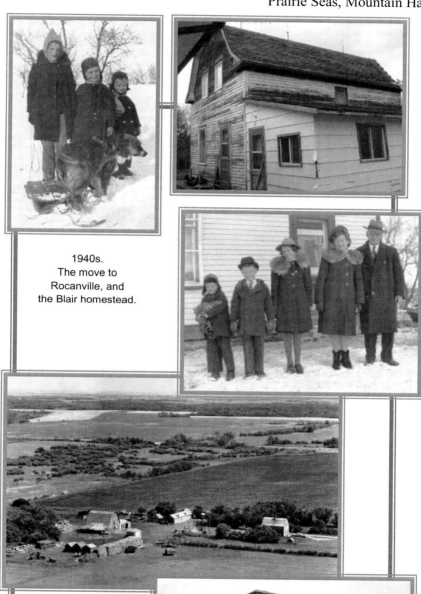

1940s.
The move to
Rocanville, and
the Blair homestead.

Shots of the house
(top right) and barn
(bottom right) taken
in April, 2005 by the
author.

1953.
Alice and Ashton in happy times.
Above, undated photo. At right, with
friend Bill on the way to Ontario and
their Grand Tour.

1954.
The wedding of Betty Lou
and Art Heeg.
Above, with Bert, and right
with Alice and Art's mother,
Emma.

1956.
Gordon River
Camp.

1956 Pontiac.
Alice's transport from the
prairies to Gordon River.
This shot taken on the
schoolground.

1956.
Two views of
Gordon River School.
Above, Alice stands
under her kitchen
window.

1957.
First day of school.
The author has her slip showing.

1958. Mrs. Marlatt and her charges. Except for Goldie.
The one and only class photo, taken by Mr. Wilmer Gold, and appearing here with
the permission of the Kaatza Station Museum & Archives, Wilmer Gold Collection.

1960.
Mrs. Marlatt has a
new desk, but we
still sit in the old
style wrought iron
models

1961. Above. Mrs. Marlatt attends a birthday party.

1962. Right. Gordon River May Day Parade. We bear our Queen to the 'fairgrounds.'

1960's.
Mrs. Marlatt in her apartment.

R.Rigsby

Early 1960s.

Above. Alice, on Vacation, stops to chat.

Right. Alice and Agnes.

Late 1961. Gordon River. The Heeg and Stephens kids

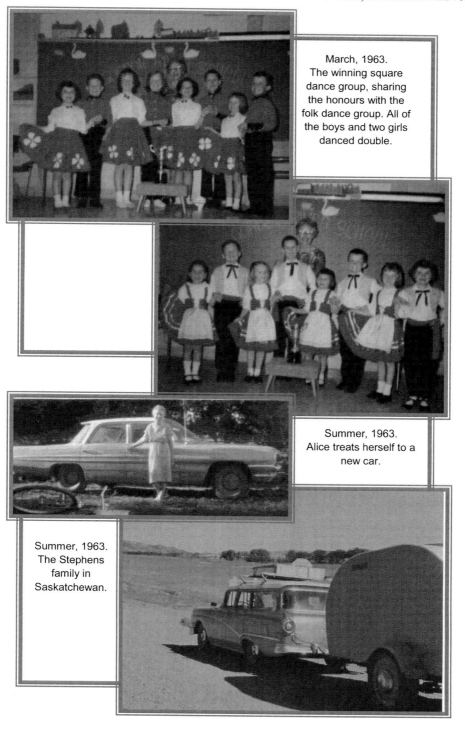

March, 1963.
The winning square dance group, sharing the honours with the folk dance group. All of the boys and two girls danced double.

Summer, 1963.
Alice treats herself to a new car.

Summer, 1963.
The Stephens family in Saskatchewan.

R.Rigsby

June, 1968.
Alice retires.

1981.
One of the last
photos. Alice,
still smiling.

Bibliography and References

Argan, William, with Cowan, Pam. *Cornerstones 2: An Artist's History of the City of Regina*. Regina: Centax.

Berton, Pierre. *The Great Depression, 1929-1939*. Toronto: Anchor Canada, 2001.

Berton, Pierre. *The Promised Land: Settling the West, 1896-1914*. Toronto: McClelland & Stewart, 1984.

Braithwaite, Max. *Why Shoot The Teacher*. Toronto: McClelland & Stewart, 2002.

Broadfoot, Barry. *Ten Lost Years: Memories of Canadians Who Survived the Great Depression*. Toronto: Doubleday, 1971.

Broadfoot, Barry. *The Pioneer Years 1895-1914: Memories of Settlers Who Opened the West*. Toronto: Doubleday, 1976.

Gibson, Bill. *Rails to Roads and The Million Dollar Camp: The Story of Gordon River*. Victoria: Island Blue Printorium Bookworks, 2010.

Gold, Wilmer. *Logging As It Was*. Victoria: Moriss Publishing, 1985.

McClung, Nellie. *Clearing in the West and The Stream Runs Fast*. Edited by Veronica Strong-Boag & Michelle Lynn Rosa. Peterborough: Broadview Press, 2003.

McManus, Curtis R. *Happyland: A History of the "Dirty Thirties" in Saskatchewan, 1914-1937*. Calgary: University of Calgary Press, 2011.

R.Rigsby

Robertson, Heather. *Salt of the Earth: The Story of the Homesteaders in Western Canada*. Toronto: James Lorimer & Company, 1974.

Savage, Candace. *Prairie: A Natural History*. Vancouver: Douglas & McIntyre, 2004.

Saywell, John F.T. *Kaatza: The Chronicles of Cowichan Lake*. Lake Cowichan: The Cowichan Lake District Centennial Committee, 1967.

About the Author

After my birth in a small hospital in the town of Duncan, British Columbia, my parents took me, and my embryonic writing muse, home. 'Home' was a logging camp then known as Camp 3, and until 1968, when I left for university, I lived all of my life in lumber industry communities on Vancouver Island. One such community was Gordon River Logging Camp where my love for a good story began.

Like many children, I had a vivid imagination, and on many nights when I should have been asleep, I visualized my starring role in thrilling episodes of my favourite daydreams. Although composition was part of our schooling, our paragraphs were related to the subjects of the day, and it did not occur to me to put my fantasies in writing. Later, I wrote essays and reports, but the topics were prescribed, and my infant writing muse remained submerged beneath the priorities of high school and then university.

Once in the working world and focussed on raising children, there was little time for writing anything but hurried letters to family and friends. It was not until the early '90s that my muse surfaced, gulped for air, and insisted that I write down the material that had been filling my head for years. I wrote plots, poetry, and memoirs, but feeling my limitations, I also attended writing classes. My muse floated free, and I kept writing and studying.

By the late '90s, I was a regular contributor to my employer's trade newsletter. I learned from the critiques of the editor–and the readership. In 2003 I decided that if a change of vocation was ever to take place, there would be no better time.

Returning to university, I launched my muse into a sea of creative writing courses, buoyed up by the guidance of gifted instructors. During this cruise through the halls of higher learning, I began the writing voyage that ended in my first published manuscript–Prairie Seas, Mountain Harvest.

10/23

Manufactured by Amazon.ca
Acheson, AB

11367617R00133